WATER~STONE REVIEW

HAMLINE UNIVERSITY

Water~Stone, known in alchemy as the Philosopher's Stone, was composed of the four elements of earth, fire, air, and water. The stone was supposed by alchemists to possess the property of changing base metals into gold, the most perfect of all metals. It was thought to combine within itself matter and spirit, or body and soul: a union of opposites in perfect harmony. *Water~Stone* connotes the dynamic, transformative power of literature, as well as the search for beauty and perfection at work in the hearts of aspiring writers. The logo type for *Water~Stone* is based on a hybrid of two ancient alchemic symbols: one for the amalgam of all elements, and the second for the element of water as a pure and dynamic force. The amalgam is a reference to the multigenre, interdisciplinary nature of the graduate writing program at Hamline University.

U.S. subscription rates for individuals are $32 for two years, plus shipping and handling. Subscription rates for institutions are $19 for one year, $37 for two years. Single copies of this issue: $18.

Water~Stone Review will accept unsolicited submissions from October 1 through December 1, 2011; all work received after December 1 will be returned unread. Work will be *read* between December 1 and April 1, 2012. All regular submissions must be accompanied by an SASE. Manuscripts will not be returned. Send one prose piece and/or one to three poems at a time. Prose should be no longer than 8,000 words, double-spaced. Please direct all correspondence to *Water~Stone Review*, The Creative Writing Programs, Hamline University, MS-A1730, 1536 Hewitt Avenue, Saint Paul, MN 55104-1284, or e-mail to water-stone@hamline.edu.

Water~Stone Review is indexed in *The American Humanities Index*.

© 2011 *Water~Stone Review*
ISSN 1520–4572
ISBN 978–1–934458–02–0
Distributed by Ubiquity Distributors, Inc.
and Don Olson Distributors

Designed by Ashley Kapaun of DesignWorks
at the Minneapolis College of Art and Design

Cover photograph by Karen Knorr,
The Aesthetic of Judgement, The Room of the Carytides, Louvre Museum, 2009

Proofread by Anne Kelley Conklin

WATER~STONE REVIEW

Volume 14   Fall 2011

EXECUTIVE EDITOR
Mary François Rockcastle

MANAGING EDITOR
Meghan Maloney-Vinz

POETRY EDITOR
Patricia Kirkpatrick

FICTION EDITOR
Sheila O'Connor

CREATIVE NONFICTION EDITOR
Barrie Jean Borich

ASSISTANT EDITORS
Steve McPherson
Stephanie Myers
Gretchen Rueth
Sarah Turner

EDITORIAL BOARD

Lucie Amundson   Michael Polak
Reneé Beauregard   Kayli Staubus
Elena Cisneros   Caitlin Thompson
Mitchell Dahloff   Jordan Wiklund
Cynthia Truitt Lynch Alida Winternheimer
Jennifer McDougal   Mary Wlodarski
Kathleen Muggli

From the Executive Editor:

Each year, when I write this opening essay, I end up writing variations on the same subject: the human condition in all its terror and beauty. Simply put, the human condition is what it is, and writers grapple with it over and over—sometimes making sense of it, sometimes not—and the work we publish captures and depicts our ongoing, mythic human journey. If that sounds like a cop-out, it's not meant to be. Because each issue *is* different; each is beautiful and haunting and transformative in its own way. But the raw material we're all working with as writers, that our authors have shaped into these winning poems and stories and works of creative nonfiction, is made of the unchanging stuff that joins us one to another—sentient and non-sentient, human and nonhuman beings.

Inspired by Philip S. Bryant's poem, we chose *How Myths Begin* as the title for this year's issue. Numerous abstract words come to mind when you think of myth, words like *epistemological, archetypal, metaphysical,* and *allegorical.* And let's not forget *sacred.* For our purposes, I'll simply say that as we reviewed the contents for our next issue, we marked the many ways in which our authors seek, in Ed Bok Lee's words, "something to believe in, bigger than themselves." These writers are embracing, revising, and exploding old myths and creating new ones.

The narrator in "Veterans Day" by Sarah Gilbert, winner of the *2011 Judith Kitchen Creative Nonfiction Prize,* chooses familiar heroes from Greek myth as models: "But for the shredding of flesh, the man-killing, I could be Achilles on any given day." Home is her crucible: "Sarah, constant, changeable, keeper of passions, bearer of woes, she of the loud voice, she who wipes the tears of young boys, wife of an Army Reservist at war."

Families in this issue re-enact—sometimes heroically, sometimes violently, sometimes in silence—the deepest struggles and decisions we face as humans. The father in Mark Rapacz's story, "Bellwether," after impregnating his daughter, reinvents himself as a father. The father in "What It Means to Be a Man" by Ed Bok Lee forces a murderous act on his son to teach him a lesson.

The questions asked in this work are important, if unanswerable. "Let us keep turning to each other," Travis Mossotti writes, "like children / pausing for answers to questions that always begin / and end with why."

What is the nature of love? How do we come to terms with, construct and reconstruct, our own identities? The narrator in Ames Hawkins's "Optickal Allusion" is mesmerized by the novel *Jaws,* which she reads when she's in junior high. Her struggles with her own sexual identity echo her father's unspoken struggle:

> But I also know that it wasn't Brody, or Hooper, or Quint with whom I identified. It was the shark itself, the great monster beneath, lurking in the open blue, always on the move . . . . This is what George, my father, and I had in common—the sense that we, too, could be hunted, tracked, and killed. We were in this wide open together, hidden yet exposed. He in his marriage and I in my gable.

Some of the questions asked are heartbreaking. Why do some women conceive and others don't—why do some give birth to a healthy baby whereas others miscarry? In her poem, "*From* Five Poems about an Apple Tree," Sarah Fox asks: "How does one hold in the mind a form / —which one intended to clutch, feed— / that is said to have existed / inside the body / which evades completion . . . "

"How did it happen that my hands came to carry words?" Lidia Yuknavitch asks in "The Work of Art," this year's *Meridel Le Sueur Essay.* She uncovers multiple roots of her avocation as a writer. One was trauma: "When my daughter died in the belly world of me, I became a writer—so that all the words that cannot name grief, all the words threatening to erupt from my belly and uterus did not explode up and through my skull and face and shatter the very world and sky."

Why are some bodies healthy and whole whereas others are riddled with cancer or AIDS, or depend on crutches and urinary catheters to function? "We come into the world naked, in a puddle of pee," writes Mary Jane LaVigne in "On Incontinence: Tim's Coming In and Out Party." "We leave shed of all artifice. In between, we clothe ourselves in personas, some chosen by us, others by fate."

Even in the womb, our bodies gesture. Once born, we communicate and miscommunicate, healing and harming, often indiscriminately. In "Signs of the Times" by Morgan Grayce Willow, *Honorable Mention* winner of the *Judith Kitchen Creative Nonfiction Prize*, a group of gang members mistake a deaf man's signal that he is waiting for a #5 bus for a "dis" against them. Morgan writes: "Body of words. Words—and signs—of the body. Whether hearing or deaf, we all require bodies to make language, bodies which then put us smack in the middle of place and story. Mistranslation can make of this gift a curse."

Characters in this issue are in the midst of mythic journeys—from child to adult, male to female, heterosexual (either in actuality or as a default condition) to homosexual or bisexual, civilian to military, single to partnered, birth to death. The personal and political are juxtaposed and intertwined. The strong pummel the weak; animals are cared for, eaten, and slaughtered. Common household objects provide meaning and comfort: the family Sno-Cone maker, the Maytag washer, a lemon, a box of oil paints.

We are caught between worlds; we yearn for wholeness; we commemorate the dead. In "Orphans in the Terrorist World," Rigoberto González mourns the death of his mother, a grief thickened by the tragedy of September 11, 2001: "I descend into solitude for a day, and ascend the next morning somehow refreshed, cleansed of a darkness that first took hold of me when I was twelve years old. But each year, it comes back, this overwhelming clobbering of my spirit. And each year, I survive it."

Our writer's interview this year is with fiction writer Richard Bausch, author of eleven novels and eight collections of short stories. In his interview, Bausch talks about his writing, his work as a teacher, the creative process, effective dialogue, characters you can't forget, the importance of reading, and much more. He also gives invaluable advice on how to live a writing life: "There's really only one thing to think about each day: *Did I work?*"

Our folio of photographs was curated (again!) by MCAD graduate Ashley Kapaun. In selecting the photographs, and the cover, for this issue, Ashley wrote the following:

My inspiration revolves around the conflicting methods and circumstances which define identity and the ambiguity of that definition, reflected in our human gestures and exchanges, our secret beliefs and hidden altars, our luminaries. The photography compares the uncertain moment to the moment of insight and hope, reflecting the continuous shift and expansion of human thought and awareness.

This year's essay review by Mary Cappello explores the "biographical impulse" in two new books of creative nonfiction: a biography of cancer by Siddhartha Mukherjee and a "life" of Montaigne by Sarah Bakewell. Both of these books newly imagine "the shape that a transcription of a life can take in writing . . . . To be able to imagine new forms of thought (literary genres) is also to be able to imagine new forms of life: not how to live, but how to make life living."

Stan Sanvel Rubin grapples with the making, and non-making, of metaphor in contemporary poetry. He looks at four new books of poetry—by Stephen Dunn, Carl Phillips, Michael Dickman, and Joni Wallace—focusing on what he calls *declarative poetry:* a poetry that by and large abjures metaphor and decoration . . . a poetry of cunning transparency."

Making sense out of the cosmos, and our place in it, is the domain of myth. We create stories to explain. A preverbal child points to what he doesn't know and gestures, "What is that?" When she's old enough to talk, she asks, incessantly, "Why?" The earth is round. "Why?" Gravity keeps people standing upright. "Why?" Finish your cereal. "Why?" Grandpa is dying. "Why?" This "Why" can drive a parent to distraction. We writers do it, too.

"If we are going to meditate on the purpose of existence," writes Eleanor Lerman in "Mysterious Interventions," "then we might as well start / with Life As We Know It, into which / we were born confused." Even if there is no answer, the compulsion to know, Lerman says, "does not diminish." So what do we gain by such questions? An occasional clue perhaps, "The night of a thousand falling starts / The mysterious intervention that / changed what you think of as your life / but may be something else. And if / so, that is where the real work begins."

I hope you find your own "occasional clues" on the pages of this new issue of *Water~Stone Review*. Where the real work has begun, and is continuing.

Mary François Rockcastle

From the Creative Nonfiction Editor:

When I was a nineteen-year-old undergraduate, yet to imagine herself a creative nonfiction writer and editor, my first college-level creative writing class was in fiction. In my 1978 Midwestern university's English department, the offerings were fiction or poetry, and to a young pre-journalism major who really wanted to be a literary writer, but knew little about poetry (and had not yet heard of creative nonfiction), the fiction genre, ironically, seemed the most "real" of the available choices. I received, in that class, my first-ever formal critique of my work, yet of all the critique-worthy comments my vaguely fictionalized rendition of a memory deserved—my story's emotional naiveté, its clichéd plot, its complete ignorance of craft, and most problematic in that context, my inarticulate disinterest in making things up—I remember only one of the professor's responses, perhaps because his were the same words so many as-yet-to-become-nonfiction-writers heard then, and have heard since.

The professor sat grimly in front of the classroom of young people, all of us convinced we needed a higher power (such as the professor) to grant us a right-of-way into literary production. He made his way through the stack of student manuscripts, publicly praising or denouncing each in turn, and as he read mine aloud he paused to say, "If this writer wants to be political, she should write an essay." These were the days when the crusty, opinionated, thinking-on-the-page essay was an artifact of the past, considered in literary circles artful, but not quite an art form. Of all the fair points the professor may have meant to make, the only parts I was able to hear then were his opinion that art and social concern must not mix, that my interests were not appropriate to the realms of art-making, and that I had committed a serious crime-of-the-art to suppose anything different.

More than thirty years later, though creative writing pedagogy has improved considerably, I try to always remember the negative impact that message had on my own first writings, and how long my defiance of the seemingly tyrannical aspects of his message kept me from the study of anything but politics. I can now, and often do, enumerate in the classroom myriad socially engaged art forms, crossing all genres and disciplines. And yet, what's also happened in literature since that time is the fresh re-emergence of the essay, in effect a constitutional remaking of what seemed to a neophyte in 1978 (despite the availability of the work of radical, and then under-taught, game changers such as James Baldwin and Adrienne Rich) a marginalized, elitist, and even stuffy non-art form. Today's literary nonfiction—including the ruminative, Montaigne-like, circling, questioning, attempting, and beautifully rendered essay in its current renaissance—is nothing if not art, but also a reimagined form of art, a symbiotic web of lyric, story, history, empathy, experiment, and yes, as often as not, some form of political exploration or opinion.

I would never say the only way to write political is to write an essay, yet I do suggest, to those drafting political works now, that we consider what else their essay could be, in addition to political. What is the author's distance or proximity to events she witnesses? What is the music of the body politic in relation to the music of one's own body? What does he see when he turns the interrogatory lens back, on himself? Where is the myth in the commonplace, and how might language itself contain, or transport, experience? The contemporary literary essay, in all its hybrid flexibility, may not be the only form to allow us to enter the personal-as-political realm, but is a genre that allows readers a relatively unmasked relationship to actuality, which can help us see the volatile aspects of our world through an ever recalibrating lens.

The first-ever honorees of *Water~Stone Review's* brand-new *Judith Kitchen Creative Nonfiction Prize* are just such nuanced, personal-public political works. Our final judge, Poe Ballantine, best known for his essays published in *The Sun* and collected in his Hawthorne Press books, *501 Minutes to Christ and Things I Like about America,* chose works that grapple intentionally and inventively with both the daily news and the forces at work behind the news. The winning essay, "Veterans Day" by Sarah Gilbert, is about the domestic side of America at war, as experienced by the wife of a deployed soldier, and the honorably mentioned essay, "Signs of the Time" by Morgan Grayce Willow, is about the urban American wars some encounter daily in such contested territories as a city bus.

About the winning essay, Judith Kitchen—old friend of *Water~Stone Review* and bearer of the nonfiction prize's name—writes: "'Veterans Day' is wonderfully complex as the author tries to struggle through the day-to-day life of a military wife and mother . . . a modern-day Penelope, vibrant in her fierce and faithful waiting, which turns out to be another definition of 'active duty.'" About the honorably mentioned essay, Kitchen writes: "'Signs of the Time' employs a fascinating device as the author doles out piecemeal the story of the beating of a deaf man. Her technique demonstrates for the reader what it is like to know partially, to be able to 'hear' only half the facts." Both these essays illustrate the ways in which social witness can meet engaged, complexly considered, and deeply felt prose, seeking to illuminate and even politicize the journalistic fact, from the commonplace to the colossal. And both essays engage an entwined personal-public eye, allowing us insight into both the exterior and interior of lived experience.

With the contest winners as our lead, all of our nonfiction selections this year take on some aspect of social identities, positions, and transgressions. One of the pleasures of serving as the creative nonfiction editor of *Water~Stone Review* is the opportunity to work democratically with graduate students to explore the formal range of contemporary creative nonfiction literature, as the work is being written now. Each year my creative nonfiction board knocks me out with their willingness to stretch beyond their personal affinities and see the power of forms that defy conventional genre parameters. So to that professor who instructed me, and surely many others, to write our politics as essays, I can only say, "Thank you." Because, as *Water~Stone Review* readers will see in these pages, indeed we do write essays, and in doing so continue to reinvent not only the essay but also the worlds our essays seek to describe.

Barrie Jean Borich

Contents

FICTION

POETRY

CREATIVE NONFICTION ⌁

PHOTOGRAPHY ⚚

INTERVIEW ☀

BOOK REVIEWS ✺

Judith Kitchen Creative Nonfiction Prize

Veterans Day

SARAH GILBERT

On Veterans Day, it is not even a week since my own soldier has boarded an airplane, returning to Kuwait after his fifteen-day leave, and I spend the slow morning with barley-rye pancakes, with cold-pressed apple cider, with Cartoon Network for my boys. On Veterans Day in my muddy, coffee-steeped neighborhood in southeast Portland, what do I celebrate? There are no veterans here; my grandfathers and great-grandfathers are stories too old to tell these boys. Grandpa Green—Grampy to us—was a mapmaker in World War II; he carried the shrapnel from an errant bomb in his hip to his grave. Uncle Mike was in Korea, and all I know of that time was his gravelly voice, grown in the war, I was always sure, until my cousin Shawn (he, the gentlest adult man I could ever have imagined) grew it, too.

I have no ritual of celebration, no communion of Army wives to gather around, no cultural context for this holiday. I dimly think, *It should be mine, but how? What should we do?* I gather my breath, gather my thoughts, but nothing comes to me. I look at the boys, huddled under blankets watching boy-heroes fight aliens and monsters and bad guys with thunder, with fire. I leave them be; I sweep the floor. When it is bedtime, when I have read them all to sweet, rain-speckled sleep, I find my own place in this war effort. I stand in my kitchen. I survey my battle landscape.

There is honor in the locking of doors; there is pride in laundry started, shifted to dryer, folded piece by inside-out piece; there will be great rejoicing whence cometh the erranding hero, fresh from her victory over things broken and now fixed, pantry shelves depleted and now refilled, books required and now secured!

I am standing tall on the wind-whipped cliff, having scrambled rough to the midpoint of my husband's 400-day deployment to Kuwait, and I am doing my homework. I have been reading records of war; I have been reading missives from sorrowful wives on the homefront; I have been standing in my kitchen, head cocked, listening to my husband's quiet, introspective voice, faraway, faraway. I am the keeper of photos; I am the teller of family tales; I am the donner of coats. I live a legend's life, if your legends come straight through the ages from classical epic, Greek myth, the evenest of recountings of meals eaten gluttonously, vessels storm-tossed, flesh stabbed and torn ungodly.

Take a Greek legend, if you will. Hector, Agamemnon, Menelaus, Athena, Andromache, every grief-wracked last one of them. Achilles, say: man/god, legendary warrior, godlike ideal of male beauty, valor; deeply wrong, deeply wronged, ripped with woe, petty, anguished, alone. But for the shredding of flesh, the man-killing, I could be Achilles on any given day. Pierced through with the strife of it all—the boys, refusing shoes with a puckish laugh, screaming and kicking when I tell them, "Go this way!"—I growl, stomp, shout, grab wrists so hard they shine red, rage so that I want to rip out my own throat, hold it pulsing over the sidewalk battlefield. I catch myself, give remorse a chance, apologize and, hoarse, crawl into my hollow chest a minute, sorrowing that I've fallen into the tragedy of this.

With days left before my husband will come home on leave, I sit in an intimate theater on a rainy Friday evening. Sister-in-motherhood at my side, I prepare for a few hours' revisiting of *The Iliad*. I watch a man playing Homer, Achilles, Hector, and the modern every-veteran tell a story of war. The very fluids in his body are actors; they drip, spurt, sputter, trail down his cheekbone, his chin, with purpose and wrath. His weapons are coat, wooden chair, dried flowers; they are no less fearsome. When he plunges dried chrysanthemums into the imagined gut of Hector, I flinch, I pale, I lurch sickly. I see myself, too much.

He speaks, shouts in the voice of Andromache to her husband, breaking from the battlefield, "Have you no pity for him, our helpless son? Or me, and the destiny that weighs me down, your widow?" Widow already, she blames him with flashing eyes and guilt that boils up into his throat, choking him, holding him down. That helpless son.

"What can you say about a good man?" the actor asks, and that is the heart of it. All I can hear is that war does things to people, even mild wars, even good people. It is a steamrolling, roiling, terribly right thing to say to a military wife, she who wrote this, even. Who wants to hear this? Not me, not me. Yet I know it—to the arches of my feet, to the tips of my ears, to the ache in my hip muscles. Rip out my gut, too; you'll see it—entrails trail behind your carriage. If you eat me, Achilles, you'll taste how it is that I know. War changes a man.

And the woman? What of the woman? If you are to read the flag-draped memoirs, the essays in magazines for "thinking mothers," she storms with tears of love and loyalty; she lies to her progeny with smiles, with cheerfulness, with laughter. She stands beside the window, huddles beneath her voluminous, half-empty covers late at night past bedtime; she counts up the stepping-stones (Thanksgiving, Christmas, a trip to her college friend's); she writes letters at her desk and listens to her husband's recorded voice reading a bedtime story to her child. She wrestles with snow blower, blown furnace, furniture movers. She pushes her children in shopping carts to pass the time; she gets so lonely she turns inward, sits sobbing in the locked bathroom, cartoons turned too loud. She dreams vivid dreams of her husband's death.

That's the woman I've been reading of—she's not me, much, unless you count the dreams. Mine came coldly. I dreamed he was dead one morning in September at a minute after the hour. Time, in its sinewy way, rippled so that I learned the news in local time. Six a.m., a firefight. That's how he died. I did not wonder how I knew before the two soldiers arrived at my front door to knock— sober, steady, upright in the face of a sinking, melting wife. I had been told in books, in movies, in television shows: I would know before they found the words of notification on my porch. I'd hear the knock and scream silently in soul-emptied grief. But I knew earlier, before even the soldiers are sent. As we scrambled through the day, I thought, *We should go home. Is it too late? We want to be there when they knock.*

But first, I thought, *We must tell Truman,* the middle son. We—the oldest, Everett, and I—sat him down; we said it in the simplest words: "Your daddy was shot, this morning in Kuwait. The firefight began and he was caught in the middle. It was over as soon as it started. We're sorry. He loved you, loved us." My son's five-year-old face was so blank I could not see his eyes, his lips; it was a skin-colored shape, whiter even. In a chilly instant I could see him, my husband, far more clearly than the boy a few feet away.

This must have been his first real combat experience. His job as a driver has him driving major generals and Fulbright scholars and entertainers—rap artists and country singers and Olympic hurdlers—down Kuwaiti highways at maximum speed. He told me he sometimes points his weapon, not at insurgents with bombs, but at Kuwaiti citizens and third-country nationals who have inexplicably stopped their vehicles in his path. His mission is escort, security guard, chauffeur. If there was real danger, the major generals and Fulbright scholars and rap artists wouldn't be passengers, not like this. His vehicles are armored; he is not the only soldier aboard toting a weapon; I often wonder how many more dangerous jobs there are, back home. He must have been so scared and so ready to use his years of training and anticipation. What discouragement. One time to face the enemy, and it's over, for always.

I dreamed I tried out the knowledge, the phrase "my husband has died," and found the clothing of "widow" too natural, fitting better than I could ever have imagined. I tried to remember what it was I'd get when the soldiers arrived—money, my husband had said, cash, many thousands. This I could not imagine: holding, in my hands, the life of my husband, represented in dollar bills.

I shouldn't know, I thought. *This should be a secret.*

At 6:59 a.m., a minute before the alarm, I woke next to my youngest, Monroe; the room was dim, a cloudy morning; on the radio the top-of-the-hour news was about to begin, again. I crept over to turn off the buzzer and heard the familiar NPR reporter's voice describe a firefight, in Baghdad. It happened several years ago; the soldier's family was seeking justice. For what, I didn't hear; the drone of fear in my head snarled until it howled.

It wasn't just my dream of his death that had me menaced; it was my deft acceptance of the news. And on a chill, foggy day in the fall, one like today, I'd dreamed my dispassion in detail. How I'd pushed a cart through the doors of New Seasons, the grocery chain committed to providing the best local farmers had to offer. How I'd bought the darkest fair-trade chocolate, a loaf of organic whole-wheat bread. Sourdough, probably, and I'd watched the shoppers maneuver their bikes and hybrid SUVs through the tiny southeast Portland parking lot and wondered blearily, *What do they know?* No accusations, just curious. *What? What do you know?*

They know a lot, my people, here. They know which fish are rated 'Green, best choice' and how to brew an IPA. They know what, exactly, Barack has done and when George W. lied. They can recite lyrics of songs of bands whose names you've never heard; they can wind a skein of yarn, and spin, and dye it, too. I know a woman with three recipes for deodorant. I know a man who catches swarms of wild bees.

They don't know soldiers. It's a foreign war and there are foreign people in it. The military wives I find in books, in newspapers, on my Twitter stream are textbook models, forever buying a new couch in a new city, used to cold temperatures and the empty looks in their children's eyes as they drive across the interstate to another home. They know all the acronyms and that you're supposed to keep a power of attorney form in the front of your family file folders. They have words for departures and reunions that are better than mine. "Hail and farewells," I read, "the singular distinction of loving, and being loved by, an American soldier." These women are heroines, leading ladies; their faults belong in a job interview: "too loyal," perhaps, "loves husband more than self." I read how much they ache for their departed soldiers, how when they look at their children and see their father's eyes, their knees go weak, their lungs deflate. They call them "my man," they scramble for the phone, they stock an admirable care package.

Not me. I made a package once this summer and put brownies in it I'd made with maple syrup and spelt flour and barley. I put in drawings the boys had made, two shirts from his dresser drawer, and a note I wrote hurriedly, complaining, probably. The postal worker gave me a stack of ten, flat-rate military boxes, which I toted up a long hill home on my bike, proud of my feat of strength. If I ever send anything inside, I'll save two dollars a pop. Self-absorbed, distracted by my domestic theater from the one overseas, wrapped up in the passions of three boys, who ask for pumpkin pie, who ask for hours on the playground, who ask for honey vanilla mint ice cream. Me, I'm all hero.

Like my forebears in the epic tales of war, I have fatal flaws by the bushel. Was it Achilles's heel that sunk him? It made him mortal, sure, but it was his hissy-fit that nearly buggered the Greeks. Agamemnon, selfish to the bone, won the war but lost his friends, his life, all for the sake of a slave girl. His wife murdered Agamemnon, king of men, in a rage. Even Hector, breaker of horses, swift of foot, with a helmet that gleamed in the sun: he killed the wrathful Achilles's friend; he would not listen to his wife's remonstrations; headstrong Hector of the quenchless fury was chased, caught by Achilles, slashed through the neck where the end of life comes the quickest. No helmet, bronze and glancing in the sun with all its brightness, could save him then. Struck, pierced, ripped, lopped, belching bloody meat, they all die in the end—fair-haired, valiant, strong, and powerful, every godlike last one of them.

My hair is fair, my arms are white and freckled, my heroic epithets are plentiful. I am Sarah, keeper of chickens, washer of dishes, peeler of tomatoes, she who scrubs the floor of its stains of mud, chocolate, pee. My heroic tasks are more plentiful than any Eurystheus could devise. Here is what I am doing for the war effort: making jam by the pint-dozens, scrubbing mold from the icebox drawers, lugging compost in buckets and shovelfuls, slicing apples, tying shoes, putting up two-and-a-half quarts of a rich onion beef stock. For you, America, I meet with teachers and counselors and principals and occupational therapists; my patriotic duty demands I keep full the bin of thick-cut oats.

Serving my country with my carrot peeler, with whisk broom, heady with the glory from picking up two boys from school, I have no time to count the days until his return. Epistolary romance is limited to the photos I put on his Facebook wall, the moment of flush when my oldest says, at wrestling club, "My dad taught me this and I'm GREAT." Everett is indeed great at the Army crawl. His dad would have liked that, were he here, I think with pride unhampered by longing. In many ways it's good, our separation: he's spectacularly competent at his job; he's decorated and well-loved; he understands the nuances and internalizes the procedures and fits, round piston-peg in round hole, in the Army's engine. At home, he is the tragic hero, or even the archetype's antithesis, unable to find his conforming spiracle in our chaotic machine. Boys vibrant, spinning in bursts of never-spent energy, jumping on and off things they shouldn't, making demands on love, patience, self-assuredness, shoulders, the small of my back—demands more than we ever could have conceived. Kicking, poking, shouting, grunting, wrestling, hop-hop-hopping with rage and joy and fluster and a subconscious zapping need: they take everything a mother has, and twice what their father does. It's easier apart; the play at home is writ for one bard only. I sing it with gusto.

I sing it with a peculiar kind of grief.

Looking for my lost loneliness, I rend, tear flesh, devour bits of the lives of other military women-at-home. I find some wives get wrapped up in rank; they look down their noses on the families of a private first class. I didn't know this until my husband was already a sergeant, a noncommissioned officer in charge, proficient in driving an armored GMC truck faster than is strictly allowed by military protocol and with full authority over the Word document whose fields are populated by the Excel sheet his commanding officer maintains on the shared server in his office. Should I lord it over the specialists' wives? It doesn't come easy, this; I tip it all into the bright and thunderous sea.

Am I cut from a different cloth, am I a wandering stranger in this foreign realm, have I any right to claim the trope of the waiting wife? I cast off the shroud of Penelope and lift high the garments of a thousand women and men, Aegeans and Acheans and Trojans and the pioneers from the Oregon Trail. Piecing together a cloak of many virtues and flaws, textures and hues in comforting chaos, home in my lyrical, unepic battle arena. Sarah, constant, changeable, keeper of passions, bearer of woes, she of the loud voice, she who wipes the tears of young boys, wife of an Army Reservist at war.

Bone Flute

KARINA BOROWICZ

We find things, change things. A flute
from a bird's hollow bone. Slanted through
braided hair, a long white feather.

How fascinating our early selves, their leavings
in display cases. Our tarnished
Roman coins. The red shards
of our pottery. Our first attempts
at glass, the small perfumeries peeling in layers
of mica. An iron key, like a lost tooth.
The lid that it fit still buried,
locked in the earth.

How many other things a museum can't contain—
not one vivid dream of the Illyrian girl who wore
this bronze spiral bracelet survives. The soft tissue
of a laugh. An intricately woven song, popular
among the women of her village, frayed and lost.

Emptied of the purpose that once breathed
through it, the bone flute
has come to rest. Here, upon a mound
of black velvet.

Brush and Ink Herd of Horses

KARINA BOROWICZ

Here is a man who has run
his hand along the neck of a horse
watched the streaming mane
gallop away

learned a poem of hoof beats
copied it down in bold
fluid strokes
on the unrolled sheet of rice paper

and with the horses he suffers
the bit burning his mouth
the slicing whip against his thigh
the nails pounding
up through his bare feet
as he drives the horsehair brush
over the blinding tundra of paper

this is how he comes to love freedom

Goldfish and Palette, Matisse, 1914

RICHARD JARRETTE

It is said to have begun as a self-portrait
after Cezanne, but Matisse
erased himself from the scene
leaving an empty balcony, some Cubist
abstractions, two goldfish in a bowl, and his thumb
hooking a white palette.

I believe that his mind was flowing out over
the balcony as he disappeared
because thirty-seven million people
were about to die in a war,
close by more millions of horses and mules,
carrier pigeons, dogs,

and that the self-portrait of a great artist
in his moment
would be the fragment of a man
and two fish, one studying the tangerine,
placed against the bowl,
with its left eye.

Living in Perilous Times

RICHARD JARRETTE

Six inches of the seas have lifted
into the sky and rain down.

Reuters

Shafts of late light pool on the path.
Woodpeckers nail evening shadows
to trees and telephone poles.

I was the baby of the family and never
knew what was going on, or why.

John Coltrane said he would ask
Thelonious Monk questions with his horn
and get answers to questions
he never thought to ask.

The doe with the split ear listens
in three directions while foraging
under the oaks.

I once heard William Stafford say,
"Maybe some things happen because
we're paying attention."

Do you think this means we're going to be
alright, little cabbage white?

Maybe if I just calm down
birds will land on my shoulders
and the one-eyed yellow cat
will leap into my arms and talk.

Bellwether

MARK ROBERT RAPACZ

The sheep had trouble crossing the crick. It'd been flooded since early spring and the foot boards had washed downstream with the winter melt, so they had to ford it. My sister Louanne crossed to the other side first, and with her breeches soaked she made no sign that the icy chill bothered her.

"Paul, Goddamnit! You stay over there and guide these sons a bitches. Count 'em going in. I'll count 'em going out."

I could barely hear her on account of the rushing water. It was muddy gray, iron gone liquid, like one long rail gliding to forge somewhere down south. The bank had softened so much that the sheep sank in to their knees. They squealed as I slapped them on their rumps to jump in. The crick was narrow at this point, so it didn't take them more than a few steps to reach Louanne, but the water rushed through in unexpected heaves, as if something sizeable were getting in and out of this tub on some unseen far end. Every so often one of these heaves caught a sheep, tumbling it in the water. Either Louanne or I hopped in and righted it, usually by lifting the dripping critter up and out onto the bank where it scurried off like a spooked mutt.

We worked like this for the better part of an hour as the sheep collected in a clearing in the trees and munched on foliage that would more than likely give them the skitters.

"I'm gonna smack Horace good for that one, you varmint!" she yelled as one sheep nipped at her. She was pulling it out by the ears. "Ya told Pa that this weren't a good idea, didn't you?"

"Yeah, I told him and he told me how else they gonna eat."

The next, she yanked by the throat. "Not every good pasture is on the far side of the crick." Eventually impatient with our progress, she asked, "How many you at?"

"Twenty-seven."

"Good, good. That's what I got, too."

A few of the sheep were still off to my side, and I could hear them tugging at leaves and snipping off twiggy branches as they rustled about. One came and the next, then I hustled three more into the crick. They all looked the same: happy as mules until I booted them into the drink, and then it was all hell and dark loneliness as they floundered blindly into my sister's unforgiving arms.

"I could let them drown while freezing to death, or I can do it my way. Jesus never said saving would be painless."

I turned back, looking for our last one, the thirty-third, but it wasn't to be seen.

"Lou. What're you at?"

"I'm at thirty-two. Send the other over."

I looked back up the path, the one we'd trampled down through the light undergrowth to reach this narrow point in the crick. Then I scanned the foliage reaching off the banks and peered back into the deeper forest that hugged our makeshift trail. Not a black or white thing was seen.

"Count again!"

Louanne cursed me right after she cursed our pa—but before the sheep—which meant her most unpleasant thoughts lay on me. "Get off your ass, Paul. We only got thirty-two."

It wasn't her command that made me stand, it was the thought of our pa and the knowledge he'd have after we penned the sheep for the coming night. Someone would have to tell him before he went drunk.

Louanne had an answer before I could ask her anything. "There ain't a damn thing we can do about it. By the time we find it, it'll be drowned and bloated and on the other side of Buckthorn Township. Sheep ain't dumb enough to go running off."

She stood a moment longer, ruminating. True to her nature and true to her being the eldest, she said, "I'll take it this time."

It was getting on late morning, the sun already burning the cool out of the trees and the dew out of the grass, by the time I found Louanne. Pa was in his room off the kitchen, asleep and sobering. Outside, the sheep looked scared, likely taking their demeanor from their leader, Horace. I couldn't place him in the bunch since they all looked so wretched. Sheep don't have faces that tell they're worried. It's more a feeling they give off, something Louanne and I had a talk-through concerning.

She was in the barn. The only reason that matters is there was no work to do in the barn at this time. She wasn't crying any, but she was beating the hell out of a horse blanket with the handle of a spade. Dust and bits of hay flew off. Nearby, a pile of rugs and work blankets was draped off a bench, never looking so clean.

She stopped when she heard me come in.

"We oughta kill him while he's asleep," I said.

She beat the blanket a few times more and then chucked the handle toward the nearest corner. The spade didn't quite make it. It slapped down, startling us both. She waited a breath before she spoke. "That's the air that makes the crack. It's going faster than time." She was talking quiet, barely to me if at all, like she had a habit of doing when she was alone in the fields with the sheep.

"He's dead to the world already. We go in there with a pitchfork or an axe. We could have it done before lunch and have him buried by supper. Hell, we'll cook Horace for dinner. Use his bell as a servant's call."

Floating in a way I never seen her walk, she drifted to the open door and leaned against the thick oak jamb. Her tendency was to lope along, dragging her heels one moment and nearly skipping the next. There was no logic to her movements, but this time she moved like she did when she showed up in my dreams.

"He didn't hit me, Paul. He didn't do nothing of the sort."

"Then what's this all about?"

Looking back at the pile of beaten and bedraggled coverings, she said, "Cleaning up is all."

"Pa wasn't mad about the sheep?"

"Nah."

"He knows about the sheep, right?"

"Yeah, he does."

"Then where's our punishment? Where's the justice he always talks about?" I paced between the horse stalls, kicking up dust. "He was drunk, Louanne."

The sheep pen stretched out in front of the barn, the fence an extension of the northern wall. Their black heads snuck through the middle rungs one-by-one, sniffing what was going on.

"I just got tired of the beatings, Paul. We figured another way."

To ease the tension, I spoke more on his murder while those beady-eyed sheep tottered their heads back and forth like they understood human situations. Louanne did not delight in my gruesome plots to kill our father. She just stared off and said that'd be nice every so often. The sheep soon tired of our fantasies and snuffled and guffawed amongst themselves. Eventually, I also tired of my descriptions of exposing my pa's entrails to the world by hanging them from a weather vane. The silence broke the air fragile.

"I thought that one would get you going for sure," I finally said.

Louanne smiled and said, "Your ideas always do, Paul." She drifted toward the sheep pen and gently lifted the latch, but she did not yell and call them all good-for-nothing bastard coots, as was her way. They were guided out, not by slapping and hisses, but by her open palm. Horace timidly licked her hand to see if she tasted safe. After a moment of quiet expectedness, as they huddled at the edge of the fence, they all shuffled through the gate and moved silently down the road, following my sister.

A few weeks later, Pa helped me to tend the field and livestock while Louanne stayed back to prepare a meal. This usually meant he had no money, so the day would go on fairly well until sure enough there was a sheep that didn't look right. Something in the eye, he'd say. Something in how it couldn't keep up. According to his expertise, such an animal was only days from coming down with a deadly illness. Selling it off now would do us all some good.

"See that there. See the gimp in her step. That ain't right." He jogged a few paces to catch up to the sheep meandering away from us, up a shadowy crest, heading toward the fading light still blazing on its southwestern side. He caught one right before the crest, a sheep that looked as sure-footed as the rest. He then flipped her over in the usual way. He could always set them better than me or Louanne, smoother and quicker, a skill I attributed to the extra length in his arms.

She was down and splayed, bleating her warnings like a grinding wheel jammed with oil-gunked rust. It was unnatural if you'd never seen a sheep sheered, but Pa had his way and his way was in his bones.

"Come 'ere," he said. "You got a knife?"

I gave it to him. He had her head crooked under his armpit, as if he was about to sing her to sleep. Her foot was folded up and he was inspecting it, scraping off the mud and detritus with my blade. As I came close, he looked up in a way to place blame.

"What?" I said.

"These sheep are yours and Louanne's, ain't they?"

"They're all ours."

"Well, I entrusted them to you."

People always talk about the eyes in a person, whether they're there or they ain't, whether they can see through you or not at all. Well, our Pa had all those eyes that people talk about and it was difficult to meet them full on.

"Sure. She ain't lame, though." I had grown four inches over the summer. Not quite filled out through the chest and back, but Pa wasn't much taller than me at that time. "Me and Louanne know what you want. You don't gotta go through your show anymore. We know you want money for booze. Just say it. We don't care no more."

Pa slid the knife between the toes to continue with his cleaning. From her heel to her toe, he scraped off swaths of her black foot, trimming it down to the invisible cause of its rottenness. Every so often she would squirm and scream louder than I heard a sheep scream before. A few sheep stopped at the top of the crest and looked back, but they couldn't see us. We might as well have been stumps and rocks to them.

"You got me pinned, huh, son? You got me pinned like I got her here?"

I moved close to inspect his handiwork and to show him I could back up the things I say. The moment I stood by him, Pa stopped abrupt, the sheep making a strange pig-like noise, and I found my own knife only inches from my nose.

"I'm well aware of who you think I am."

The blade was a breadth away, and a gash wouldn't have been anything new.

Still, I did not move. We remained like this until it was clear the sheep could no longer handle our human peculiarities, so Pa returned the knife to its purpose with a quick slice between her toes.

A smell rose out of that sheep's foot. I did not pinch my nose, but I must've made a look.

"You smell that?" Pa asked.

"Yeah." It was the smell of cheese decaying in a bog.

"And that's the smell of a sheep that's right as rain?"

The noises increased in that poor beast and her twists, more violent. Pa squeezed tighter, putting her in an off-kilter sleeper hold meant only for a four-legger since the joints of a sheep don't move like that of a man. "You hold her hind legs now. She's not gonna appreciate this right off."

I gripped her tight as we laid her flat on her back. Pa stood over her and crouched, hovering above her chest as he got a better view of the lame foot. He pierced the blade in and a fluid oozed out, but she made no noise. All this field surgery my father did as the light begun to fail us and the herd traveled farther from us.

When it was done, the sheep leaped up like a playful dog. At first she was careful how she stepped, then went on regular-like.

"When's the last time you checked for rot?"

I couldn't answer him because I don't believe we ever had.

"That could infect the whole herd, you know." He still held the knife as if he were a doctor curing the world of all its disease.

"Louanne mentioned something about that—the foot rot—just the other day."

"Did she?"

"Sure, she did."

He slapped the hilt back in my hand as if he knew I was looking to stab something as well. My arm went dead, nearly paralyzed with shame as Pa went after the herd that was somewhere down in the gully by now or lazing on the other side of the hill. He loped the way Louanne used to, skipping toward the setting sun, pleased that he'd brought one sheep from florid decay. I could have rushed him and stabbed him in his back if it wasn't for him turning to tell me one last thing.

"When we get back, prepare a zinc bath for that ailing foot so we won't have to sell her in town. Make up for the one you lost."

He disappeared on the side of the hill before I decided to catch them. I could hear him whistling.

Louanne was getting bigger. She was filling out in her chest and belly and bottom, curving like a woman and becoming how I supposed our mama would've looked. One afternoon we were in the kitchen, Pa was snoozing, and it was drizzly outside. Wind picked up unexpected and chilled the air, turning a summer day into straight fall with a few quick breaths.

"You eatin' more?" I asked.

She was by the stove, mixing in flour to thicken up a lamb stew. "Excuse me?"

"You. You're fleshenin' up. You eating more?"

Her womanly tasks became slower for a while, contemplative. "I suppose so."

"Just wondering is all."

Her spoon clanked the edge of the pot softly, resonating like a bell as she scraped the bottom to keep the potatoes from sticking.

After a while Louanne asked me to go wake Pa for our meal.

His room smelled so much like Pa it would make you gag. Sour with man sweat unless the windows were open, which let in the boggy smells of the wetlands and deadened the sourness in the air. This neither worsened the room nor made it better, it just mingled two different fumes of decay—man and earth.

"Get up." I nudged his shoulder. He made no sound or movement. "You been drinkin'? Get up!" I dug my finger deeper between one of his shoulder blades.

His arm raised toward me and lazily swatted at me.

"I mean it. Louanne's got stew on."

The groggy son of a bitch rolled. "Oh, Paul," he said and continued with a few indecipherable mumblings. Finally wiping his face down a few times with his dry palms, the stubble making crackly noises as he did it, he said, "I had a dream."

"So what." He always had dreams.

"Would you like to hear it?"

I turned and walked out.

Everything was set at the table and we even had heifer milk because we ended up selling the gimped-up sheep, anyway. After her zinc bath and a week of healing, she still had the signs, as Pa said, so it was better that she ruined someone else's herd than our own. Plus, we'd come away with a tidy profit.

The stew was in the big cast iron and the bread was all cut up and warm and slathered with lard. There were plenty of root vegetables softened in the stew, and the lamb was tender. The milk was fresh and made talking difficult. Despite the goodness that Louanne worked so hard to provide for us, she could not take a bite.

"Louanne," Pa said. "Eat some of this. You worked hard and it's marvelous. What a meal. I had a dream of this very meal not a moment ago and here it is." His face was creased with self-satisfaction, as if his genie dreams and not Louanne's hard work was the thing that made the dinner so.

"Paul's noticing I'm getting bigger," Louanne said.

Though he spoke to her, he turned his attention to me. "Really? Well, who wouldn't notice that you're becoming a woman. We should be happy. It's about time we had another woman around the home."

The silence in her became a whimper and then a sob and then my pa was yelling at her to shut it and save it for another time. "Not this. Not now!"

Louanne's sobs became bleating wails, and soon she left and went into Pa's room, the bread still on her plate.

I reached for Louanne's bowl after I finished mine, but as I touched her stoneware, my wrist was caught and twisted. Pain shot through the joint.

"Women are sensitive about their bodies," Pa said. "You should know this as a young man." He held my wrist a moment more, taking a few nibbles of bread with his free hand. Crumbs tumbled down his chin, some getting stabbed and caught in his two-day growth.

My eyes had trouble looking away from my hand. Something messy was happening with its fleshy color. "I know why she's bigger, Pa. I know it ain't no Christian magic that's bringing another child under this roof."

He flung off my hand as if he were tossing it away into the sand. His own chapped hands pawed at his watery eyes. I went in to check on my sister, who lay in the room full of foul smells, a room that had borne us into this world, and soon would do the same for my own flesh-and-blood sibling.

For months we got along fine. It was the winter months, and though we were miserable and cold, we spent much of it indoors and together. Pa was withdrawing from the booze, changing himself for the better through deprivation and fits of illness. During the time of Louanne's magic growth, as he maintained outright, he determined that being a father and grandfather, melded as one, meant something more profound than being alone or drunk.

While Louanne nursed him, I did the sheep raising, the wood chopping, and the brunt of the chore hauling. The home ran its fire off my sweat and the sheep stayed healthy off my aches, and all the rest was done from Louanne's goodness. Most especially, making Pa whole again. She grew as the cold wind blew. Many nights while Pa was in his delirium, we warmed ourselves near the stove.

"This must've been how it was," Louanne said more than once. What she meant was what it must've been like with our mama and our pa before she passed and Pa became the man we knew.

"I should be drunk."

"No, Paul. No, you should not. You spend one second in that room with Pa, sick as he is, and your lips will fall off your face from fright."

The wood shifted in the stove.

"We always wanted to kill the man," I said. "We could right here now. You spend so much of your energy trying to save the bastard when you know he's just gonna take to drinking soon as the child can crawl and then what'll he do to it? Same as he done to you?"

"Not no more. Not this again, Paul." She shied away from me. "Things are different. I told you then and it's the same now. Now we just head on."

"Head on to what?"

Them heavy logs were being eaten ragged by the fire and I wondered where their heaviness went after the fire ate it. All I could figure was it went to nothingness, which was about the same place we were all going to in the end.

"It don't matter," I said.

"What don't?"

"That you and Pa don't know where we're heading and you don't know how it's all gonna be when the child comes."

"I know how it's gonna be."

Glow light came out of the knobs and switches and from the creases in the stove. It lit her up in beautiful ways. She carried herself like she always had, like the flesh was always in her. "It's gonna be like the fire in the stove. Everyone knows fire burns away all the unnecessaries around a thing and leaves only the Jesus dust it took to make it." She stared at me in the half-light. "Shush, Paul. Forget it. Right now Pa's in bed sweating out a past he don't ever want back and we're in here sweating for a home we finally find desirable. We're burnin' off what we never needed."

"What's that supposed to mean?"

"Jesus, Paul, I could draw it on a length of string and thread it through your eyes and you still wouldn't see it."

The logs burned down and the stove begun to cool before either one of us spoke again. Little noises reminded me that the world gone unseen can never rest. The heat whirled in the stove like a fiery twister, its metal dinging and tapping in agitation. The creature noises outside were drowned by the needle rain that spackled against our window panes. Words hung on our tongues.

This moment collapsed. Hackles exploded from the darkness of Pa's room. Quick rustles and the creak of his bed were followed by confused murmurings that sounded like a game bird felled and warbling through its blood.

"Maybelle," the voice said. "Water."

Louanne's body stiffened, which somehow—by the power she's always had—made clearer the sights in our little house. What once was dim now was bright. What once was concealed by the foggy smoke was dispersed. It was as if a quill-covered sun suddenly rose to the peak of our ceiling and shone down, burning away what Louanne would call the unnecessaries.

"He's had a terror," she said, staring toward the door. "He's just a sick man coming off a life of booze. He ain't ever been more than that."

She hucked up her dress, filled a basin with water, and disappeared into Pa's room. A few muffled things were done to him in the darkness. Then a match was struck and a gas lamp lit. I only had a partial view of Louanne and Pa, framed as they were by the twilit doorway. She sat by him and felt his head, then wet the rag and dabbed him.

"It was that dream, Maybelle. That same damn dream," he said.

"Shush, shush, Pa … This here's Louanne."

Pa's voice had dropped somewhere below the vocal box, somewhere deep in the chest. It pained him to talk.

"Maybelle," he called her again. "Hold my hand."

Louanne did so.

"Like all them terrors before—Oh, Jesus!—I were reading the Book of Eternity!"

"Now there, Papa, just a terror—just a dream. You rest and warm yourself. Here." As Louanne lay down beside him, her head disappeared behind the doorframe. Only her legs were visible. "'Tis nothin' but the dead playing tricks with the thoughts of the living."

Pa was quiet, still stuck between worlds.

"Pay them dead souls no mind," she bid him.

I did not move from my stool. Some unknowable force had reached us. This here was the death of our pa as true as the ice flecks that had begun to scratch like hobnails on our panes, truer still than the light that danced from dark corner to dark corner, looking for space to hide. No longer would Pa force my hand, making me the murderer I expected to become. The booze that drained from his veins, out his pores, like the wine out a ragged thin bladder, created in me a sense I had not known for some time. I was happy.

His voice went on, becoming clearer with each hack and wheeze. He was saying things to Louanne that she seemed to understand.

I crept nearer his door to hear the words of Pa, which filled him with greater intoxications than the booze leaching from his skin. After months of draining, you'd expect he'd be shriveled like a dried slug, but here he was, virile and energetic as ever after weeks of cold sweats and delirious rants.

" … I dreamed of that book. Of scripture. A hundred times I must've had this dream. God Fearers alive!—My dream is true."

"But, Papa—" Louanne said, nuzzling into him.

He rolled to face her. "Dead or no, we brought this world new life, Maybelle. A glorious sight if there ever was one … All regrown from the earth here." He motioned around as if our decrepit and failing farm was the very place of the Beginning. "And the man and woman started again with child." He left it at that, supposing it sufficient for forgiveness, and perhaps for Louanne it was. But to me it only furthered the mystery of his fever dream and the treachery this family let grow like rotten gourds.

I walked out into the cold drizzle, my hatred for Pa receding some and settling on Louanne. There was nothing in her that had changed as far as I could see. She did not move. She did not say anything to my father. I had a feeling, a wave of movement descending on our household, as if the threads that tie this world together had suddenly tightened—or snapped—I cannot say, but I knew Louanne as its cause. As she lay next to my father with their unborn in her belly, she changed from one thing to the next as if her deeper spirit was a pile of tattered clothes. This child of theirs was to be raised without shame. All eyes would be averted from our farmstead for good because it was she who had chosen, who had rescinded the rightness we were born with.

Some of the sheep were standing at the fence. The sleet collected on their backs and glistened in the moonlight. Their black heads bobbed and they mewed in protest of the cold or the dark or both. I petted Horace, acting dog-like, nuzzling and licking, his teeth scraping at my palm as if I held a bit of carrot.

Finding none, he nipped me. I walloped him with my open palm, sending the whole herd scurrying to the far corner of their pen. Disappointed in myself, I turned to go back in, but my home was no longer one I recognized, the candlelight flickering like beast eyes guttering in a hollow.

Well before daybreak I awoke still in the sheep's pen. I was alone but for Horace, who jumped up the moment I stirred, a noticeable gimp in his movements as he scuttled toward the rest of the stupid creatures that had left us some time in the night.

In early April, Louanne went to bed with labor pains. She spent a week in Pa's room, telling him what to do and how to do it. She screamed, he soothed, and I was in the pasture when it was born.

Pa didn't go out much to do the heavy work afterwards. He preferred to work in and around the home—puttering as I called it. He'd fix wobbly stool legs and build little shelves. If you went around back he'd be there scrubbing the wash, coming in with cold, blue hands that he'd warm by kneading dough or rolling tallow into candles. His hair had lost its shine and dark color, and wrinkles crept across his face. His posture matched the position his chores put him in: hunched. Where once he did his duties mean-spirited and crudely, he now accomplished them lightly, carefully, as if each were part of one long task never to be fully done.

After an evening of chores, I found him straddling a bucket, his hat pushed back and his sleeves rolled up. He moved a paring knife dexterously across the curves of a potato, hardly looking at what he was doing. Peels dropped limply into the bucket or stuck to his forearms, hanging to him like leeches.

He looked up. "You been out long."

"Broken fence post down near the road." I moved toward Louanne's room.

"Don't," he said as he wiped down his arms, leaving slicks of white slime. "They're both finally sleeping." He stood up, not fully, but as high as he could and he worked the creaks out of his back. "How 'bout if I make Louanne some marrow broth? We need her spirits up for the baby."

"That'd be good," I said. "Probably should give her more than old bones and potatoes, though."

"Yeah, yeah." He sat back down on the stool and straddled the bucket. "Horace has been limping."

"Been gettin' worse," I said.

"Caught it just in time, then." He thought a moment longer and then resumed his work.

I left him to begin a miserable evening of slaughter, eviscerating the only sheep we'd ever given a name.

Masonry

GRACE BROGAN

Pick the stones first.
Lotta people go t' the quarry.
We've got some piles 'round the yard
from what the field's turned over.
When you're pickin' stone
pick 'em to fit.
Not match.
Fit.

Dig a li'l ditch—
not much deeper
than the one we dug for the fence post.
Pour the footing:
one part cement—
four parts gravel—
two parts river sand.

Need some lime in the sand
for the mortar to be flexible.
Mix it till it's like Ma's butter.
Just smooth 'nuff to spread.
Firm 'nuff to sit in its place.

Base stone.
Bed stone.
Don't forget the weep holes
for the wet days.

Use a trowel to spread the mortar.
I just use my hands—damn near a trowel now.
Do it single wythe.
Lay the stone staggered.

Can't build a stone wall too high
or it'll be dead weight.
Build it to hold
things together;
not keep 'em apart.

If We Are Human Then Let Us Be Fools

TRAVIS MOSSOTTI

I.

If my father had told me the secret
I'd pass it on now.

Instead,
I'm just another abandoned zinc mine
in the middle of the country,

gladiolas on my wife's Sunday dress,
liver spot on the left wrist

of the dead bartender
who baptized me five nights a week
for nearly ten years. I was devout.

My father told me not to hoot with owls.
My father told me to soar with eagles.

I ordered chicken wings and called it
a compromise.

Even if he hadn't been off hopping
from city to city
selling kitchen implements,

even if he had been a fixture
on the couch each weekend:
lazy bastard, womanizer, creep—

anything. My father told me
that dedication and spite
were tributaries emptying into the same river.

My father told me that love was just an axe
that can't chop wood for shit.

II.

Because you've failed to notice the orchards
dropping their bayonets each autumn,

you've come here for advice.
If we are human then let us be fools.

Let us keep turning to each other
like children
pausing for answers to questions that always begin

and end with why. When winter comes,
you'll know it's your wife's birthday.
When spring shows up, buy it a drink.

Spend the summer watching a field of wheat
fill its golden lungs
with soil.

III.

He stares out from a hotel
towering some strange city

and thinks of his wife
and children. He follows

the smokestacks littering
the industrious part of town

all the way up until they hit
clouds and begin to dream.

He recalls what his father
told him and feels the metal

in his chest grow brittle.
He sinks back into starched

linens and disappears each
night, just like that.

Leaving Home

GEORGE FRIEND

After the last six cows were loaded on the trailer
And after we took a breather in the clear, cold sunshine,
　　Our feet numb in our spattered Wellingtons and
　　The weak winter sun still leaving everything frozen.

After he asked to buy the cattle directly from me
Instead of taking them on to the auction,
　　And I had agreed, and we'd found a price.

After he wrote me a check for my last few girls,
And I took it and looked up at the rolling eyes
　　Peering out between the aluminum slats.

And after we'd had our handshake, and I was leaving
To walk down the lane from the empty barn,
　　My friend turned, and smiled, and softly said:

"Well, George, now you're out of the cattle business."

The Great Flood of Crawford County

GEOFF COLLINS

After many years, the father returned home at dawn from his high, cold mountain. He brewed a pot of strong coffee and moved his bishop to trap the queen's pawn. Waiting for his next move, he revised the final stanza of his song. As the sun rose, he went to repair the porch railing, but his oldest daughter met him near the mailbox and asked, "Where have you been?" While he thought of an answer, she turned into a butterfly and flew away. On cue, the spring peepers emerged from the mud, singing their love songs. He took the claw hammer from his belt and drove a nail.

Breathing once, another year passed. The ink pen he used to butcher spring calves suddenly changed color at dusk. He could not go through with it. His enemies were strangers who had known him since before he was born. They gathered from all the villages and townships to stand beside him in the hickory pews and sing the old-time hymns. His wife at the porch railing held out her hand. He climbed toward her for many days, reaching out across the dusty hills, praying over the bones of his ancestors, and swallowing the many cold rivers that ran swiftly out onto the prairie.

Finally, there was peace. The middle daughter knit him a threaded heart that would protect him forever. When his dead son came striding up the long driveway, the father's smile reached the heavens. Everything was forgiven and they sent for the fatted calf. Time was just a knotted bracelet on a thin wrist, black and purple, a bit frayed at the ends. It was nothing more than good oak wood chopped and stacked near the back door. Nothing more than a single red leaf falling through the cold air. One morning they awoke and he was gone. The littlest one cried for weeks. Her tears flooded the entire county.

Optickal Allusion

AMES HAWKINS

> *Colours in the Object are nothing but a Disposition to reflect this or that sort of Rays*
> *more copiously than the rest; in the Rays they are nothing but their Dispositions to*
> *propagate this or that Motion into the Sensorium, and in the Sensorium they are*
> *sensations of those Motions under the Forms of Colour.*

Sir Isaac Newton, *Opticks,* 1704

WHITE Colours

> *Lichtenberg says that very few people have ever seen pure white. So, do most people use the*
> *wrong word, then? And how did he learn the correct use? He constructed an ideal use from*
> *the ordinary one. And that is not to say a better one, but one that has been refined along*
> *certain lines and in the process something has been carried to extremes.*

Ludwig Wittgenstein, *Remarks on Colour,* 1950

Before the spectrophotometer, now found in any home improvement store paint department, brought us the gift of color matching, there was my father. He had the same ability to translate the color of an ordinary object—a dish, a shoe, a stuffed animal—into a formula for paint. He was better at this than the machine, because he measured not with math, but with his eye—by what other people would want to see, not by what the fluorescent light revealed. He wasn't just reading color; he was translating human perception, seeing whatever it was that fiber optics, an LED light, cannot. My father conjured and cajoled color, brought it to life—*into* lives—in order to reinforce their meanings.

After reading *Invisible Man* by Ralph Ellison, I never again looked at my father's ability to match paint, an ability I thought of as a kind of trick, the same way. He would add tint to a gallon of white, and I would think about Optic White, the color that the protagonist (a character who never gets a name) is assigned to mix at Liberty Paints; the color used on all of the government buildings and monuments; the white that becomes ultrawhite, überwhite, with the inclusion of a dollop of black. My father had his special formulas, too: Grosse Pointe #1 and Grosse Pointe #2. GP #1 was white with $1/32$ of an ounce of yellow oxide; GP #2 doubled the recipe. "Why yellow?" I once asked him. "Because," he told me, "white all by itself needs to be tempered. White alone is cruel."

RED Object

The first challenge in writing about colors is that they don't really exist. Or rather, they do exist, but only because our minds create them as an interpretation of vibrations that are happening around us. Everything in the universe—whether it is classified as "solid" or "liquid" or "gas" or even "vacuum"—is shimmering and vibrating and constantly changing.

Victoria Finlay, *Color: A Natural History of the Palette*, 2002

I grew up in a three-story, red-brick colonial in Grosse Pointe Park, Michigan: 1262 Whittier, where my father, an interior designer, enacted a particular version of normalcy by constantly redecorating the rooms. My favorite room in the house was the first-floor half bath. I really can't remember the wallpaper, but my father tells me it was a Chinese print. I know the sink had a marble basin, the toilet an oak seat, and the whole room itself was no bigger than a closet. If you turned the water on before you sat down, you could wash your hands while you peed. The most distinctive feature of the room was the ceiling. Using twenty-five yards of a faux moiré, a polyester fabric woven to look like watered silk, he suspended tension rods on all four sides of the ceiling, gathered the fabric to the center in a sort of reverse canopy, and hung the fabric in plenteous folds from the edges to the middle. At the focal point of the gathering, he hot glue–gunned a long-petaled, rosette-style flower that had to have measured eight inches across. The color (the name of which he still remembers: Beach Plum) was a deep red with yellow undertones. Those with a perfect color wheel—a sort of artistic counterpart to perfect pitch—can picture it. For everyone else, let's just say it was a kind of dark red that complemented, yet did not match, what you know to be Chinese red.

The reality of this ceiling treatment was that it lowered the eight-foot ceiling about a half-foot.

It was here, before I thought anything about my own latent lesbianism, that I sat on the toilet until my legs fell asleep, reading in various news magazines about "the Gay Plague" and "the Gay Cancer," the deadly disease of and for homosexuals, heroin users, hemophiliacs, and Haitians. It was here, in a room without windows, with a scarlet sensibility, that I imagined HIV and AIDS as Poe's Red Death: "No pestilence had ever been so fatal, or so hideous." I imagined the seven chambers in the Imperial Suite as rooms in our own home, imagined death coming to a party at our house, blood spilling on the floor of every room. Somehow I already knew that what I was seeing in the photos of the emaciated, purple-blotched men in the magazines was a party to which my dad, years ago, had been invited yet had never arrived, having chosen, at least for now, to leave no forwarding address.

ORANGE Disposition

We said at the beginning, not without reason, that our environment appeared to be colored to us. We did not claim that it was colored. For appearances are deceptive: the world as such is completely colorless. The visible world consists of achromatic substances and electromagnetic vibrations, which are also achromatic and differ from one another only in their wavelength.

Harald Küppers, *Color: Origin, Systems, Uses*, 1972

My father's minivan sat in the driveway, the Design Detroit insignia on the glass nearly invisible in the sun's glare. An unusually warm spring day had lured him into the backyard, where I knew he would be weeding or pruning or planting something. He hadn't yet removed his suit; my mother would be furious if she saw, an exhaustingly familiar complaint of hers that he never paid any mind. His jacket was off, shirtsleeves rolled up, shovel in hand. He dislodged great chunks of earth near the side of the garage. He excavated and uprooted tiger lilies— day lilies some people call them—wrenching them from their home under the eaves where they had thrived long before we moved in. He vigorously shook the long, slender leaves, fibrous stalks, and carroty flowers to free the rich black dirt, the "keeper" in the maneuver.

He felt me standing behind him. Without turning around, he said, "So hideous, aren't they, these outhouse lilies? You have to really dig to get all the roots. These damn things are insidious."

His favorite plants sat only feet away: peonies replete with large green bud-balls covered with ants, whose job was to eat the botanical "glue" in order to free the frilly white flower; the over-splayed remains of tulips—yellow, red, and white— he had intended to crop, only to be sidetracked by the lilies. Pachysandra and ivy were revered, tended, understood. The daffodils dedicated, roses regarded. I didn't understand what he had against the lilies. Was it their lack of respect for other plants, their tendency to grow anywhere? Was it the fact that he didn't really need to tend to them, couldn't trim them? Or, I wondered, as I looked around the yard, did he not like their color?

When I finally read Jeanette Winterson's novel about a lesbian girl in England, and so learned that *Oranges Are Not the Only Fruit*, that all colors of the spectrum are important, I smirked because orange is my favorite color: I own seven orange shirts, orange socks, an orange phone, orange running shoes, a set of orange golf clubs. When, years later, my partner Corrine and I buy a house where my father will move in and criticize the "outhouse lilies" near our front porch, I consider removing them from my yard. When he moves out—I have to ask him to leave— I decide to keep the lilies. Only then do I recognize my love for orange as a starting point for love at all.

YELLOW Rays

Our sensations of colour are within us and colours cannot exist unless there is an observer to perceive them. Colour does not exist even in the chain of events between the retinal receptors and the visual cortex, but only when the information is finally interpreted in the consciousness of the observer.

W.D. Wright, *The Rays Are Not Coloured*, 1967

Why I let my father dye my hair blonde only days before I left for Italy in June of 1984 had something to do with the wordless understanding that I did not possess innate desire for boys, for the male form. I unconsciously decided that looking more "female," whatever that meant, might help with this cultural disjuncture. So, despite my absolute hatred for the way he regarded me as a gender-art project, a way to recraft his masculinity, I assented and presented him with my scalp.

"Hold *still*," he commanded as he worked to fish a lock of hair through one of the many holes in the blue plastic cap with the crochet hook–looking tool. My head pressed down, I stared at the space between the Wolmonized pine planks on our deck and recalled the contractor showing my brother Chad, though I was watching, too, how to use 16d penny nails as spacers between the boards before screwing them into place—"Ya gotta have space for the rain to get through, space for the natural expansion and contraction of the wood." Sunlight diffused through a layer of stratus clouds caused a glare characteristic of a February day, but I still felt the warmth of the sun's rays.

I wasn't moving, I wanted to tell him. His own motions were pushing my skull around. I couldn't anticipate his next move and therefore couldn't brace myself. I wanted to grab his wrists, wrench them away from my head, and thrust them back at him. But for some reason I wanted my hair dyed more than I wanted his hands off me. So, I submitted to the pressure of his fingertips, the desperation in his grip as he turned my hair from pedestrian mouse brown to the more glamorous L'Oreal color: ash blonde.

This would be the first and last time we'd use the cap in the ritual, going all out from that point forward, plastic nozzle pressed directly to the scalp, ill-fitting, plastic-gloved fingertips massaging the foamy blue into the root-line— a practice I'd eventually take over once I went to college, one I'd not cease to practice for four more years, not even after reading *The Bluest Eye*, not even after writing a paper in which I recognized that the blonde, blue-eyed beauty was fucked differently than Pecola Breedlove, but fucked all the same.

GREEN Dispositions

Decorators and designers sometimes tend to be guided by their own subjective color propensities. This may lead to misunderstandings or disputes, where one subjective judgment collides with another. For the solution of many problems, however, there are objective considerations that outweigh subjective preferences.

Johannes Itten, *The Elements of Color*, 1970

My mother stood in the dining room staring at two strips of green wallpaper, two lone pieces that my father had hung before walking away. When she asked about the incomplete status of the job, he said, "It isn't incomplete to me. I can picture what it'll look like now. That's enough."

The two strips of paper created a commotion in our house. It wasn't only the stress that the wallpaper caused, the tangible, visible flashpoint for the tension that always existed between my parents. It was the strips themselves, situated together in the corner, abandoned. I stared at them on a daily basis, pleased by the depth of green, enamored with the silk-patterned print, impressed by my father's skill at matching the seams so that the two strips became one, astounded that he would abandon the project regardless of what my mother said. I remember how they looked in the corner of the dining room, how you could see them from the kitchen, how you also from the kitchen could see a bit of the front door. The spot for experimenting with the paper had been chosen on purpose. My father wanted to know what it would look like from the kitchen, too. He already knew it would work with the living room paper across the foyer; it was the other angle he needed to understand. Interior design as one-night-stand.

My mother tried, for about a month, to get him to finish hanging the paper. "George, this is your business." Or "George, we make too much to have this be half-done." Or "George, can you please just do it because I ask?" Nothing moved him. It was green wallpaper; we all knew it was green. But for my mother, this was "The Yellow Wallpaper," strips of decorative design that had the potential to drive her mad. She was not Charlotte Perkins Gilman, but she *had* been an English major. One day, in order to keep his emerald wallpaper from turning an infuriating shade of ochre, she hired a paperhanger and took care of it herself.

BLUE Sensorium

Blue suggests the form of a circle or sphere. It is cold, wet, transparent, atmospheric. It is further retiring, is poorly focused in vision and usually creates a blurred image on the retina—particularly from a distance. While it may have bulk, it does not lend itself to sharpness or detail.

Faber Birren, *Color, Form and Space*, 1961

On Sunday afternoons in junior high, when my homework was done and I didn't have soccer practice and we weren't driving around looking at houses for sale, I would sit in the small gable in my bedroom and read. For the most part I read horror, stuff by Stephen King, and other titles like *The Keep*, *The Exorcist*, and *Rosemary's Baby*. I particularly remember reading *Jaws* by Peter Benchley, the late-twentieth-century, now-famous story about a giant killer shark off the coast of New England. A story about the crisis in masculinity and the last vestiges of overt sexism before we could admit that either existed.

I am not sure why I sat on the hardwood floor inside the gable rather than in my bed, or on the rug only a few feet away, the blue rug, appearing as cerulean, indigo, cobalt, navy, sapphire, midnight, depending upon the time of day. I loved the rug because it was one of the few aspects of the room I had chosen that represented who I was and what I wanted. I don't know that I wanted "blue" or what that even meant; I do know that this carpet felt solid and secure. Maybe it's because of what my father said about carpets, rugs, and floors: "Ground your room in dark color. Give people something they know they can count on."

Our house stood not quite a mile from the shores of Lake St. Clair, a little body of water that connects Lake Huron with Lake Erie, a decidedly freshwater lake replete with fishflies and freighters, with sailboats and sunsets. There wasn't anything particularly scary about Lake St. Clair—no sharks lived here. But I couldn't help imagine "what if?" What if a shark came to Lake St. Clair? What if a sleek, pewter, prehistoric fish began terrorizing the parks and clubs? What if I came face to face with it, just like Brody, or Hooper, or Quint?

I read the book from cover to cover that day, thrilled by the use of profanity, the blood-scented sex, the intensity of the hunt. But I also know that it wasn't Brody, or Hooper, or Quint with whom I identified. It was the shark itself, the great monster beneath, lurking in the open blue, always on the move. I fit well enough but never felt as clearly delineated by cultural norms as I needed to be, as sharp as is vital in a 1980s heteronormative setting. This is what George, my father, and I had in common—the sense that we, too, could be hunted, tracked, and killed. We were there in this wide open together, hidden yet exposed. He in his marriage and I in my gable. We were nothing and everything alike. We were blurred beneath the blue, at sea.

PURPLE Forms

On the divide between the reddish-yellow and the reddish-blue values sits a color in which Goethe was very interested. It is purple, a bright red color that resolves the polarity between yellow and blue. Words can barely describe purple. It is often called "the color of peach blossoms." The question is whether purple is realized in nature and as a pigment color, or whether it is a theme that nature plays upon, a goal for which it strives. Purple is the zenith of Goethe's world of colors.

Torger Holtsmark, *Goethe's Theory of Color*, 2007

My dad loved television and spent a great deal of time, through the 1970s and '80s, in the family room with me and my brother, watching any number of sitcoms. Among his favorites: *Happy Days, Laverne and Shirley, Bosom Buddies,* and most memorably for me and my brother, *Three's Company*. Jack Tripper (a straight man playing a gay man so that he could share an apartment with two women) prompted from our father a grin so disturbing that we actually gave it a name: the perpetual. "Look, look!" we'd goad one another, bouncing on couch cushions, yelping and pointing like chimpanzees. "Look at Dad. He's doing it again!" My father sat glued to the television, eyes electric, cheeks raised, lips tightened in an upturned crescent, watching John Ritter trip over the couch for the millionth time. "Dad, stop it!" we'd shout. "Dad, you're doing that creepy perpetual grin thing." He'd tell us to be quiet, wave us off, or simply cry out, *"So what!?!"* Sometimes we'd stay and continue to harass him, sometimes we'd leave the room in disgust, sometimes we'd give up and pretend not to notice. Always we wanted it to stop.

Maybe because I was trying to be a straightforward bad-ass like Jo Polnecek or Buddy Lawrence, maybe because I was trying to figure out the answer to a mystery like Velma Dinkley or Sabrina Duncan, maybe because I was trying to illuminate a particular aspect of philosophical/biological truth like Peppermint Patty or Jaime Sommers. Whatever the reason, one day near the end of *Three's Company*'s eight-season run, I asked him the question, simple as that, "Dad, are you gay?"

He answered with a story that could easily be transformed into the plotline for a sitcom. "I am not gay," he told me, because he was cured. He entered re-programming because of pressure from his father way back in the early 1960s. He offered my mother and my brother and me as evidence of the success of his resolve. "I am not gay," he said, "not anymore."

I remember being relieved but not necessarily reassured. None of this felt natural. None of it was funny. I had no language for his denial of our lavender connection. But I did keep watching. I watched and watched. Finally, I recognized what I had been watching for: the apex of honesty in a purple predawn.

BLACK Colour

Black is the color without light, curtain dark, the portcullis-dropping color of loss, humility, grief and shame. Although to the human eye everything visible has a color, where color exists as an optical phenomenon, with a place already constructed for it in the human imagination, what can be said of the color black? Is black visible? Is it even a color? Or in some kind of grim, somehow ruinous thunderclap and with a sort of infernal ghastly force does it somehow smother color? Wholly destitute of color, is it the result of the absence of—or the total absorption of—light?

Alexander Theroux, "Black," *The New American Essay*, 2002

In the basement of our house, a dimly lit, never-decorated space, you could find a world of treasures: tins of buttons, boxes of bows, yards of fabric, jars and jars of homemade pickles, jams, mincemeat. There were bottles of booze from birthdays and holidays at the ready for my brother to pillage when the time came. There were a heavy bag my brother used in order to vent his frustration, and a tool bench my grandfather had made for him. There were a carpet with a brown pattern reminding me of hamburgers, and the radio on which my mom listened to WWJ as she ironed our shirts. There were the cat litter box and an extra stove, a sewing machine, and an old milking stool. Decorations and dishes, tools and thread. Laundry and lace, paint and pillows. Bats and books, suitcases and stain. Unremarkable and undeniable, a mass of things that mattered.

Among these items were what I believed to be the most powerful object in the house: my father's box of oil paints. The box was shaped like a little suitcase with two brass latches, blond in color, plain, without varnish, most probably made of pine. Save for the sixties-esque flower decals on one side, if you saw it today you wouldn't be able to tell whether he purchased this box more than forty years ago—as he did—or just brought it home from the art store yesterday.

I was never, ever allowed to touch the box, or to open it when he was not around. I was never allowed to play with the paints, to experiment with them myself. They were *expensive*, I was told, and messy. If any of them got onto the carpet or my clothes, the stain would not come out.

Recently, as my father lay in his single bed, staring at the ceiling, talking and waving his arms out in front of him, recovering from radiation treatment for cancer, which had spread as a result of advanced AIDS, I was overcome by the urge to rifle through his closet and find the box, to rescue it from its ultimate fate. The box compelled me, not because of the colors, but the caps. The black caps. I wanted—needed—to know whether I might be able to run my thumb along the tiny ridges of the black screw caps and finally remove them to see what was inside.

It was as compelling an action for me as I imagine it had been for dear Pandora. White may be cruel, but black unveils. Desire denied, cravings cauterized, wants wasted, we—my father, mother, brother, and I—lived in our house full of colors, collectively vigilant to keep the bright rays from shattering the dark.

"We Walk through a World Continually Disappearing from View"

—Steven Millhauser

REEVES KEYWORTH

A passage is deleted; the room is out of work.
Seawater laps at the legs of the red chair,
the chair muffles its responsibility to uphold
the little girl, who was in fact a marred and
minor character, best discarded. The red blurs,
north melts into south, and brimming hate collapses
into doubt which vanishes. The painter's brush
falls from her hand, the window goes blank.
There's no point in hoarding odd pieces of wood,
assorted nails, old curtains—it all falls away
at the breathing-edge of the future. Erasure comes
to everything; at the end there's always *fade to white*,
but thanks are offered for the room left bare,
dissolved and dissolving, and the red chair.

Mole

REEVES KEYWORTH

Because he undertakes
to know the illimitable
darkness,

because darkness & dirt
are his sufficiencies,

I choose him.

His hidden progress
writes the Sutra of No-Self
on the illegible earth;

he is unfettered
by nostalgia
for starlight.

Let me study the thrift
of his expectations.

Yellow Post-It Note with the Message: "What If?"

KATHLEEN M. HEIDEMAN

Suppose we avoid mentioning darkness for a while, okay?
No bad dreams, no caverns, nothing to fear, bury, or excavate today . . .

What if it's a relief? We agree on this. Suppose we keep sunlight on overhead
like CNN, but no cathedrals collapsing like failed loaves of bread, no Haitian dead

— *Deep Time?* Abstractions are fine, but no salt mines, no trapped miners,
no rare-earth ore, no ecstatic spelunkers dangling in Yucatan cenotés on slender

cyan threads of poly-static rope, no extremophiles or feathery speleothems
poised to be destroyed by their boot or breath or bacteria, no fission theorems

theoretically abandoned in blasted desert bunkers. No mossy Nordic tombs.
Seriously, who likes reading your dark poems? No catacombs, no karst rooms

strewn with Paleolithic brushes, no master Tenebrists of creosote and tallow.
Trust me. Breathe deep. We'll speak no more of the hand-prints of Lascaux.

Never mind hieroglyph'd mummies, forget Mayan child-sacrifice and intercourse-
with-moon-goddess depicted in deepest Naj Tunich. *Obliterate Dark!* Of course

that's what the vandals cried, we think, the ones with flashlights, using knives
to scratch away soot-painted scenes of prehistoric lives

and vandalize the galleries of Naj Tunich, smearing what scenes remained
with mud as they left, as midnight gangs tag insignia over rival names.

No regrets. Neither Hades nor Minotaur. Give Ariadne back her spool still full
of thread and tell her to cross-stitch something sunny but instructional:

pastoral tapestries with innumerable sheep-paths threading labyrinthine
up the summer hillsides, so many plausible routes for reaching heaven!

What if. No dark burrowing, no worm. Only lambs, fleece still white, a sky
so bright we can't bear looking up, where golden birds are circling, O circling high!

As if some lamb limping far below has caught their eye.

An Easter Poem for Christopher Smart

FRANCINE MARIE TOLF

*The eighteenth-century poet grieved over cruelty to animals, referred
to flowers as the poetry of Christ, and died in debtor's prison.*

Christ's poetry blooms in your garden, Kit,
bluebells and hyacinth, crocus, pinks.
Soft paws of pussy willow climb new branches
as Jeoffry washes his face in a puddle of sun
and the lowliest toadstool sings.

Every ring has been removed
from the nose of every ox.
Bears baited in London theaters
roam mossy forests now, and slaughtered sows
praise God as sows should,
rolling on hairy backs and grunting joy.

This is the heaven I imagine for you,
Christopher. I believe that in Bedlam,
abandoned by all except one small cat,
you heard the tide of that great river
animals cross to come home—
sea turtles and parrots, work horses,
lambs. Vanquished or beaten,
turned into hair combs and glue,
they have risen with you
into nectar light.

Can this kingdom exist?
Let our longing create it.
Somewhere, you are reaching
toward your Savior's outstretched hand.

Paradiso

L. ANNETTE BINDER

His parents took him to Hawaii when he was little. He was only eight, but he remembered the turtles and the heat from the sand and how all the clouds were silver. Even the rain was warm, and he ran into the waves and they were warmer still. This was before his father lost his job and before he went to jail. His mom tried to hold his hand, but Thomas raced ahead. "Be careful," his mom shouted when he went too fast. "Be careful where you step." There might be glass or jellyfish on the sand, and he'd have to see the doctor if he got stung. Her voice was sharp, but he didn't slow down. He went even faster, chasing the waves and falling back when they broke, and she ran with him at the end. She held her sun hat down and moved beside him with a speed he didn't know she had. She looked so happy, happier than he'd ever see her again, and the air was soft from the salt. It raised goosebumps the way silk did. His father was waiting for them on the towel. He cut a mango with his folding knife, and the juices rolled down his fingers. "Try it," he said. "You'll never taste a better thing. Not if you live to be a hundred," and Thomas reached for that sweet fruit.

God rest his father, who died in jail. God rest his mother, too.

He drove in circles from Pueblo up to Denver. He worked his way to the Walmarts and the Targets, the convenience stores on I-25, and he signed the papers they gave him. He showed them his ID or one of the others he carried. Sometimes they gave him looks. One clerk made him wait twenty minutes before she unlocked the cabinet. She was fat with dimpled arms, and her bangs stood up from her head the way girls had worn their hair twenty years before. "Don't come back here," she said. "Buy it somewhere else."

It was getting dark when he came out with his bag. The sky was orange, and he wanted to follow the sun behind the mountains. He'd go to Wyoming if he had the gas. He'd go to New Mexico or the Kansas border and buy his cold medicine there, but nothing was close and nothing was easy and he only had ten packages. After this, there'd be no more money for ingredients or food, nothing for his baby girl who wasn't even one. Danielle had stopped asking about the checks because he wasn't going to send them, and she was with an electrician now who made good money. They lived together in a split-level house. They had everything they needed. Circles up and down the state and he felt a burning behind his eyes. She'd told him once that we're made of stardust, all of us. She watched those astronomy shows on cable. "Every part of you was a star once," she said, "when the world was born." He knew these things from her. The stars grew and collapsed and were born again, and now they were racing apart.

He was careful when he worked. Even when his hands were shaky, he put away the bottles. The lye went back to its spot and the cold compresses and the starter fluid. He reduced things to their elements and flushed the muddy brown water, but sometimes his attention wandered. He thought of Danielle and his girl, Kira. He thought of their dark eyes. He'd missed both their birthdays and Mother's Day, too, and now he'd waited too long. It was too late to send them a card. He shook the tank and let it sit. He shook it and vented it when it was time, and some of the lye hit his skin. Just a few drops along the top of his right hand, and it brought him to his knees. It bubbled up in rivulets. Water made it worse. He scrubbed the blisters with soap, poured vinegar over them, and wrapped them in strips from an old T-shirt. The pain was an anchor he pulled with him to the bedroom. It would be another two hours before he could make it go away.

The neighbors watched him. Some days they said hello and others they walked on by, and there was meaning in this. They were telling him something with their waves, with their laughter and their fights, their crying babies, and how they honked their horns out in the parking lot. He covered his windows with tin foil because the blinds weren't enough. The blinds and the curtains and the Thrifty Nickel newsletters he taped against the glass. They saw through it all, especially the widow across the courtyard. She stayed home all day and watched Jerry Springer reruns with the volume set on high, and she walked around with a parakeet on her shoulder. "I named him Marty," she said, "like my husband. Bless his soul." Sometimes she forgot to put her dentures in, and her face looked like a shrunken apple. She used to bring him brisket and spinach and whole roasted chickens, but she stopped from one day to the next and now she didn't say hello. It was because people were talking about him in the laundry room and down by the mailboxes. They huddled together and told lies.

Nothing mattered and nothing touched him when the batch was ready. His infected hand stopped hurting. Hurry hurry to get it going. Hurry and slow it down and the sun is shining and they're by the water again and all the air is touched with silver. He saw a falcon once flying over the freeway. Riding the updrafts, it hung in the air like a crucifix. That's how he was, every muscle tensed, and nobody knew the effort it took to stay perfectly still.

He lived on Paradiso Circle just behind the Garfield School. Every morning the little girls walked together in their uniforms. He watched them from the balcony, and sometimes he had to hold the railing because his legs were shaking. There was one who looked like Danielle with her shiny black hair. One day Kira would look like that, too. She'd swing her books around and the crossing guard would tell her not to run, but she wouldn't listen. She'd be like him that way. His mother told him to stay away from the stovetop coils and the neighbors' barking dogs. "Be careful with those scissors" and "stay away from your daddy's folding knife." None of it stopped him.

In summertime they went to the Royal Gorge to walk the suspension bridge. He loved to feel it sway. He could see down to the water through the rotted knot holes in the planks. He went to his knees sometimes and worked his fingers through. "Keep moving," she'd say. "You're holding up the line," and she took him by the hand and didn't let go. "We'll go walking on the other side. Maybe this time you'll find a fossil. You can show it to Daddy when we go visit." He wanted to stay there above the water. One thousand feet down, it was only a silver ribbon. He wanted to climb the railing. He always felt the pull of things when they were forbidden. Maybe that's why Danielle was able to stop and he had to keep on going.

He walked around Palmer Lake in the rain. He didn't mind the thunder. The city was draining the water because the concrete had sprung a leak. Halfway to the bottom, they'd already found old steamer trunks and a 1973 VW Beetle. The rain turned to hail, and he kept going and his hand stopped hurting. He wrote her letters while he walked the path. He saw the words as if they were already written. He told her about the trips they'd take when she was older and how the ocean was warm and there were turtles in the water. They'd go together, and she'd see how big they were. Enormous things that were nothing like the box turtles people caught in the sandhills east of town. Not even fifty yards out and the turtles were moving around him, graceful as birds when they turned circles. They came so close he reached out to pet one, but his father pulled him back. There was fear in his father's eyes. He could see it behind the mask, and his father squeezed his hand so hard Thomas felt the bones in his fingers crack. He talked to her about the mangoes and the sun dropping below the water, and every beautiful thing he ever saw he remembered, and he wanted her to hurry. Hurry up and grow because he had so much more to tell her.

The management company posted the notice outside his front door. They taped it over the peephole. He had three days starting tomorrow. They'd file an eviction suit if they didn't get their money. They'd go to the court and get an order, and then the sheriff would come. Thomas took the notice down. The fingers were stiff in his right hand, and he couldn't tear the paper. He went back inside and saw vapors in the air. He noticed them even though the bottles were all closed. They were settling on the walls and in the sofa cushions and he felt them on his skin, too, and they stayed after he took a long shower and rubbed his skin with a towel. Red streaks were rising upwards from his hand. They worked their way around his arm like rivers on a map.

Danielle was waiting at the park. She was sitting at one of the redwood picnic tables by the BBQ pit, and this time she didn't have the stroller or the diaper bag. Teams from the high school were practicing down in the field. Running to the forward line and back again and farther out. They slid because the grass was muddy. In another month the ground would freeze. The coaches shouted and blew their whistles, and their voices carried all the way to the tables.

"Where's Kira?" He sat down across from her. She had a paper coffee cup, but she didn't drink from it. She warmed her hands against it, and she was wearing a ring he hadn't seen before. A gold ring with a round diamond, and when she saw him looking she rubbed the stone with her thumb as if to polish it.

"She's home. Her bottom teeth are coming in." She worried the ring on her finger. It was loose, and she turned it round and round. "She fusses all night and she won't take her bottle."

Thomas looked over her shoulder. The boys were jumping tires now, hopping from hole to hole. One of the coaches pumped his fist in the air. "I was hoping you'd bring her with."

"I've got some pictures." She opened up her phone and worked the buttons. "We went to the dunes last month."

Danielle was in the photo holding up little Kira, and there was nothing but sand around them and the clear September sky. "She looks like you when she smiles," he said. "She already knows where the camera is." He looked at all the photos. Kira in her sun hat and sleeping in her stroller. Danielle was in some of them and the electrician, too. He held Kira against his shoulder, and he looked proud as any father. Thomas gave the phone back. Both his hands were shaking.

"What did you do?" She reached for his right hand. His bandage was loose, and he'd forgotten to hide it under the table.

"It doesn't hurt. I don't even feel it."

She unwrapped the dressing, and she blinked hard when she saw his skin. "You better get to a doctor. I think it looks infected."

"I need a little help this month." The sun came out and went away again, and he could feel the gold from her ring against his wrist. "Five hundred if you can do it. Five hundred and I'm set." The words settled between them.

She set his hand down. "I've got a first-aid kit in the car. I'm going to get some gauze."

When she came back, there was a tightness in her jaw that made her look older than she was. She squeezed some antibiotic ointment onto the gauze, and she was gentle when she wound it around his hand.

"I look like a boxer," he said after she was done. "I guess I'm ready for my fight." He held out his good hand. "You better do this one, too."

Her face was even tighter now, and something was working its way out. "I need to go. Our sitter leaves at five." She pulled her purse up to the table and took out her wallet. "I've got eighty right here. Eighty-seven and that's it." She took out four creased twenties and some singles and pushed them across the table. "This needs to stop," she was saying. "You need to see a dentist. Promise me you will. You need to cut your hair." He knew what she was going to say and what he needed to say back, and these things made him tired. He took the bills she gave him. He held them in his left hand and pretended to listen. They were the only thing keeping him afloat.

He stayed after she was gone and the football players had started packing up their gear. They looked so small without their padding. They looked like boys, and their mothers were waiting with hoodies and water bottles. The park emptied itself and even the dog-walkers left, and he would have slept there if he could. He wanted to lie there and watch the stars as they came out because one day they'd be too far away to see.

There was a man who had to fill his water buckets even though they all had holes. His mother didn't know the names, but she told him all the stories. She told them in the kitchen and when she drove him to school. About the man who pushed the rock and it always came back down and the man who was cursed to be hungry. He ate his children, and he ate his own arms and legs, but he was never full. His body was gone but the hunger remained, and there was no greater curse than that. We have to be happy with the little things, she'd say. We have to be grateful, and her voice shook sometimes. Promise me you'll never steal. Promise me that. He knew then all the stories she told were somehow about his father.

He lived in a trailer with three other people. He couldn't keep things clean. Three people, five people, sometimes six. A group of house painters with dented trucks. A mother who was losing her hair. The faces kept changing, and they didn't put away the bottles. Nobody bothered to tape the lids. The first flakes were falling outside. They were drifting downwards soft as ash. Giant, whirling flurries that melted against the ground. He was cold even when he stood in front of the oven. People complained how it was hot like a jungle in the kitchen. Water ran down the windows and he sweated and shook, and his down parka was heavy from the steam. Danielle didn't answer when he called. The phone rang and rang and the machine didn't pick up, but there wasn't a recording, either, telling him the number had been changed. He took that as a good sign. If he still had his car, he'd go by there. He'd wait outside their door, and maybe he'd play with Kira. He'd show her how to catch the flakes. In fall he'd take her to see the aspens the way his mother had taken him. "Your father needs a reminder," she always said. She pressed them in wax paper and brought them on her visits.

He sat by the window with the phone in his lap. Maybe Danielle was out walking in the snow. Maybe that's why she didn't answer. Of all the seasons she liked winter best. She said it cleaned the system. The coldest January on record five years back, and she'd made him go on walks. They cut through the playground and past the Texaco station and the convenience store that always smelled like chicken fat and potatoes. Mr. Kask, the Estonian, was in there, and he didn't say hello or smile. Up and down the length of Paradiso and he shouldn't have complained when she wanted to keep on going. She was telling him about the constellations. She knew the stories behind their names, and he didn't slow down to listen. That was his problem. He was in a hurry even though he had no place else to be.

He had a black eye, and he didn't know why. He always had new bruises. He took the mirrors out from the trailer and dropped them in the Dumpster. The bathroom mirror from the medicine cabinet and the hand mirrors on the coffee table. They were crusty, all of them. They were losing the silver around their edges. They made a musical sound when they broke. He sat on the stoop when he was done. They were fighting again inside. "I told you what to get," somebody said. "You never listen; that's half your problem. Now I have to go myself." He leaned against the trash can. The trees were black in the falling snow, and behind the shouts in the trailer and the cars over on Fountain he heard the rushing sound of water. A woman was talking somewhere between the trees. Thomas tried to make out the words. All these years and he knew his mother's voice, even when she whispered.

It took three buses to get back to Paradiso. The voices on the drivers' radios all sounded like his mother. The ladies with their babies looked like Danielle. Black hair and blacker eyes and he watched them until they changed seats. He couldn't keep still. His mother's voice was a thread, and he'd follow where it led. He clenched and unclenched his fists. Everywhere he looked there were spiders. Some were fast and some turned lazy circles, and his arm was too big for his jacket sleeve. He held it close against his side. The shivers were gone and now he was hot and nothing hurt him where he was. He could walk for days through the falling snow. It wouldn't stick, not just yet. The ground was still warm from summer. He changed buses once he got downtown. There were lofts up in those old bank buildings and restaurants with their windows lit. The only thing that was still the same was the Virgin Mary billboard. She promised peace if you called the number. It was only a dollar a minute. Her eyes were closed, but she wasn't sleeping. She held her baby boy.

He went to the convenience store when he came to his stop. The Estonian folks were gone. They used to have their flag over the register, three bands of blue and white and black, and old Mr. Kask would curse the Russians if you got him started. "Forty years of the Russian boot and now we're a free republic. But here we've always been free." He would tap his chest where his heart was. The flag was gone, and there was a calendar instead with pictures of the beach. Colors so bright they hurt his eyes and snapshots of dark-eyed babies. Mangalore, the calendar said, and the water was green and blue. He leaned over the counter so he could see it better. There were mothers in the picture walking along the sand.

"Samid," the lady behind the counter was saying. "Samid, you need to come." She moved away from the register. She turned toward the back door, and her braid was thick as a rope and threaded with gray. There was music in her voice. Thomas could listen to her for days.

The husband came running. He was a little man. "Can I help you?" he asked. "Can I help you, sir?" His voice was musical, too. He stepped in front of his wife, who was reaching for the phone. Thomas kept his right hand in his pocket. It didn't belong to him anymore. Dead as a brick and his heart pounded through it. It carried the poison through his veins.

He moved toward the water. Toward his baby girl who was watching him from the pictures. The man told him to stop. He was reaching for something beneath the counter, but Thomas didn't listen. He heard only the waves breaking and his mother's voice and other children shouting.

His mother ran ahead. She was faster for once, and Thomas raced to catch her. The water was silver in the light. It was as warm as he'd remembered. "Hurry," she said. She stopped and waited for him to come. "There's people waiting behind you." They were going to see his father, and she led him by the hand.

Today, The Lake

FRANCINE WITTE

Today, the lake is a mirror. You can bend over and see yourself. You like yourself like this, this angle. You are balanced.

Tomorrow, the lake will be a swimming hole. You will watch your children, Buddy and Jane, in their bathing suits, streaks of sunscreen on their noses. You will watch your husband watching as they play.

The lake will also be a postcard. "Hello from perfect!" it might say. You will wish it all could freeze like this.

Next week, the lake will be a memory. "Nice summer," you will say. "We had fun."

You will look into the bathroom mirror. That will be your lake. You will look dead on and uneven. As if something could knock you down.

It's something that has been coming. By spring, your husband will leave you. You have been noticing his absences, his muffled late-night phone calls.

Your children, too, will start to leave. Each day, school will teach them something else about the world. Explorers and geography. One day, they will bolt in, plop their books on the counter. They will tell you that even though they like the lake, it's boring—there's nothing to do. They will ask to go to the ocean instead.

Washing Boys

REBECCA FREMO

The oldest sits naked
on the toilet seat,
then rises like steam
to hack at the shower curtain.
What the middle boy fears
the oldest craves: hot water
pelting back and shoulders,
my voice thwarted
by the locked door.
The middle boy leaves
the bathroom door open
wide as the arms gathering
new bathtub crayons.
Stay with me, he says.
His freckled body lies
submerged and I know
he hears me now like
he heard me then, before
all our cells split apart.

Night in Winter

RAE GOUIRAND

Suggest: that the candle is not the light itself, but
the enduring, the space of the darkness around,

no matter the moving flame, no matter the spill
that hardens again, unmade. In the watching of

the flame, suggest: that what has been forgotten
was never really lived. Ask: *was it ?* If the candle

forgets itself as it spills over, does it ever exist
again? Follow: does it grieve? Is there room

in the letting for a loss that gets felt? Nothing
stops the burning except the breath. Nothing

stops the dreaming except the sharp bell. Talk:
with the candle, can you talk with the candle

without talking with everything? With something
that outlasts your own letting and lets that too?

Choose: what we get to choose, what we feel,
what we make in the growing dark, a healing.

Lemon

RAE GOUIRAND

The notion, the wholeness, glows in fog,
its own envelope. The first firm one

scenting the tree, lucid in juice, thick with
cold pigment, rich in heady oil, its own

argument. So the lemon carries the season,
the moment, shows back itself and not

my own question, not my own deep inhale
and high-pinned thinking, *what is this,*

this emitting. For a time, it is good to be
alone, to not have to share the new fruit

or particular number when thoughts blur,
eyes set on the basket again. Here the girl

reaches sweetness, acidity—hand weighing
one thing only—and takes it in: matte, finite.

An Interview with Richard Bausch

SHEILA O'CONNOR & LOREN A. TAYLOR

Richard Bausch is the author of eleven novels, including *Thanksgiving Night* and *Peace,* winner of the American Library Association's W. Y. Boyd Prize for Excellence in Military Fiction and the Dayton Literary Peace Prize, and eight collections of stories, including his most recent, *Something Is Out There.* In 2004 he was awarded the PEN/Malamud Award for Excellence in the Short Story. He co-edited, with R. V. Cassill, *The Norton Anthology of Short Fiction.* Since Cassill's death in 2002, he has been the sole editor.

An acknowledged Master of the short story form, Richard Bausch's work has appeared in *The Atlantic Monthly, Esquire, Harper's, The New Yorker, New Stories from the South, The Best American Short Stories, O. Henry Prize Stories,* and *The Pushcart Prize Stories.* His stories also have been widely anthologized, including in *The Granta Book of the American Short Story* and *The Vintage Book of the Contemporary American Short Story.* He has won two National Magazine Awards, a Guggenheim Fellowship, a Lila-Wallace Reader's Digest Fund Writer's Award, and an Award from the American Academy of Arts and Letters. He currently serves as the Moss Chair of Excellence in the Writing Program at the University of Memphis.

This public interview with Richard Bausch was held in front of a live audience on March 7, 2011, during his visit to The Creative Writing Programs at Hamline University. The two interviewers were Sheila O'Connor, a member of the faculty and the fiction editor of *Water~Stone Review,* and Loren Taylor, a student in the M.F.A. program at Hamline.

TAYLOR: I'd like to start by congratulating you on being named a finalist for the *Los Angeles Times* book prize for your collection, *Something Is Out There.* Your career continues to be illustrious, but apart from your ongoing success, what keeps you returning to the page in general and to fiction in particular?

BAUSCH: Habit. It's just how I do my days. I get up and do it. The thing that keeps me going back to this is not success. Success is when somebody whose work you respect says something kind. That is the thing you work for, and the public kind of stuff is . . . business.

TAYLOR: Is there something that your stories give back to you as you're writing or as you're revising?

BAUSCH: The surprises are what I get back. I don't trust the work unless it surprises me. If I know too much about a story as I'm writing it, I get bored and I really don't want to finish it so I usually just set it aside until something comes up to complicate it. I keep telling my students: add trouble. Good writing is about serious trouble, so you start with that, whatever that is, then you start writing through it and when it surprises you, that's the reward.

TAYLOR: In the Master Class today, you talked about the need for writers to maintain empathy for the characters in their stories and empathy for the reader. Is that something you concentrate on during revision, or do you focus on it from the beginning?

BAUSCH: I think it's there from the beginning. The revision process is only you trying to be clear, trying to be good, so that the lines are not getting in the way of each other and they're all giving forth something. If it's dialogue, you're trying to make sure the lines are doing more than one thing. That's usually true of all the other lines, too. Here's an example of a line of dialogue that's only doing one thing: "They'll never find you in this logging camp we've brought you to against your will." You get lines like that from student work; that's actually a quote. But the line of dialogue that's doing more than one thing, like these lines from *Cool Hand Luke,* when Luke says, "I don't know, I just can't seem to find any elbow room," and his mother says, "You always had good jobs. And that girl in Kentucky. Oh, I taken a shine to her." And Luke says, "She sure took off with that convertible fellow."

Everything they're saying gives information about who they are, but it's also doing more than that. "Your father wasn't much for sticking around, Luke, but, damn it, he made me laugh." I mean, I *heard* that. I went to see that movie in 1967 and I knew when I was looking at it that it was something I could learn from. It's still to me one of the best examples of dialogue in which every line is doing more than one thing.

TAYLOR: In your fiction, and in your short stories, in particular, you create an enormous range of characters' voices. Do you use techniques, perhaps reading aloud, for example, to help you with those voices?

BAUSCH: Well, I do read aloud. Mostly when reading aloud I'm just trying to hear the prose, trying to hear how it sounds. It is finding a voice, but I'm not in a rational conscious state—it's a kind of daydream. I'm not really thinking about anything, just trying to spit it out, trying to get it to be vivid.

TAYLOR: One of my favorite stories in your collection is "One Hour in the History of Love." Among other things I was impressed by the control of the omniscient point of view. Omniscience is not a frequent choice in stories these days. Do you have an opinion of why that is?

BAUSCH: A great number of us have probably ceased to believe in any kind of omniscience—or an omniscience that we can trust in fiction. You know, Tolstoy will take you into the minds of the hunting dogs and when you read Tolstoy, it's as if God is telling you the story, and I just like that. I mean, I don't want to do that all the time because the culture doesn't really sit still for it much, but I really like doing it.

TAYLOR: When you are revising a story, does the story ever say, *I need to be in a different point of view?*

BAUSCH: Oh, yes, many times. I mean, god, the revisions are so many. I have written stories with revisions that go up into the forties and fifties in terms of times through it, times working it and reworking it, and then discovered that it's in the wrong point of view and so tried another way. One of the great things to teach yourself is stubbornness—you're going to stick with it until it blesses you.

The truest thing about writing is that it's done in confusion and doubt most of the time. And almost nothing that's ever been written that's worth reading was ever done in any other state except confusion and doubt and working your way through it and being confused and understanding that that is the territory. That's what I teach. I teach the life. You're *supposed* to be confused.

TAYLOR: A sense of place is prominent in your fiction, and your work often includes beautiful descriptions of the weather. Could you talk about that sense of place and what it means to you as a writer? Do you have that in mind when you begin a story?

BAUSCH: No. It's interesting. I'm often criticized for not concentrating much on the place. As a so-called Southern writer—I'm not denigrating that term— it's just that there are often people who say that someone is Southern just because there is a lot of place in his work. But I don't often get categorized that way because of the sense of place. To me, the place is interior. It's the characters, the identity. I've placed stories in West Africa, in England, in Duluth. I think if you consciously set out to be a thing like a Southern writer, if you consciously do that, you're making a terrible mistake. You can't escape where you've been or who you are. Although, well, no, you can. (Laughter.) You can escape your own experience, but your experience is a wide thing. You can experience things in a number of ways.

O'CONNOR: I admire so much of your work but if I could reference a favorite, it would be "All the Way in Flagstaff, Arizona," the story of an adrift, alcoholic father who has lost his wife and children. This is a story I've read countless times, and each time, I have profound compassion for the struggle of the alcoholic.

Compassion that transcends judgment—which is something that happens to me so often when I read your fiction. For me, this is one of the greatest gifts of fiction: the call to understand what we might otherwise judge. Can you talk a little bit about how you use fiction to understand?

BAUSCH: That's an amazing question. I remember Robert Penn Warren in an interview saying, "I'm just trying to make sense of my own experience." I began to realize that all literature is really about experience. It's not about philosophy. It's about experience. Felt life. Travel—that's what the beautiful Emily Dickinson means when she says, "There is no frigate like a book." In books, you can travel anywhere, to any time or place. For me as a writer, I always believe that, and want to take part in it, and I believe in what the French said, that in understanding there is forgiveness.

If you can get into the reasons for any behavior—and, of course, you have to do that if you're writing fiction—there's an amazing reasonableness to the world's fictional characters. We know why Gatsby stands at the end of that dock. We know why Anna Karenina jumps in front of that train. We know why Emma Bovary kills herself. We *know*. But in life you don't know. And the big mistake that the inexperienced writer will make has to do with the ability to be mimetic effectively, so s/he will concretely and with great detail deliver somebody sitting at a dentist's office. I don't want to sit in a goddamn dentist's office, even if I'm not a patient. The mistake is to put the reader there without it meaning anything. Because what you're doing is inventing reality. It's not what you're supposed to be doing even though it's supposedly realistic. It's called verisimilitude. It isn't supposed to be merely realistic; it's supposed to be realistic with a purpose, creating this otherworldly thing.

The example I use is the hospital room. Context creates story by what's going on in that room with the people in it. So there are certain objects in that room to describe and you describe them in terms of their circumstances and their character. So, it's like E. M. Forster's wonderful line, you know, "The king died, and the queen died." That's nothing. They're facts. If you say, "The king died, and the queen died of grief," you've got a story. You've got something to deal with. How does that manifest itself? How does it show? For me, the thing that you start with is compassion for the people in the circumstance because you're visiting trouble upon them and seeing how they're going to behave in the face of that trouble, whatever it is. And they usually behave better than you ever will. I mean, that's the other thing. Usually I would fail the tests my characters go through, oh my god, so many times. The stuff my characters have to go through, I wouldn't last five seconds. I'd say, "That's it for me. Give me the pills. I'm gone." But, you hope they have courage.

O'CONNOR: Authorial voice is a term that's often mistaken by writers to be the equivalent of the narrator's voice—but what I'm thinking about is something much larger, which is the sense of the writer's presence that moves through all of the work, what Raymond Carter called the writer's fingerprint. A sense of the writer's beliefs about humanity, about the way the world works, about love and death and faith and chance, all of that. I'm wondering if you're aware of your fingerprint and whether it has changed?

BAUSCH: I'm not conscious of a central theme or fingerprint. I believe that it exists, but again, it is something that exists in the same way my actual fingerprints exist. I don't really think about it. I don't have many theories about anything. I think I know pretty well what's good when I see it, and I'm an advocate of good work, and it's always good work if it moves me and if I get pleasure out of the actual process of going through the lines I'm reading.

When I'm writing a story, I don't really think about anything thematic. I'm only thinking about being clear and being involving. Trying to make it so a reader will want to turn the page. I'm using whatever tricks I know, but I don't actually think of them consciously.

O'CONNOR: Let's talk about Bob Dylan and JFK—you mentioned they're the reasons you became a writer.

BAUSCH: Well, Kennedy was killed when I was eighteen and I was going to pick up the torch. I wanted to follow along behind him. I looked at all those speeches—I know some of them by heart. I learned that Kennedy had read *War and Peace*. To emulate him, I would be a politician with some substance who knew some stuff. So I read *War and Peace*. I couldn't get enough of it. I never saw anything like that. I'm reading that book again, for the seventh time. I love that book. There's so much in it, moments that are so astonishing and penetratingly human: the little princess is dead, they're burying her and she has a look on her face: *I'm such a nice person, why would anyone put me through this, I didn't do anything to deserve this.* And Prince Andrei is standing there seeing that. Prince Andrei, who has been unhappy with her, annoyed by her, as his wife with the silly opinions and moods. Or, there's Natasha at her first ball and Tolstoy writes, "She was at that pitch of happiness where it is impossible to imagine an ungenerous thought in another person." And you think, *My god, I know how that feels. I've been there!* Or there's the scene at Borodino when the men are blown up and Pierre has this thought, *Surely now they'll stop.* I mean, it's so brilliant and so beautiful in that way, the way of felt life, *that* kind of full truth, that it's a book you can live in. I like to go through the book with students; I read little sections just to say, "This is how much life is in here. You want to write fiction, you're serious about it, then you should have this book under your belt, the same way that if you want to write plays you should have *Hamlet* and *King Lear* under your belt."

At the same time I was reading a lot of poetry and I heard about Dylan. I started looking him up at the record stores. I remember reading the back of an Odetta album—she just passed away last year, a great singer and writer. But I read the lyrics to "Mr. Tambourine Man" before I heard the song. I was so impressed with the rhyming of *chasing* and *facing.* So far apart, with all those rhymes in between. So I had this idea that if I could get famous as a songwriter, they would let me write novels. That's how little I knew about any of it. So I started learning to play guitar.

O'CONNOR: You've talked about ear, and certainly there's musicality in your prose. How do you encourage students to develop an ear?

BAUSCH: By reading. The more you read, the better the ear. In every single instance in my life, and I can say it's a long life now, I've never met a writer whom I considered better than me who wasn't also better read. They knew more. I don't mean knew more information. They had been exposed to more; they had run more through their minds. The brain is an astounding recorder. It records everything, *everything.* You have in your memory, as brilliant and absolutely present as now, the memory of bending over in a hallway at three years of age to pick up a sock. Every single instant of your life is recorded there. And so when you read, the more you can fill it with, the more resources you have to draw on and the better your ear is.

A good ear is not something you're born with; it's something you get from reading. You can't make someone do that, but you can encourage them and say, "Look, take it in, take it in, read, read!"

O'CONNOR: Do you pay attention to sound when you're leading a workshop, when you're looking at a student's work?

BAUSCH: Oh, yes. Some of the stuff you get is so funny because the sound is so off. If the ear is off, there's lots of stuff that's off real bad, too. "Jack Smith's eyes skyrocketed shut." No. "He looked across the veranda and thought of friends and dogs from long ago." No. "He tweaked her nipple and grabbed it as though it were the arm of a small child." No. These are real lines. "Dawn came early to Auschwitz, but Jacob didn't mind; he was a morning person." Now, dawn came early to Auschwitz. Look at it. When does dawn not come early? It's dawn. "Dawn came late. It was five o'clock in the afternoon before it arrived." And of course the business about dawn is only the tip of the iceberg concerning what's wrong with the tone and sense of that passage.

O'CONNOR: You've said that your job as a teacher is to prepare students for a writing life. I wonder if you would share what that means to you, and if you feel an obligation to prepare them for the publishing world.

BAUSCH: Well, the writing life does have to do with the publishing world, and so we talk about it, but you shouldn't spend time worrying about it too much. You've got to work *not* to think about it too much. There are things in this life that take discipline, and one of them is trying not to think about that stuff. There's really only one thing to think about each day: *Did I work?* If the answer is yes, no other questions are necessary. If you do two pages a day, that's more than 700 pages in a year. Of course, you will think about it, and you have to try to make yourself not do it, the same way you have to try not think about, I don't know . . .

O'CONNOR: Dying.

BAUSCH: Dying. Or sleeping with your next-door neighbor. Writing is simple in the same way that virtue is simple. Which means, it's incredibly difficult, but it's simple. And it really is just those things.

I have a room full of people who I know have talent. I don't take a second seat to anybody in knowing talent when I see it. When it's there, it's alive. It's coming off the page, whether it's grammatical or not. So what I have as a teacher is a room full of talented people who have a complete set of misconceptions about the whole thing, the same misconceptions I used to have. The misconception that as a writer you have to have some sort of superintelligent theoretical imagination, and, you know, all that. It's bull. You just have to be someone who wants to tell stories, and who loves to read them and is continually soaking them up. You don't have to have a tremendous amount of smarts. Just the appetite for it all—everything in print that's worth keeping and remembering.

One of my favorite lines in movies, and I use it all the time in class, is from John Wayne's last movie. He's a gunfighter talking to a younger gunfighter and he says, "You don't have to be fast—you just have to be willing." That's *it* for a writer. You don't have to be terribly intelligent or supersmart, you just have to be willing. You're working on a story you're going to have to write seventy-five times. Believe me, after seventy-five times, you're going to be real smart about that story. About anything else, you can be as dumb as I am about all that stuff. I couldn't remember how to spell *Tennessee* today. Couldn't remember whether it was one "n" or two, and I *live* there.

O'CONNOR: I love your Ten Commandments for writers and I've used them for years. Probably my favorite one is "Don't think—dream." You talked quite a bit about this tonight, about trusting the dreaming part of the writing process. The second one is "Accept failure as a part of your destiny. Learn to be willing to fail, to take the chances that often lead to failure, in the hope that one of them might lead to something good." Could you talk about moving forward after failure?

BAUSCH: It's the day's work. I feel good that I worked. It didn't go too well, but I worked. You put in the time, like any other good citizen. There will be times when you feel like you can just point to the sky and say, "Rain," and it will rain. Because you feel that powerful. But then there are other times when it's just work, and you did it. You messed with it for a little. Next day, maybe it will go better, easier, whatever. But you don't allow yourself, and this is something you can teach yourself, to worry about it too much. It's just a day's work.

Now think about this. Let's say that this is a symposium about playing golf. All of you want to play golf. All of you have a golf pro that you go to see. You take a swing and the golf pro says, "Left arm's way too bent, you're shifting your weight, your knees are bent, you're moving your feet. You're moving your head, your head was up—did you see your head? That's why you miss things." And what do you do? You say, "All right. Let me try it again." With writing, somebody says that stuff about a story you wrote and you say, "Oh, I guess I better quit. I don't have any talent!" It's just a fuckin' swing of the golf club. I tell the students, "Look, this is what we're doing. You're not trying to produce a masterpiece in this workshop. You're just trying to get your swing right. That's all. You might not write a story worth publishing the whole time you're here, but you're going to get your swing right, and then the stories will come."

Judith Kitchen Creative Nonfiction Prize—Honorable Mention

Signs of the Time
MORGAN GRAYCE WILLOW

I

Sunday evening. A cold northern city. A young man waits at a corner bus stop. Five other young men drive by. They call out to the one on the curb. A bus arrives at 8:33. The first young man boards. The driver closes the door, pulls away from the stop.

Murderopolis. It's 1995 and *The New York Times* has dubbed the city where I live Murderopolis. By the end of the year, the number of homicides will reach an all-time high: ninety-seven, a spike from sixty the previous year. Minneapolis police attribute the sharp increase to gang activity, especially on the north side.

Sunday evenings, my partner and I tend to settle in for the evening in our cozy south Minneapolis bungalow. We each have early work hours on Mondays. She checks in with dispatch at 5:30 a.m., or earlier, to get her run number and inspect her bus before she pulls out. Sometimes she drives the number 5 line that goes through the north side. I need to be at an urban high school by 7:15 in order to get to homeroom to interpret rapid-fire announcements from the loudspeaker to a classroom of deaf and hard-of-hearing students. By 8:30 p.m.

on Sundays we've usually walked and fed the dogs, cooked a simple dinner, and settled in to watch *Murder, She Wrote*.

II

Sunday evening. February in Minneapolis. A young black man waits at a corner bus stop. A carload of five other young black men drives by. They call out and gesticulate to the young man on the curb. The bus arrives at 8:33. The young man boards. He is agitated. The driver senses something is wrong. He closes the door, quickly.

The north side. The first community on Minneapolis's north side was created by Jewish families. They'd been prohibited by covenants from buying property in other areas of the city, so they settled the area known as the Oak Lake subdivision. German Jews who'd come in the mid-nineteenth century were later joined by Eastern European Jews, refugees from the pogroms. By 1910, a community of nearly 8,000 Jews was thriving on the north side.

Those same covenants that restricted Jews from owning property also applied to African Americans who'd moved up to Minneapolis during the Great Migration. Though jobs were more plentiful in cities like Detroit and Chicago, Minneapolis attracted its fair share of African American job seekers. Between 1910 and 1920, their numbers on the census rolls had increased by more than 50 percent. Many of them began to make their homes in the Oak Lake subdivision as well. As they did so, some Jewish families moved out, extending the city boundaries further north. Each community had developed its own social service agencies to address family, social, and cultural needs. These, too, rolled over as patterns of segregated housing moved northward. On October 17, 1924, for example, the Phyllis Wheatley Settlement House opened in a building that had previously been the home of the Talmud Torah.

Patterns tend to persist. The north side of Minneapolis was not immune to the civil unrest of the 1960s. In July of 1967—the same year as disturbances in Watts, Detroit, and Newark—a conflict between two African American women at the annual Aquatennial Torchlight Parade escalated into a full-scale riot. A group of some 250 youths smashed windows and started fires in businesses along Plymouth Avenue, many of them owned by Jewish families. Koval Furniture and Appliance alone lost more than thirty TV sets to looting in the fracas.

Initially, Minneapolis firefighters refused to respond without police backup. The police had been warned not to intervene for fear of further escalation.

Eventually, however, the police did receive orders to clear the street, and Governor Harold LeVander called up the National Guard to assist in restoring order. Hoping to quell the disturbance before it could continue through a second night, Minneapolis Mayor Arthur Naftalin directed his staff to set up a bandstand, hire a band, and arrange food booths along Plymouth Avenue. At least 150 young people, mainly African American, participated in the street dance that evening. The violence of the previous night faded into—and for some, out of—history.

III

Sunday evening. February in Minneapolis. A young black man waits at a corner bus stop. A carload of five other young black men drives by. They call out and gesture to the young man on the curb. The bus arrives at 8:33. The young man boards. He is agitated. The driver senses something is wrong. He closes the door against the shouting young men, who are now out of their car. He pulls away from the curb but is forced to swerve past one of the shouting young men who stands in front of the bus.

According to Lieutenant Michael A. Fossum, gang activity in Minneapolis had been on the rise since the mid-1980s when crack hit the streets. Once that happened, violent crime increased about four times faster than the city's population. The primary working gangs in Minneapolis in 1995 were the Vice Lords and the Disciples, both of whom originated in Chicago. They'd migrated to the Twin Cities via Gary, Indiana, attracted by a strong market for crack cocaine and the nickname "Moneyapolis," a moniker coined by earlier arrivals who'd found ready access to the Minnesota public assistance system. The Vice Lords (VL), who referred to themselves as "People," traced their origins to Chicago's west side; the Gangster Disciples (GD), who referred to themselves as "Folks," traced theirs to Chicago's south side. Both organizations date back some four generations. In the Twin Cities, each would develop its own identity distinct from its parent group. During the early 1990s, the Vice Lords maintained primary control of sales of crack, though conflicts over control of Minneapolis's north side—especially of Plymouth Avenue—persisted. Other gangs, though less prevalent, competed for territory as well. The Crips and Bloods, both L.A.-based, tried to make inroads into the Minneapolis market in the mid-1980s and early 1990s. Nevertheless, by 2000 a research team led by John Harrington and Kate Cavett concluded that the Gangster Disciples was the largest gang in Minnesota.

IV

*Sunday evening. February in Minneapolis. A young black man waits at a corner bus stop.
A carload of five other young black men drives by. They call out and gesture aggressively to
the young man on the curb. He signs back. The bus arrives at 8:33. The young man boards.
He is agitated. The driver senses something is wrong. He closes the door against the shouting
young men, now out of their car. He pulls away from the curb but is forced to swerve past
one of the young men, who stands in front of the bus.*

Driving bus is a dangerous way to make a living. One of the lucky ones, my
partner has not been sucker-punched from behind or shot at, though this has become increasingly common. She has been spit on, sworn at, called a "cracker," and,
once, a "honkey-assed, blue-eyed bitch." One time, a group of youths displaying their
"colors" got on the bus and began to bang out rhythms on the bus stanchions with
chains, chanting rap lyrics. Another time, a couple of young riders dismantled
some of the metal stanchions and swung them as weapons.

Drivers train themselves to be on the lookout, to notice things. They develop
a good memory for regular riders and their stops, both boarding and departing.
Drivers notice when trouble gets on; they notice where trouble gets off. They develop an instinct for danger, though sensing danger is never enough to protect
themselves, or their passengers, from harm. While the bus has a call button to
signal transit police, usually, by the time the cops arrive, the damage has already
been done. One of their few defenses is to close the door.

Each route has its own character, each run its own victories and failures. The
commuter runs have traffic to deal with, bad roads in snow storms, ice, tornado
threats, flash floods. The regular city routes have all this and, often, challenging
passengers. In 1995 the toughest line in the city was the Minneapolis 5. The 5 line
connects the north side of Minneapolis to the south side, Vice Lords to Disciples.

V

*Sunday, February 26, 1995. Latell Chaney waits for the 5 line at Lowry & Penn in
north Minneapolis. Five young black men in a 1987 dark-blue Pontiac Bonneville pull
up alongside him. They begin yelling and signaling to him. He signs back to them. The bus
arrives at 8:33. Chaney, clearly agitated, boards the bus. The driver realizes something is
wrong. He closes the door against two of the shouting young men, who try to board. The
driver pulls away from the stop but is forced to swerve around another of the car's occupants,
who has taken up position in front of the bus. Later, recognizing that Chaney is deaf, the
driver writes a note on a bus schedule asking if he knows the guys who'd tried to board.
Chaney writes back, "No, just saw them today."*

Latell Chaney, at this time, is twenty years old. He lives in north Minneapolis. He's on his way to visit his girlfriend, who lives in south Minneapolis. He'd moved here with his family within the last few years. Chaney has been deaf since childhood, a result of a series of ear infections that went untreated. He has recently graduated from St. Louis Park High School, where there is a deaf and hard-of-hearing program, much like the one where I work on the opposite side of the Twin Cities.

Early in the school year, my colleagues and I are required to attend a staff in-service training day. Listed among the scheduled workshops is one called Gang Awareness. The blurb explains that officers from the city's Gang Strike Force will talk about how to spot evidence of gang affiliation among students. Our supervisor has encouraged all interpreters to attend this session, a rare acknowledgment of the fact that we have, by virtue of our physical position in the classroom, a unique vantage point from which to see what's going on among the students. Unlike teachers who write on the board, we never turn our backs on the class. We also pass from classroom to classroom in the halls during the same five-minute breaks students have. We see student interaction, including the usual fist bumps, casual shoving, and banter. We see the passing of notes, and possibly other things, from hand to hand. We see signaling of various kinds. We're trained to recognize when gestures assume linguistic significance and become sign language. I have often suspected that some of the other signals I see are ritualized throwing of gang signs, but these are signs I am not trained to read.

Not that we haven't been privy to conversations about gang members. In an auditorium in an inner-city high school, a colleague and I, on a day's assignment, have been interpreting for students in a theater program. During a break, while another group is rehearsing its scene, our students are chatting. Part of the job is to interpret chitchat between deaf students and hearing students who do not know how to sign. The students have created the play they're rehearsing out of stories from their own lives. One of the characters gets messed up with a gang. In a small conversation circle off-stage, one of the deaf students asks the hearing students whether anyone they know is a member of a gang. One student shares that her brother is a GD, but she claims they don't "do none of that stuff," referring to the violence the character in the play gets involved in. Another talks about her cousins in Chicago and how the gang is just like family to them. They take care of their own, she insists. My colleague and I are obliged to voice both questions and answers. We are also obliged, by strict adherence to a professional code of ethics, not to divulge the content of the conversation to anyone. Our deaf students are well aware of this.

When the Gang Awareness workshop gets under way, the cops distribute a handout. Almost the instant we get these papers in our hands, all the interpreters in the room exchange glances. The handout outlines graffiti insignia, color codes, historical background, and primary constituencies of the most populous gangs in the metro area. What grabs our attention, however, are the rough sketches of gang hand signs. The first one, the sign associated with the Vice Lords, looks exactly like the American Sign Language handshape called the "3 classifier."

One doesn't need to know ASL to recognize the gesture hearing people use for the number *2*, or its use when the palm is turned away from the body to signify "V" for victory or, since the sixties, "peace." In the ASL manual alphabet, the same handshape constitutes the letter *V*, or the numeral *2*, depending upon which way the palm faces. It's also easy for nonsigners to recognize the handshape for the letter "L"—extended index finger and thumb, the remaining three fingers of the hand curled into the palm. This is an iconographic handshape; it looks like the letter it shapes. It's commonly used by nonsigners to indicate an "L" shape, as when describing an L-shaped room, for example. It also has the derisive slang usage "Loser." When the finger points horizontally instead of vertically, it suggests a gun—a smoking gun, if the person making the sign first blows on the finger tip. When in ASL it signifies the letter *L*, it's used vertically.

When these two signs are used together—that is, two fingers raised in the number "2" or "V" shape, with the thumb added to shape an "L" from thumb and index finger simultaneously—even nonsigners recognize the letters "VL." According to the handout, this is the hand sign the Vice Lords throw to signal affiliation and affirmation. The strike force cops elaborate further: flashed in a vertical position, the "VL" shape is a salute, an emblem of both recognition and respect. The same shape displayed in a horizontal or downward position constitutes a "dis"—a sign of disrespect to the Vice Lords. The shape and position may also signify affiliation with a rival gang.

VI

The bus continues on its route. Meanwhile, the five men climb back in the Bonneville, drive to a convenience store to get exact change, then drive on to the bus stop at 7th Street and Bryant Avenue North. They wait. When the bus arrives, they board. They pay their fare. They then begin beating on Latell Chaney. One of them swings a beer bottle and breaks it over Chaney's head. He goes to work cutting on Latell Chaney's face.

In their report, *G Is for Gangsta: Introductory Assessment of Gang Activity and Issues in Minnesota* (Hand to Hand Productions, 2000), researchers John Harrington and Kate Cavett made it clear that not all gang violence is just about business. They quoted one young Latin Queen as saying:

> It's like a big rush. You get all excited. You get hyped when you're throwing up your signs and you're like throwing down somebody else's sign. It gets you hyped, like a rush and you're ready ta, represent.

It's about wanting to signify, to be significant, to be somebody. Sign. The word comes from Latin *signum*, a distinctive mark or figure, seal, or signal. To signify is to have meaning or importance, from the Latin *significare*, which is *signum*, or "sign," plus *facere*, "to make." Or, as the poet Patricia Smith puts it in "CRIPtic Comment" (*Close to Death*, 1993):

> If we are not shooting
> at someone,
> then no one
> can see us.

Perhaps the young men just wanted to matter, to have significance, to leave their sign on the world. To write their legend on Latell Chaney's face.

VII

Two and a half miles farther down the line at 7th Street and Bryant Avenue North, five young black men, quarters in hand, board the bus. The driver would report later that he had no reason to suspect these were the same young men who'd harassed Chaney at Lowry & Penn. They boarded calmly. They paid their fare. Then, they began swinging on the stanchion poles. They approached the passenger they'd signed to at the earlier stop. One of them swung and broke a beer bottle over the seated passenger's head. He cut Chaney's face so badly that surgeons would have no alternative but to remove his right eye. They stole Chaney's ring and $2 cash. Two others attacked a nearby passenger, having taken him to be Chaney's friend. From this passenger they stole two gold chains. A witness later reported hearing one of the attackers shout, "G.D. killer and Crips cuz" ("Deaf Bus Assault Victim," Star Tribune, March 7, 1995, Sec. A).

Before the 1960s, ASL was not considered a real language. At best, it was considered a crude, visual variant of English; at worst, mere, primitive gesture. William Stokoe's linguistic research, however, shattered these suppositions. A linguist at Gallaudet University, Stokoe undertook a careful comparative analysis of ASL and verified that ASL embodies all the linguistic features of any natural language. It has a consistent syntactical structure, and ASL sentences do the same work that sentences in any spoken language do. As described by Deaf-culture historian Harlan Lane, ASL language includes syntactic units that perform each of the four primary functions of any sentence: "the agent responsible for the action, the act, the person or thing acted upon, and the person or thing receiving what has been acted upon" (*A Journey into the Deaf-World*, Dawn Sign Press, 1996, 49). The only difference is that these units are manually signed instead of voiced. The linguistic structure is one that's compatible with the physical instrument of the hand rather than the physical instrument of the larynx.

ASL has a very flexible system of pronouns. They are unlike English pronouns, which are concerned with the category or class of the noun to which they refer. For inanimate nouns, we use "it" in third person, for example. If a noun is animate, English demands that we specify a gender and use "he" or "she." In the case of ASL pronouns—which are called classifiers—category or class is irrelevant. ASL pronouns are more concerned with expressing shape or size.

There are many such classifiers in ASL. One of them is the handshape used for the number *3*, or 3-CL in conventional notation. In ASL the "3" handshape uses thumb, index finger, and middle finger. In other words, it's the very same handshape used to make the gang sign for the Vice Lords. In ASL, classifiers— or pronouns—refer more frequently to things than to people. Skillful use of classifiers is perhaps the most versatile, most creative feature of the language. The 3-CL, for example, is frequently used to designate vehicles. Once a vehicle is established in a conversation, that handshape indicates that specific vehicle throughout the rest of the conversation unless, or until, a different vehicle is clearly identified. The 3-CL handshape may be used for a variety of kinds of vehicles, including a bicycle, an automobile, a train—everything except airplanes and boats, for which different classifiers are used. Latell Chaney would have used the 3-CL to refer to the number 5 bus. When the 3-CL signifies "bus," it is signed horizontally—not vertically, as it would be if the handshape meant the number *3*. Also, Chaney would likely have moved the 3-CL through his signing space, reflecting the direction he anticipated the bus would come from—or the direction it had gone, if the bus had recently left the stop. Chaney may simply have been signing: "Hey, man, I'm waiting for the bus." His five attackers may have mistranslated his 3-CL as a Vice Lords dis.

VIII

Latell Chaney had been deaf since childhood. He'd moved with his family to Minneapolis from Kansas in late 1992 or early 1993 in order to be nearer relatives who were ill at the time. He graduated from the deaf/hard-of-hearing program in the St. Louis Park high school in 1993. He relied on the visual language of ASL to communicate. On Sunday evening, February 26, 1995, he was on his way to visit his girlfriend in south Minneapolis when he was attacked on the number 5 bus by several youths. One of them cut up his face with a broken beer bottle. His cuts were so extensive that surgeons would need to remove his right eye. After the surgery, it would take several weeks before he would know whether sight would be fully restored to his left eye.

Enough reports of the misinterpretation of deaf people's signing as gang signs have surfaced for the phenomenon to be logged in the category of urban legend. Newsgroup postings affiliated with the AFU and Urban Legends Archive cited articles from the *Los Angeles Times* that reported shootings of deaf victims in gang-related drive-bys or other incidents. Commentators noted, however, that none of the articles provided clear proof that sign language, in fact, had been mistaken for gang signs. They point out that speculation about the connection most often comes from police officers investigating the cases. Nevertheless, the discussion itself suggests a level of anxiety worth noting about the possibility of being misunderstood or of being harmed or killed as a result of a mistranslation. Minneapolis *Star Tribune* writer Margaret Zack, covering the court appearance of one of the young men, reported that "others involved in the attack have said they thought Chaney had made a gang sign" ("Deaf Bus Assault," Sec. B).

IX

Police report that the young man who waited for the bus at Lowry and Penn on February 26, 1995, is deaf. They speculate that his hand gestures actually may have been ASL signs that were misinterpreted as gang signs. The Deaf community agrees. Doug Bahl, then president of the Minnesota Association of Deaf Citizens (MADC) and an acknowledged leader of the Deaf community, expressed grief and shock about the incident in an interview. He asked to talk to gang members to determine which gang signs are similar to ASL signs. "We would appreciate knowing . . . so we can work it out with them" ("Deaf Bus Assault," 6A).

According to newspaper accounts, all five suspects in the beating of Latell

Chaney had gang affiliations. One newspaper feature read, "Police believe Chaney's signing was misinterpreted as gang gestures" ("Deaf Bus Assault," 1A). A police sergeant called it a "vicious, brutal, senseless attack" (6A). Gary Sudduth, leader of the Minneapolis Urban League, called it "tragic." Reporters made some attempt, at least for purposes of their coverage, to involve members of the Twin Cities Deaf community by consulting Doug Bahl of MADC. He responded that he wanted "to know what kind of signs Chaney was using and why they may have been interpreted as gang gestures" (6A). Bahl put out a call for a meeting with the gang members to discuss their signs and to educate them about ASL. No such meeting ever happened.

Following a series of lawsuits and appeals, the Minnesota Court of Appeals ruled that Chaney could not sue the bus company for damages. The driver, they determined, had followed all appropriate safety and incident response procedures. Police apprehended all the suspects, and each of their cases completed its circuit through the justice system. Nothing further was heard about Latell Chaney beyond the fact that he and his family had moved out of the area in fear for their safety.

Other passengers riding the number 5 on that trip—all able to hear, none able to sign—reported hearing the attackers call out, "G.D. killer and Crips cuz" (6A). This they could understand. Chaney's signing, however, no one understood. Sgt. Robert Tichich reported, "He was trying to communicate—by pointing to his mouth and his ears and mixing sign language in with it to get the picture across" (6A).

X

Five suspects were apprehended for the assault on Latell Chaney. All, according to police, were known to have gang affiliations. One was convicted of aggravated robbery and assault. The other four defendants pleaded guilty.

Penn and Lowry Avenues North meet in more than place. Their intersection is one of story, history, and language. Latell Chaney was apparently beaten precisely because he could make neither the right sounds come out of his mouth nor the right signs come off his hands. His experience can be read as an act of literature—literate-ture—an act of misreading of language on bodies.

XI

On November 17, 2006, Deaf activist Doug Bahl was on his way to visit his soon-to-be wife in a Twin Cities hospital. He was pulled over by St. Paul police on a routine traffic violation. Bahl attempted to communicate with the officer in writing, but the officer refused to let him. An altercation ensued. The officer sprayed Bahl with a chemical irritant and pulled him from his vehicle. He then booked Bahl into the Ramsey County jail, but not before taking him to Regions Hospital to be treated for injuries he sustained in the "scuffle." Despite state and federal laws requiring that law enforcement officials provide effective means of communication, neither the police nor jail personnel arranged an interpreter for him. The incident happened on a Friday. It wasn't until Monday that jail personnel offered him use of a TTY to communicate with friends, family, or an attorney. Meanwhile, his fiancée, also deaf, had attempted to file a missing persons report on him. What began as a routine stop for a red-light violation ended up with Bahl being convicted of a misdemeanor offense.

By the time I read about Doug Bahl's arrest, conviction, and three-day incarceration with no means of communication, my partner and I have moved out of south Minneapolis to a quieter neighborhood in northeast. As I skim the headline in the *Star Tribune*, I can barely breathe: "Deaf activist sues county, city over arrest, jail stay" (Aug. 2, 2008, B1). The cutline under the photo of Doug identifies him as "Deaf activist Doug Bahl." The attribution under a highlighted quote from his attorney yet again describes him as "deaf activist Doug Bahl." Why, I wonder, this attempt to make him seem like a threat to society?

True, Doug Bahl is the very same community leader who, after Latell Chaney's brutal beating, called for a meeting with Twin Cities gang members to share information about ASL signs and gang signs. He'd hoped that by meeting face to face with gangsters, he could raise awareness and prevent the mistranslation of ASL signs for gang signs. His faith in the sheer possibility of communication across language barriers to resolve and prevent problems made him then, in the days and weeks after Chaney's beating, a visionary.

Doug Bahl was my instructor in advanced ASL classes when I was in the sign language interpreter training program at St. Paul Technical College. He was an avuncular, bright-smiling presence in the classroom each day. He was firm and demanding, as the best teachers always are, qualities I have learned to appreciate all the more since I myself have swapped roles in the classroom and, instead of interpreting, am now teaching. Doug was very strict on exams, which were administered one-on-one. He insisted on precision as he observed our construction and execution of the sentences we were asked to perform in his presence. He was also kind. His strong code of ethics prohibited him from giving away anything about the results of the exam until the appropriate time after we had all completed the protocol. Nevertheless, his warm smile or light touch on the shoulder was often enough to reassure us that he knew how stressful it was for us to perform, in this new (to us) language, those basic, sturdy sentences in the presence of a master.

For Doug Bahl is a master of language. In the Deaf community—nationwide, not just locally—he is known as a skillful, delightful storyteller. It is not possible in these English sentences to relay the nuances of his narratives, the artful construction of his ASL sentences, his miraculous use of space to convey action, character, and dialogue. This is the man who apparently so frightened a St. Paul police officer by his request to communicate in writing—which would have been done via hand motions miming writing with a pencil on a hand—that the officer deemed it necessary to spray chemical irritant in his eyes and drag him out of his car. Quite possibly, such utter refusal of any translation or communication is even more frustrating than mistranslation. Certainly it is just as dangerous.

XII

In March 2006 a thirty-three-year-old African American man was arrested in Fairmont, Minnesota, following a scuffle with his ex-girlfriend, the mother of his two sons. The fracas involved a car chase between the disputants. It ended in a crash, after which the man was charged in Martin County with two counts of criminal assault and two of criminal damage, all felonies. The man was deaf. He was refused an interpreter at the time of his arrest and again at the Nobles County jail where he was transferred. He languished in jail for several months without an interpreter. He was convicted by an all-white jury, who were improperly shown an inadmissible police report. He then served five and a half months in a state correctional facility, after which he was released from prison pending a new trial. Though the conviction was eventually overturned, he nonetheless spent eleven and a half months behind bars. That man is Latell Chaney.

Eleven years after being beaten and badly cut, after losing sight in one eye and sustaining permanent injuries to his throat, Latell Chaney was again being mistranslated, or worse, not translated at all. The first time around, he'd been misread by gangsters, themselves living in tense relation to the law. His more recent experiences, however, were perpetrated by those sworn to uphold the law. Officials at the Nobles County jail refused to provide an interpreter for him because, they claimed, he could read lips or read written English "well enough to get by" ("Justice May Be Blind," *Star Tribune*, Aug. 4, 2008).

Lip reading—or speech reading, its more accurate name—in the popular mind and in popular culture is known for its accuracy, as when HAL 9000 discovers through lip reading that Dave Bowman and Dr. Frank Poole plan to deactivate him in Stanley Kubrick's *2001: A Space Odyssey*. In embodied, spoken-English environments, however, the accuracy rate maxes out somewhere between 30 and 40 percent. On the face of an English speaker—and assuming no visual obstructions such as a hand in front of the mouth or a moustache—the expression "Where there's life, there's hope," looks identical to the question "Where's the lavender soap?"

As for reading well enough to get by, the arresting officer's method of Mirandizing Chaney was to hand him a Miranda card. Remember, Chaney has lost vision in one eye, and has some vision loss in the other. In addition, the Miranda card merely reprints the Miranda law. It does not elaborate what the law means in terms of actual, lived rights. It does nothing to break the structure of sentences designed for legal text down into a syntax understandable to someone whose knowledge and experience of English are minimal. An ASL interpreter skilled in court interpreting could, and would, have performed both these functions.

In 1990 the first President Bush signed the Americans with Disabilities Act (ADA) into law, making it mandatory that law enforcement officials provide whatever means necessary for effective communication. Such means might include sign language interpreters, TTY devices, and relay services for making communication over phone lines accessible, even paper and pencil for writing messages back and forth. Two decades later, and some law enforcement agencies, whether from ignorance or malice, continue to refuse some deaf persons the right of translation.

As to Murderopolis, the 1995 peak in gang activity and murders abated. The numbers fluctuate from year to year but have trended downward, except for a spike between 2006 and 2008. Police spokespeople noted that many of those arrested and convicted during the Murderopolis surge were being released from prisons, having served their time. Others claimed the numbers were compounded by a generation of sons of those who'd been taken out of action in the mid' 90s. Latell Chaney's attackers would likely be among those long since released. One was convicted of aggravated robbery and assault. The other four pleaded guilty.

After sitting eleven and a half months behind bars himself—some of them possibly in the same cell block one of his attackers might have occupied—Latell Chaney was released. His attorney identified significant irregularities during his arrest and trial, separate from concerns about violations of his rights under the ADA. As a result of these irregularities, his conviction on the domestic charge in Martin County was overturned, a retrial scheduled, and eventually a plea agreement struck. In a separate civil case, Chaney and both Martin County and Nobles County jails agreed to a settlement. In addition to monetary awards, each county will improve communication access for future deaf inmates.

XIII

lan-guage n. 1) The body of words and systems for their use common to a people who are of the same community or nation, the same geographical area, or the same cultural tradition . . .

The Random House Dictionary, Unabridged Edition, 1973

Body of words. Words—and signs—of the body. Whether hearing or deaf, we all require bodies to make language, bodies which then put us smack in the middle of place and story. Mistranslation can make of this gift a curse. When this happened to Latell Chaney, language *became* the story. If time and place are coordinates that locate us in a world, then language is the coordinate that lifts that world to its most translatable dimension.

Killing the Snake

KERRY JAMES EVANS

In the beginning, I was angry, my apartment's backyard flooded with the leftovers
    from my neighbor's divorce:
                bicycle without chain,
          bookshelf cockeyed
                  at the joints,
    a forty-year-old woman, three children—
one, a boy with a cowlick
              similar to mine,
                  backpack strapped to his shoulders.
                                  I know this boy.

            He will forget how to ride on the handlebars,
    pumping fists
                to a godless sky.

                          His mother walks
                without swinging her arms,
      and when she waves each morning,
                  leaving for work,
        I recall my mother's sad knuckles.
                        Her complexion—
how the shame steamed on a plate of gravy
                with each man she brought home.
There are words for this shame.

There are words for my anger.
For offering my neighbor a home-cooked
      meal: pan-seared lamb,
          potatoes mashed
  with garlic and onions—
      this after potted meat on white crackers.

      Mine too. No heater and the house unfinished,
I followed my father into a bar,
      throwing darts to make rent,

leaving my mother to raise my brother and sister,
       to overdose in the projects,
in back alleys and single-wides—
    beyond the washed-out gullies
        of gravel roads.
I've left those stories for the moon to decipher.

      But my neighbor's not interested
    in my mother—
she needs help moving a television
      through a crowded hallway
        to her bedroom, which is packed in boxes.
   She grabs my forearm:
        Let me pay you. How much?

No room for leftovers.

        Nowhere to hide the remnants of her shift
at the nursing home, where she massages bedsores
              from bony thighs,
      thinking burial,
   her own skin
      stretched like the back
         of a bald cat.

Call the landlord, I tell the gardenias.

But the only landlord is the diamondback coiled like a noose,
    rattling behind a gas grill
        sinking into mud.
          And in this yard we share,

     a diaper bag
       molds beneath a hanging tomato plant,
whose leaves have shriveled,
      whose buds
        have flowered and died.

Her children will do nothing with their lives

but grow angrier at their father
who has left them to rot
in a backyard where mosquitos
nesting in empty storage bins
buzz ancient and indifferent.
I should know.

I never owned a bike that wasn't broken.

But I owe it to this woman:

A man can love—
even in this world.

I drop a hoe's steel blade, slicing the head
clean off the body, and as the blood
clumps in the dirt at our feet,
I ask her for a mop bucket,
and when she says,
Now what?

In a quick, charring moment,

   I throw the snake on the grill,

  scales crackling
     on the grate.

Moth Boy

HERSHMAN JOHN

Moth Boy's life, a cliché for the flame
Born in First World, the Black World, with no noon, no midnight
Who told me to write this poem on Valentine's Day
Now flutters about like a lost wish

Who hopes that someone will wreck a ship
Hopes that snow will touch the world all at once
Hopes everyone's lips will sing and kiss
Whose language is being overrun by a virus
      Who says my blood is tainted too
Who is there every night waiting for the porch light
Who watches through the window
Who loves to bake sweets and fry bread
Loves to watch the supernatural on television
Loves to shop for expensive leather shoes

Moth Boy elucidates like Las Vegas every evening, burning and fizzling
      out with a vampire's and Navajo's sacrilege: no sun!
He loves the feel of cashmere on his colossal marble form, eight-pack
      abs, steel cables, two percent body fat, big "guns," an imperviable diamond
O Narcissus can never pass a mirror, his wings dazzle Sirens
Who sees the glint of gold, of a candy wrapper, and buys a Swiss watch
Whose Blackjack buddies are ethereal wisps, ghosts, and the moon
Who hates onions—they smell of all that is dead and unholy

Who once whispered help in Born for Water's ear, who forgot how
      the story ends or begins, but knows it goes on
Who's become a mortal bulb, whose life will burn out like a birthday candle
Who goes to the gym five times a week, maybe Cupid is real?
Moth Boy, whose stories are no longer told in coming winters
Who reads romance novels and dreams of a wedding by the ocean
Always thirsty, drinking from desert flowers and icy cans of Coke,
      always thirsty for his mirror image with blue or green eyes

Who has never seen the ocean or even met a Jinn
A girl from Kansas, with pretty red shoes, is slowly poisoning him
Who bought an orange sports car to fit in, who can never drive home
Who has never been in love and wants a mother-in-law
Who told me he will never have a child—never see his face in another
Maybe one night a star will fall for him but it never does
Who never wears a seatbelt, it wrinkles finely spun linen shirts
Moth Boy is lost in the Glittering World, the Fourth World

June 14, the moment of your death, only the rain spirits will remember
      you, your death will summon a hurricane

AIDS Ward, City of Angels, 1995

MADELYN GARNER

for Omar

Now as his thrush-full,
pith-white throat
numbs to water—you

sit on the sweat-stained bed,
cotton swabs in ungloved hands,
pulling viscous ropes into a tissue

as if this were no more a chore
than mopping figure-eights
along endless corridors.

You brush his teeth and rinse until
the mouth is infant
and ready for your sleight-of-hand trick:

sweet orange removed from
your pocket, peeled and pin-wheeled
over the tray table,

each pulpy wafer placed
on his tongue with love's ease—
you husband him.

Blue Thumb

ALISON MORSE

Luis Jimenez remembers the dream
and the dollars he gave the coyote
to smuggle him north under indigo sky,
but he doesn't recall the bluegrass
Florida lawns he mowed
and weeded to pay for a future acre
of Guatemalan loam in his homeland
mountains of Cuchumatán,

or his blue Chevrolet, smashed
by a bourbon-filled, insuranceless
American driving a stolen van.
Luis's skull now uproots—with every seizure—
a memory: *calabaza azul*, the name of his wife,
how to defecate in a toilet, how to stand.

He doesn't remember the Florida hospital
where he lay curled like a bud
wrapped in forget-me-not blue hospital wool
while the staff debated, *do we pay*
this illegal alien's bills, or don't we;

holds no image of the ice-blue sky
out the window of the American plane
that delivered him to Guatemala
as if he were a highland orchid
transplanted north for exotic display—
tossed back bloomless.

Luis's land is the Maya Blue
blanketed bed in his mother's home
in the mountains of Cuchumatán,
where no public care exists
for a withered seed pod, scattering.
If his mother dies before she returns
from town, who will remember
to water and feed him

What It Means to Be a Man

ED BOK LEE

We were driving down to Hastings, Jorge and me, with a trunk full of six four-day-old puppies in a cardboard grocery box. Pit bulls. The whole way down 61 you could smell and hear them, whining away through the Camry's back seat, or more like they were singing out of tune. The day was cool and gray. Only when we hit one canyon of a pothole somewhere just past Cottage Grove did the dogs finally quiet down.

I was taking Jorge to Hastings to show him what it means to be a man.

Dawnita and Jorge's mother was dead, and neither had ever known either of their fathers. I have always been attracted to women who've needed me around, found me useful. Back during this time, I'd somehow learned to seduce single, beleaguered women with dead-end jobs and small children. Prior to Dawnita, for two years when I was twenty, I'd dated an older woman named Yolanda who had a toddler boy and infant girl. I looked after them while Yolanda worked at an Ethiopean restaurant. In the end, I found out she was sleeping with a woman bartender named Daria she'd sometimes lock up with. Yolanda was half Ethiopian, and for a time I forgave her because I could see how if you've never dated your own kind, you might always wonder. And because we'd talked about marriage, it sort of made sense, the need to get this kind of question out of your system . . . until I learned she and Daria were planning a trip to Hawaii together—and I was supposed to change a thousand diapers in our one-room apartment while they sipped piña coladas out of live coconuts on paddleboards.

The pit bulls were going to be a peace offering to the farmer whose dog Jorge had shot and killed six days before. It was Dawnita's idea, despite my misgivings. I was worried about what the farmer, a well-off man named Reiner Toleffson, noted for his unpredictability, might do when he saw Jorge again. I was also worried about what Jorge was capable of, despite my and Dawnita's having sat his ass down to explain the situation in the kitchen.

We'd just finished the chili I'd heated up for dinner.

"I thought it might be rabid," Jorge said, about the man's dog he'd shot. It was a lie through the little gap in his front teeth. But Dawnita has certain ideas about her little brother that don't allow her always to see such things.

"Then why even let them fight in the first place?" she asked.

Dawnita is an impressive woman—still a few inches taller than her gangly, fourteen-year-old brother, and a good ten pounds heavier. But, more, it's the sharp, harsh features she can bore into you with, accentuated by pencil-drawn eyebrows and sometimes also lipstick liner.

"I don't know." He half-shrugged.

Jorge had shot the farmer's pit bull after it had torn open his own favorite dog's throat in a cramped, moldy basement match in Frogtown.

"I won't do it again," Jorge muttered, slumped in the cracked orange plastic booth. Under the kitchen's single fluorescent light, you could already see what his face would look like in middleage.

"We don't know that," I said to Dawnita. "Maybe he will, maybe he won't."

"I just don't know what to do anymore," she said, rubber-banding her black, bronze-high-lit hair into a ponytail behind her head. "How many times I gotta cry over you?"

None, I thought, but kept my mouth shut.

"I didn't know it was loaded," Jorge said, making no sense.

Jorge is a typical teenager, except with a skin condition that splotch-bleached a third of his otherwise dark brown face to three basic colors: brown, reddish pink, and off-white. People think it's an acid burn, and he likes to make them believe it is, so he seems harder than he really is. But the truth is he was born with it. Hyperpigmentation. Sometimes he uses it to cull pity. Other times like a weapon his eyes steel themselves behind.

"Can I go now?" he said, eying us like we were both frothing at the mouth and in his pocket he still had that .22 he'd picked up from a meth-head neighbor a few months earlier.

"If you climb out that window upstairs one more time," Dawnita said, "don't bother ever coming back."

"I pay rent," Jorge said, half under his breath.

"You contribute to this family," Dawnita corrected.

Now Dawnita was standing over him. This, her typical method to try to psychologically break him. In the past, he might have shrunk. But now that he was making good money fighting his dogs, he just tinkered with the plastic flowers in a vase, ignoring her stare.

"I guess we all better take a chill pill," I said.

"Take this little shit out of my sight," Dawnita finally said. She walked past the garbage can overflowing with paper plates and stopped in front of the sink. I could tell she was really upset, in part also from the fight she and I had had earlier that morning.

"Fuck you both," Jorge muttered, stomping down the hall and out the front door.

"Little motherfucker." Dawnita used a spoon to clean a plate with macaroni and cheese on it that had turned to granite.

Suddenly, I felt overwhelmed with sadness for both Dawnita and Jorge.

They are only half-siblings by an affair her father had with their mother, who was from Shreveport, Louisiana. Jorge didn't look Mexican. Dawnita did. Mexican and something. Not Asian, though, unlike me. That was the only thing she didn't have in her. She often made sure I knew that.

For the record, I don't condone dog fights. I don't even really like going. Lately, they can't open the windows in those two or three basements, so the smell begins to burn. I only took Jorge that first time the summer before this incident because I was supposed to be watching him, and a friend needed me to work security at the very last minute. It was going to be our secret. A week later, a neighbor sold Jorge his first pup, and then another man gave him a second mongrel, and what do you expect from a mean brown kid who doesn't have any friends or parents and a splotch on his face like Australia the color of bacon?

I didn't think it was a good idea for Dawnita to let him keep training them. But after the kid won almost a grand from his first fight, giving her half, I knew she'd eventually cave.

And I knew I wouldn't say anything.

The boy had a way with the dogs, knew how to move with and talk to them.

"I don't hold you responsible," she'd told me in bed one hot, rainy night. "I just don't want to know any details. If anything bad happens, it's on you. And keep those mangy things away from my damn tomatillos."

Reiner Toleffson. I got the name of the Hastings farmer from Warsame, the dude who'd hosted the Frogtown match. Warsame was cold to me on the phone over the shooting. "Why you want to know about that farmer? Believe me, he don't want to know nothing about you." But we'd gone to middle school together, and by then I was taking my third class in refrigeration technology at St. Paul Tech and knew Warsame was trying to get out of the game. So I hinted that as soon as I got my own business going, I'd personally train him.

"I just got to right this wrong," I explained. "You know how Dawnita can get."

"Leave that farmer alone. Shit, man. He's a pussy. He started to cry. Like he was a tiny child."

I'd had a Pneumatic Controls class that night and so missed the whole shooting incident.

"Do me this one favor."

"Just like a baby," Warsame continued. "And then the crazy man takes his cash and picks up his dog in his two arms, never mind his nice jacket, and then he just goes. That's it. No words."

"Silent type."

"Don't go out there, my friend."

"It's for the kid's own sake," I said. "Unless you want him to turn out like you and me."

Rural Minnesota has never done much for me. Fields. Silver silos. Chipped white barns. Water towers like armless giant robots. Sky on this afternoon like a giant oil spill with thunder in the distance.

The whole hour-long drive southeast, Jorge didn't speak much. I took it as a good sign that he'd finally accepted the fate of his pups. Or, at least, one pup—whichever one Toleffson wanted from the lot as restitution.

"Remember," I said, as we pulled into Hastings proper. "Just say you're sorry. I'll do the rest."

Jorge's Afro was out of control. Slouched in the passenger seat, he looked like he was balancing the car roof on his head.

"I feel sick to my stomach," he said.

"Drink some more water."

"I hate the taste of water."

"Think of it like medicine."

Maybe the pups had accepted their fate, too. Now they were completely silent. I jostled the car, which got a couple of the feistier ones yelping again.

"If he cusses you out, don't say shit," I said.

"Whatever." Jorge slipped on his headphones.

The gray day smelled like earthworms and fish and big, wet buckets of wind. In the distance, a formation of geese was veering northward and, suddenly, I could see what my and Dawnita's lives together would be like for the next decade. We'd get married, maybe rent a house. I'd have my own business and a few employees by then, and she'd hopefully be a nurse, or at least back in school. Fast-forward fourteen, fifteen years, and I'd be sitting in the same place, having the same conversation with our own child, who, like Jorge, might be staring out at all the farms and fields in passing, wanting either to be more like or to kill me.

"You know how I feel about your sister, don't you?" I said.

Now he was pretending to sleep while listening to his headphones.

"Not everyone would make you do what you're about to do," I said, "but she loves you and wants you to know shit like this. That's not just a good sister, or woman . . . but a good person. You come from good people. Don't forget that."

He'd forgotten to buckle up from where we'd last gotten gas and breakfast sandwiches with the money Dawnita had given me. But I let it slide.

Reiner Toleffson's land, five miles south of Hastings, sat on at least twenty acres. He was doing well—all new equipment: a Chrysler, a Ford pickup, and a silver SUV on the gravel driveway winding up to his house.

Clearly, dog fighting was just a hobby for him.

I pulled the Camry up next to the Ford in the grass and turned off the engine.

Because I hadn't been there on the night of the shooting, I figured I had about thirty seconds standing in front of the farmer to say things right before he laid eyes on the person who'd shot his best dog.

"Stay here," I said, closing my door. Now it was starting to sprinkle. You could smell it, sweet like the water in a flower's stem.

Jorge pretended not to hear me, like he'd fallen asleep to the iPod he'd recently bought for himself with his latest winnings. One for Dawnita, too, and a plasma TV for the house.

I was halfway to the farmer's brick two-story when Jorge spoke up from the car. "You don't even know, do you?"

His eyes were still shut, a consternated look expanding across his forehead. "What's that?"

"Or do you just not care?"

I came back and leaned forward, propping myself in my open window. "Speak English, amigo."

His seat was reclined, but he refused to open his eyes.

"She's just with you until she gets over him."

The him, I presumed, was the fiancé she'd lost in Iraq a few months before I'd met her.

"We'll talk about this later," I said, rising from the car window.

As I was walking back to the man's house, Jorge called out: "Because you're safe, you fat chickenshit! She would never actually marry someone like you!"

I knew Jorge was planning on joining the army as soon as he was of age. He'd basically stopped going to school. I suspected it, but hadn't said anything to Dawnita, who must have known it, too. You can only handle so much at one time.

"You're a babysitter and a fucking maintenance man!" Jorge shouted.

I could have turned around. I could have gone back and pulled him out of the car by the hair and dug my fingernails into his throat and treated whatever veins that popped out like earthworms and I was a fucking fisherman who hadn't eaten in days. I could have told him how close to signing the contract at the recruiter's office I myself had been. How the four guys I'd gone to that strip-mall office with were now in Iraq, Germany, and Afghanistan. One dead. One in the brig. But how I was different because I didn't need the military to cure my life. I could save or destroy it myself.

"Can I help you?" someone called from the porch. It was an older woman holding a tin watering can. She wore an expensive-looking dress and matching jacket, like maybe she worked as a bank administrator or high school principal. Only when I saw the Bible in her other hand did I realize that she'd probably just come back from church.

"Young man, are you OK? Do you need something?"

Just then, the farmer came out. He, too, was wearing his Sunday best. The large man was older than his wife by about twenty years, and he walked with a silver-handled cane. Aside from his thick gray hair, slicked back, he was a mess: heavy breathing, humpbacked, and overweight by at least a hundred pounds. But he was sharp still. I could tell by the way he slowly fixed his faded blue eyes on me over his glasses.

It took him forever to hobble off the porch to where I was standing.

"Can I help you?" he asked, cautious but not unwelcoming.

"Mr. Reiner Toleffson?"

"You boys selling something?"

"No, sir. It's about something that happened last week, in the city."

"The city, you say."

The old woman was still on the porch, listening.

"Maybe it'd be better if we spoke in private," I said.

Something about the old man's gaze made you feel self-conscious.

"It involves that dog you lost," I said, lowering my voice. I'm not exactly sure why I said what I said next. I am only thirteen years older than Jorge. But it somehow felt right. "The dog of yours my son there in the car shot."

Finally, the farmer understood. Strolling down the drive, I explained exactly what our purposes were, and asked him if he'd like to go somewhere else to look at the pups. He finally looked back at his wife, and waved her back into the house. She turned and lingered for a moment.

"That him there?" He cupped one hand over his eyes toward Jorge, still slumped in the car.

"Yes," I said.

"I guess we better take a look at them then, since you came all this way."

I won't say I liked the old man. Any more than he seemed to like me. But I think he understood what I was trying to do, and so there was a certain unspoken respect built between us from the get-go.

When I opened the trunk, the box of six new pups looked drugged. A miasma of heat and piss rose, and I wished we'd thought to take them out in Hastings proper and put them in the back seat so they could cool off.

Reiner Toleffson stood over the open trunk and removed his glasses to clean them with a handkerchief. "Yep," he said, "I guess them are some pretty decent dogs."

I removed a plastic bag from the trunk. "These here are photos of their parents. Tough as nails."

He looked and made a face, though it was hard to tell if it was the wind and slight warm drizzle, or something about the pit bulls in the photos.

"Let's take this elsewhere," he said. He put the photos into the plastic bag and placed it carefully back in the trunk.

"Jorge!" I called, but he had the volume way up, pretending to be asleep.

"Don't do that," the old man said, looking back at the house. "Not here."

It took the old man ten minutes to return to the house, get a hat and jacket on, and finally pull his pickup out so we could follow him. Twice I spoke to Jorge and even thought of yanking his headphones off or punching him. But from the peaceful look on the boy's face, I decided to wait until we got to wherever we were going.

We followed the old man for over ten miles, long enough to make me want to pull up beside him and ask how much longer. But I didn't. At one point, I wondered if he was leading us out to some barren field to shoot us. At the same time, not once did I have an urge to turn the Camry around.

People pay great prices for this kind of feeling of destiny, or fate.

Because by now I figured that whatever was going to happen was going to happen, and so reached forward under the dash for the space I'd made for my gun and slipped it into my coat pocket. The whole time, dribble leaked out of the clouds like some great purple-gray stomach rupture would at any minute break into torrential rain.

After twenty minutes the old farmer pulled off the highway and eventually onto a gravel drive leading to a smaller, shabbier farm.

"Wake up," I said, pulling the Camry up behind the old man's SUV. This time I pulled off Jorge's earphones. "We're here."

"I'm up," Jorge said, groggy.

"Remember, just say you're sorry. I'll do the rest."

"OK." He was dazed, had really fallen asleep, and so, very briefly, was his truest self.

"If there's any trouble, just take off. Here, take these."

For the first time all afternoon, maybe all week, he looked me in the eyes. Finally, he reached out and I dropped the car keys into his palm. As the old man got out of his vehicle, I popped my trunk and went around. One of the pups had almost completely chewed the collar off another pup.

"Mind bringing them around this way," the old man called, "so we can get a dry look at them?"

"You can see them fine like this," I called back.

"That pole barn right there should do the trick," he said and began hobbling toward it, as if I hadn't spoken.

You may have gotten in the car and driven home. Maybe you would even have lied to your girlfriend and told her the farmer didn't want any stupid pup. Or thrown one out of the car on the highway and said, "Yeah, he took one," and left it at that. Or just dumped the whole damn box in a river, gotten your record albums from her basement, and never turned around again.

"Where you going?" Jorge called from the car.

"You heard the man."

Jorge fell quiet for several seconds. "I ain't going in there."

"Then don't," I said, without looking back.

"Fuck you for bringing me here!"

"Thanks, but I already got your sister to do that. And hers is a lot nicer than your ugly, fucked-up face."

"You're making a big mistake!"

The pole barn was cramped with fertilizer and ammonia, but it was dry, as the farmer had promised. The old man had turned on a kerosene lamp. I waited for my eyes to adjust, then put the box of half-dazed pups down on a wooden table littered with several ancient-looking awls and other rusty tools. I had a pair of gloves in my pocket, next to my gun, and thought of slipping them on, just in case. Because my heart was thudding, and the pups seemed to know something strange was about to happen. They shuffled quietly, eyeing me like I was the wrong and only god.

"Get your fucking ass over here right now," the old man said behind me. "Now."

We are all of us given a destiny, like a race and parents and language and a roulette wheel of beliefs and ideas, and the best you can do is not look too hard and hopeful, as someone else with a half-smirk spins the thing.

"Goddammit, if you don't get your ass out here right now, I'll light this whole goddamn place on fire, so help me God."

As it turned out, the old man was talking on his cell phone. With his free hand, he fingered through the largest tool box I'd ever seen. I lowered my hand from the gun inside my jacket pocket, feeling stupid.

A pup with black gums started barking.

"Help me out here," the old man said, this time to me. "Fill this bucket with water. Should be a hose just outside."

It was just past three now, though by the way the clouds were, it might as well have been dusk. As I got the hose and filled the bucket, I caught Jorge watching me from inside the car. At first I thought the furrow in his brow was out of spite, but on a second look, I realized he wasn't even looking at me. A tall, thin figure was approaching from the front door of the shabby farmhouse.

"What the hell is going on?" shouted this other man. He was thin and wore white cowboy boots and leather chaps, and he carried an oversized, feminine orange umbrella. Both his arms were sleeved with tattoos, and the only significant hair he had on his head was a foot-long reddish-brown goatee. Still, he looked vaguely familiar.

"Who are these people!"

Clearly, he was in a bad mood. He passed right by the running hose in my hand without comment, trudging through the soft mud into the pole barn.

I was smoking a cigarette when Jorge finally came up beside me.

"I want to go," he said.

Finally, the trip was beginning to pay off.

"I guess they're just deciding which is the best pup," I said.

"Come on. Let's get out of here."

"Maybe if you went to school, you wouldn't need to learn this lesson." I flicked the butt and mashed it into the sandy mud. "Besides, I think you forgot about something. Your damn dogs are still in there."

That one got him. He kept looking between the pole barn and the ground.

"It's OK," he finally said. "That dog was one in a hundred."

"The one you shot, you mean?"

"Yeah."

"Because it beat yours."

He looked at me, but not with malice. "I guess."

The old man and Red Beard were in the pole barn talking in lowered voices when Jorge and I came in for the dogs. The two men could have been members of a very strange circus. The old man was smoking a cigar, and the younger one was trying pointlessly to clean off his white boots with a rag.

I guided Jorge gently through the darkness toward the two men.

"I'm sorry I shot your dog," he said.

The only problem, he said it to the wrong man.

"Whatever," Red Beard replied.

"You want one of them pups over there?" Jorge said, pointing at the box.

"I don't want your damn dog."

By now, I was thoroughly confused. I thought maybe the old man would be, too. But, instead, he joined in on their little conspiracy. "Son," he said to Jorge, "bring them animals over here to me."

A field mouse darted across the pole barn floor, but no one noticed.

I decided to keep my mouth shut because maybe I was still driving out to Hastings and had fallen asleep and if I suddenly woke up, I'd jerk the wheel headlong into a semi. And then I'd never learn how this or the rest of my or Jorge's or anyone's life turned out in the end.

"Take one out," the old man ordered Red Beard.

"What?"

"You heard me."

"I don't want one," Red Beard said, snidely.

The old man whacked the box with his cane, causing not just the pups, but all of us in the pole barn to perk up. Three of the dogs started barking.

"Reiner, if you don't take one of these fucking dogs, so help me god, I'll find them dogs you got hidden wherever the fuck they are and I'll stomp on their heads one by one. You understand me?"

Red Beard, or, as it started to become clear, Reiner Toleffson Jr., shook his head, slowly approaching the box. He picked up one of the pups by the scruff.

"Now what?" he said.

"Outside," the older commanded.

It was like the day was trying to go dark as fast as it could to prevent whatever was going to happen. Jorge held his own arms as if it were already late fall.

"Take this," said Reiner Sr., handing the other a rusty awl.

"Jesus, Dad."

Outside and up close, you could see the white strands woven finely into Reiner Jr.'s red beard. His eyes had almost as many crow's-feet as his father's. But you could also see something of his mother in him, something matronly in his weak, sunken chin.

"You like to see these animals tore up, anyway," the older said. "What's the difference?"

"You know the difference."

"Don't give me that horse shit. No one eats your damn dogs. But you raise them and watch them get slaughtered just like a damn butcher."

Red Beard turned to Jorge and me, looking like he was about to blame us for everything.

"Do you know what day it is?" the old man said. "No, because you got your orgies and your house of sin while your mother sneaks you money. Don't think I don't know."

But it wasn't until Reiner Jr. squatted in the mud and held the sleepy, squirming puppy over the bucket of ice cold water that I realized why any of us was there: A mistake had been made. Actually, many of them. And this was just the consequence, the logical conclusion to every bad thing ever done.

"I need a rock," Red Beard muttered, shaking his head.

I looked at Jorge, who was watching, chewing dry skin on his bottom lip.

"No," the older said. "Use your hands."

It took a good two minutes for the last of the air bubbles to come up. The whole time, Red Beard looked at nothing but a few white pebbles the color of luminescent bone lodged in the mud.

At one point, as a jet passed high overhead, trailing sound like a sonic tail, I thought I could maybe hear some of the other dogs in the pole barn wailing. Storms, epileptic seizures, earthquakes . . . Sometimes they just know things.

But long after the jet had passed, still nothing.

On the drive back, I kept all four windows down and the radio blaring. I could tell Jorge wanted to say something, but I didn't care.

Meanwhile, on either side of us, green pasturelands unfurled for a long time, and then scabbed slowly over into outlet malls, a water tower, asphalt, passing cars, buildings, more fields, more cars, another water tower, a faded Rolodex of billboards, concrete, parks, steeples, a far, night-lit downtown, more neon and incandescent high-rises and billboards and trash and asphalt and strip malls and bars and clubs and schools and anonymous buildings and bodies, basements and churches—and all the other hidden altars people seek, when they need to corner something to believe in, bigger than themselves.

Deep Wound Singing

MICHAEL SCHMELTZER

i.

A brown buck shot in the side.
A son who days ago said

pulling a trigger frightened him the same way thunder did
as a child. And now childhood and blood

populate the spoor, mar the blades of grass,
and stain the desolate woods

with their strange brand of harmony.

~

The father stalked the blotches, the body
of a dying beast

cacophonous, so much so the son
cried in his bed, prays

he never shuffles again
as if chained behind his father,

the world linked in a primal music
pulsing from the blood.

The anxious son
dreams in the dark of his room

as if in the middle of a field
soaked in that darkness.

ii.

The boy shudders out of sleep, the girl
beside him pale & nude. He remembers

last night's moon. Still he thinks
of the buck, how it struggled downhill

toward the river as if called. He listens
for that song until the sun ignites

the girl's yawn, her eyes open
like an eclipse passing.

He notices blood on his fingers,
on his thighs. The girl is humming

into his chest as if the heart heard
music. Her first time she warned

and even though she bled, she thanks him for it.

St. Mark and the Boat of Demons

JOEL LONG

1

Water moves like the fur of rats,
the sky mirrored. There is contagion
everywhere.
                    I am not afraid. Waves
lift my boat above the piazza
and I pull them with my oar,
my prow ticking cathedral stairs.
Lightning turns my nets to ash in water,
singes my hair, smoke hovering near
the skull. It will snatch the heart of wood,
but mine is safe, shimmering
                        in fish scales.
Clay jars rattle the boom, my chest,
the jambs glazed with storm and flash.
The wine in barrels turns poison.
The poison turns to wine the devils drink
as they shriek in the wind.
Noah's hammer knocks, and the dogs drown.

2

There is a voice in rain. There is a hand
on my shoulder. Birds hide in the arches.
I cannot do what you want me to do.
Water will destroy me.

"Here is shelter, beneath

        the finial, beneath the rib."

Your voice comes from incense and ember,
smells of leaves under leaves. *I will do*

            what you say.
I don't know from what century you speak,

          candle flame,
lighthouse. The rain goes through your words.
Suddenly we are in my boat. You smile,
and the storm tears the fabric of the hour above.
It is raining inside me. Your fingers comb small feathers
in the crow's breast, spectral

          spray of rain and oil.
It closes its eyes.
The boat does not tip, does not sway.

3

There are two more stops, two more voices
in the boat. You want
                    me in the water again.
I cannot tell the difference between water and storm,
both gray and churning tatters of the air.
There is a stench of the prophet's floor, sheep guts
and flies, stench that makes my tongue shrink.
My oar thrumbs my palm with
                        thunder and wild current.
This is your journey, and I am the hinge.
The charred ship was carved of storm, after-burn
of lightning strike. Blackness moves, waves, claws,
bleats at the center of longing and terror, the boat of demons.
Faces of dead children rattle the balustrade. Death brands
its seal on my heart. They would turn marble to cinder,
dome to dove shell golden in the heat.
                        I love them.

I want them to burn
                me, cut me. Dolphins break
waves mounted by demons. I push my oar backwards.
The boat goes toward the galley. I fear I will be flame.
How sudden. How quiet. The sail of the demons is smoke.

4

You cut three crosses in wind,
hands so white they blind. Bells in the campanile
swing, and demons dissolve.

You breathe the storm from the sky, peel gray
from blue and a wave of sunlight, every atom of marble
and water lit. A violet breeze sweeps away

the singed pig,
the goat's head. The bells bang light into canals.
Give me your ring I plead.
They will not believe you have saved us.

Festival of Mars

LEE ROSSI

How can we not love them, our great men,
who were once our children, boys who climbed
the hazel nut and pear and pelted our downcast
heads with early fruit? Early they learned

cruelty, it was so much a part of the world,
like a tree taking in the soil's bitterness
and making it flower. We could only marvel
as they scattered like monkeys at our shouts

and curses, as if they could outrun
even themselves. And now they stand
before us, all medals, oaths, and stiff uniforms,
heedless of the frail skin that fills with every breath.

Let us praise them with voices raised as one,
and curse ourselves for what they have become.

Strange Roots for Talking

ANDRE PERRY

One

My father talks of North Carolina. Getting in fights with white kids on the way to school. Throwing bricks, bloody yer teeth. Living in the nice house in Washington, D.C., with nice kids in nice schools—you don't forget that brick-tossing shit. You put your sharp kids in sharp schools. You want them to go further than the kids of the people who threw the bricks. Father shakes hands and signs contracts with people his age. They were on the other side of the fence fifty years ago; maybe their hearts are still there. Drinks wine from France while Mom charms, both of them diplomats. He comes home laughing at her for being all smiles with the white people. But he does it, too. It's all in the game. *Ducking from crackers dodging crazy spades.* If you own the place, does that make you a house nigger?

My brother and I learn the science of masks. Can never be white, would never want to be, will always carry nigger skin, but can act whiter than you can ever be. Even Brooks Brothers shirts tossed like rags on our backs look good. Girls stare at this fine dark man and you look just normal in your standard white-man suit. They'll marry you and sleep with me, set me up for the lynching, postmodern-like, kick me out of the club, render this degree and my membership card nil. Run with wolves, bound to get bit.

Choke on your white guilt: I carry the burden. Yes, me—good, safe black man from the good neighborhood and the ivy-laced halls, right shoes on. Look like the president. It's good to own land. Slaves make sense. Not a communist. Committed old boys sear-suckered and feeling good, sipping scotch, neat, in Charlottesville. Exclusive tea parties in Brookline. The black help replaced by their Central American counterparts serve food while the Earth is divvied up, a slice of cake for everybody in the wedding party. There's niggers all around the world and not every last one of them is black. There's city developers, capitalists, splitting these streets in half—white faces on one side, dark faces on the other. After all this good sex they still don't believe in mixing. Vouchers send the darkness to the outskirts. Ring around the collar. Capitalism inherently makes people do bad things. Basketball brings us all together in arenas. You trade niggers like baseball cards. Us, too. The players dress fine. You want them shoes, socks, and go 'round wearing your shorts just like Ray Allen. For only twelve percent we sure make up a whole lot of your scene. You sure poke your heads into ours. Find your own styles for once.

I wake up free but I don't do anything for the next fifty pages. Caught in a pensive, white, contemporary American novel.

Two

The next day, old Southern women—old enough to have beaten my mother in the street some fifty years ago and gotten away with it—smile at me. Ordering eggs, grits, and biscuits from them, I can't tell if they really care for me from behind those sweet, buttery eyes. Do they find it absurd that the tables are turned and they are now serving me? Sitting in the diner being served by the kind Southern women, I tell myself to stop being so paranoid: it's weak of me to ask for equality and then stereotype the *other*. But I see scars in the past and I'm sure they do, too. It's not that easy to just smile and forget. In New York, they look you in the eyes and stab you in the chest. In downtown Washington, D.C., if someone smiles at you, you're pretty sure they hate you. In Boston, you already know they hate you.

These biscuits look like the soft, resistant women you put on your cutting board. Tough at first, until you slice in. Gives in when you punch the center. Why buy them when you can make more on your own? Have fun in the process, bloody yer sheets. Mixed kids are always so beautiful. I eat my breakfast and leave a good tip. I get in the car and hightail back up to the Northeast.

Three

Tonight I dance drunken in the backyard of the Klan. If my dark skin makes you itch, just let me know and we can get this out of the way. Can't tell which ones are good and which ones are bad, so paranoia is an asset. Behind my smile is a shotgun waiting to erupt.

Thoughts of butter-drenched eggs and cheddar biscuits run through my mind. We're at a late-nite food joint called Time-Out. The line is long and a scrappy punk of a white kid starts talking shit to me as I wait to order my food. If there is a game to be won in life, he has seen me, swinging happily in Dixie-land with a bright-orange Princeton University *Go Tigers* T-shirt and knows I have won it. My tipsy happiness is mud in his eyes. The kid wears baggy blue jeans just beneath his butt. His white Nike cap is twisted backwards against a body full of Southern hip-hop fashion. After a few rude lead-ons—asking me what I am doing in his town, then doubting where I go to school, and ultimately warning me not to talk to the girls—I acknowledge him properly with a vicious scowl. He is energized. He responds, "What? Do you wanna fuckin' do this?"

I feel alone under the neon lights. The sizzling pitter-patter of frying pan oil and the whole weight of the greasy spoon calling for action. A black cop pushes up from the rear of the line and says, "Calm down, boys." I fall back into the line, finding comfort in the uncommon ally of a police officer. I smile down at the punk as I step up to place my order. This time, there's nothing he can do. *Hang that nigger!* The pleasures of North Carolina. The rest of the patrons seem unfazed by the whole event, the cop included. *Did y'all hear me? I wanna see some strange fruit up in this bitch!* So accustomed to a system of racial tension, they can no longer be bothered to care about small-time beefs. It is late, many drinks under our collective belts; it is time to feast on this hot, greasy food.

Four

All my niggaz in the house better tap them boots
Strange fruit, strange fruit!
Get that bitch on her knees
Strange fruit, strange fruit!
Hang her nigga from a tree

Five

My college friends and I move along like happy losers through the Chapel Hill bars—just glad enough that our team kept the match within eight points. A mile deep into tall, sticky pitchers of Budweiser and here I am entertaining the escapist fantasies of former debutantes. Fuck me, marry him. Her lights dimmed long ago. She bought her hair blonde like a beer special. Blue-dress Devil girls and Tar Heel mistresses are happy to smile at me, wondering what it would be like to go down on their closet desires. Considering advances, my dazed lips crack smiles full of uneasy teeth. Unhinged, I feel. The eyes of possible boyfriends stare me down, stunned by my nerve to whisper calm Yankee nothings in the ears of their girls. I am a little afraid and somewhat intrigued to find out how much I can piss off one of these guys by taking a white girl home. Friends pull me away from the fray. We take off for food at a greasy after-hours joint called Time-Out.

Six

In college at Princeton. A black tiger. 1998. Road trip down to Chapel Hill, North Carolina. You've never seen college basketball until you step into the Dean Dome. The shrine to success. MJ back in the day. Dean and his boys. The Nigger Dome. Welcome to the Terrordome. When you got MJ, you don't need another Thunderdome. Mad blacks, sweet lax, and whites cheer on.

Howie: It's a breakthrough year for the Tigers and they actually stand a chance at challenging the Tar Heels' legacy. Thanks, Howie, now back to: a Princeton fan in this place is a minority to begin with. From the moment he walks into the Dean Dome, he's catching tilted glances from white and black fans alike. Walking among his chipper white friends, he feels like a mascot they pulled down from the North. Parading him around, cheering, "Look at what we brought down with us." Admittedly, some of his friends are a little on edge, out of their element as well. No matter who you are, it's hard to cheer against a vicious athletic powerhouse on their home turf. On the other hand, his North Carolina native friends are at home, a false risk for them to pretend they're on the visitor's squad. They're just Southern gentlemen doing jury duty up North. Did you see that dunk! Damn, those niggers can play. *Who said that?* (You *know* we're putting ON AIRs.)

The Tigers, with the white-boy backdoor cut, with John Thompson Jr. assisting, put up a good fight against the Tar Heels. They threaten to seize an impossible victory. Yet the will of tradition will not allow it! An eight-point deficit. Shrug happily at the buzzer, you orange-and-black-clad Northerners. You know a Princeton victory might have spelled out a rockier evening for your personal safety in this white and blue town.

Seven

When white people smile at me in the South, I stutter on the inside. Mostly I smile back as a calculated measure. Either it'll steer off unwanted conflict or maybe they actually can see past the sad history. Maybe they can help me to see past that history and let go of the doubt that infects me. Perhaps I'm too paranoid or maybe I'm just waiting for a more formal apology, an ongoing apology, a change.

I've got different unease depending on the part of the country. In the countryside, sometimes I know I'm not wanted, but at least we have that understanding. In the liberal part of the city, they may preach the equality platform but "forget" to invite me to the dinner party. Some people are good; most are complex. I meet you at work, new white colleague, and we get along, having a good time on the job. I wonder when you go home if you call Shaq a nigger, out loud or in your head, for missing that free throw. That big ape should practice more on bending his legs. When he does, he really gets better.

Hope

JOYCE SUTPHEN

Somewhere armies have been called in,
and the government is mobilizing.
None of this is of any help to us.

Here the sun is bright. The shadow of a tree
falls across a house where no one lives.
It is of no consequence.

The sea beats down walls and floods
the coast. Millions are without power.
Darkness, darkness.

I suppose she can no longer drive.
(Perhaps there is some mistake?) No,
this is how things are going to be.

If just one bird would sing,
with a twist of its feathered shoulders,
I would hear it.

Two Young Men in Another Country

WILLIAM REICHARD

hang from nooses tied to the arm of a crane.
That's the way they execute there, the newscaster says.
No steps to the gallows, no drop of the trap,
body falling, neck snapped.
Instead, a crane, with noose
tied to the machine's arm,
rope tightened around the men's necks,
beam raised so the men die slowly,
hearing the crowd scream about justice.

If these men, eighteen, maybe twenty years old,
must die for who they are,
may they have done
what they wanted to do. May their lips
have known one another, their tongues together,
slowly turning. May they have seen one another
naked, erect, in full sun, made love in the heat
of the day, the light's rays painted across their bodies.
May theirs not be a thwarted love, a longing only.
Let their bodies, as the crane's arm is raised,
turn so they can see each other,
and leave this world with eyes open.

That Woman Who Used to Sit Here All Those Years

ALBERTO RÍOS

1.

After one war and before another—
Perhaps she had lost someone, but no one knew for sure,

Only that she wore black for all those years
Even in summer, even in rain, another of the many women

Revolution makes love to so cruelly, by not touching,
By not holding, always simply by taking away.

At first she could only look down. Perhaps
That is where she imagined her husband to be.

She could only stare with a falling attention, and rarely spoke
Though of course it can only be said that she was polite enough,

Never a bother. But they say that one day she heard
The sound of a small, passing bird.

2.

That one afternoon in the spring, startled, she looked up,
She kept looking up, she could not stop

Looking up, so much was up there, held in the fluid
Air of this place, the languorous float of plankton,

Their sea all this time above her, embers, minor diamonds
Highlit in the tide of coarsing sunlight, ferocious, thick,

Glimmering through the trees newly leafed:
A mote here, a tree in the distance, the two

Joined by the eye as belonging to each other, then more,
This persuasive Galilean trick of perspective,

This tree of stars and desire, of dust motes and sunlight
So easily seen in the moment and striking.

3.

And then, one afternoon in the spring she lifted her eyes
So much, so well, and with such reward,

Her head made itself
Rigid in its wonder, steadfast to the good,

Unbent, alert, no longer capable or happy
To be in league with things below.

The constellations at night in their height
Suited her, allowing her their direction

Even in the dark. Where they went, she went,
Though she seemed immobile on her bench.

In the fields and in the old days
Horses that looked up like this,

They were called starbucks,
And took as their direction, *Up*. It meant, *away*.

4.

These were the animals with blinders put on them,
Sometimes whips, sometimes harsh words.

They were beings thought to be lost to the work of the world.
But by looking up, she made a new marriage for herself

To them, a kinship to those not lost at all, the sky full with itself
And with them. She did not see except to see everything at once,

Her eyes impatient, her hands wanting
To reach the distances in charge of making this world.

Later in her life, looking up became an act of holding her head
Above water, and she could breathe only in this way

And in gulps, as if it were the sea beneath her legs
Readied and anxious to receive her

Though she was herself not ready.
Still, one day, after not looking down for so long

She forgot what was there, could not imagine any longer
Those things of the world that held her down.

Small-Town Cashews

ALBERTO RÍOS

Not Newberry's. I loved Kress's 5&10 best, and best thing
In that store was the first counter on the left,

The popcorn machine, followed by glassed cabinets of nuts,
Mixed, separate, almonds, peanuts, candied, pistachios—

But the cashews were the ones. Warm, served in paper cones
Sodas used to come in, paper cones that fitted into holders

In the pharmacy soda fountain where I'd get a Coke
After school, waiting for my mother to get off work as a nurse,

Sitting there with my cornet in its blue case and glad
Not to be carrying it, a Coke, into which—what was her name?

Angie. The woman at the counter with the curly hair—she'd smile,
She'd get my Coke, and then she'd spill-in some of the bright juice

From the maraschino cherry jar she normally used to make sundaes.
Cherry Coke, she'd say, all those years ago, happy with herself

And for me: *who wouldn't love that?* seemed plain enough
On her Angie face, and an invention good enough for me.

But the cashews in Kress's: I once saw an older high school boy
Buy some for his high school girlfriend—she held them

And she smiled at him, looked at him, but I looked at the cashews

And never forgot, so that every time I went into Kress's

I looked at the big cabinet that held the cashews
And I wished the glass was not there and that all those cashews

Were for me. *Go ahead,* they said, every time: *put your mouth
Right in there. Dive in. We're all for you, every one, just waiting.*

Open. Shut. Open.

A Folio of Photographs

SHIZUKA YOKOMIZO
Stranger No. 2, 1999

AUGUSTA WOOD
family to go through, 2006

ANNA BEEKE
Torre and Sailor at Bitsy's House, 2009

SARAH HOBBS
Untitled (insomnia), 2000
Courtesy of the artist and Solomon Projects, Atlanta, GA

RACHAEL VICTORIA NELSON
Charlie, 2009

RICHARD MISRACH
Untitled, 2005
Courtesy Fraenkel Gallery, San Francisco

ANI KINGTON
Untitled (Cobwebs, Lakeside, OH), 2008

ANDREA STAR REESE
from the series *The Urban Cave*, 2010

ANNE GOLAZ
L'assistance du chasseur, 2010

DEBBIE CARLOS
Sprout, 2007

CARLA ALEXANDRA RODRIGUEZ
I Loved You More (Maddie & Michael), 2008

JEFF WALL
After Invisible Man *by Ralph Ellison, the Preface,* 1999–2001
Courtesy of the artist

CHANG KYUN KIM
Silent Scream #09, 2009

DAVID GOLDES
Standing Chain Reaction, 2006
Courtesy Yossi Milo Gallery, New York

Romeo, Romeo

SIMON BARKER

It was about halfway through third form and I'd been on detention for a fortnight. As part of my punishment I had to copy out the balcony scene from *Romeo and Juliet* two dozen times because I'd shouted something in the middle of the movie and made the rest of the school laugh. Miss Pink said I'd ruined the mood.

They'd sent us to the Practical Agriculture room because the English department didn't have a detention room. With all the writing, my hand was beginning to ache so I started fiddling with the instruments in the glass case on the wall. There was a big scissors thing called a de-horner and something with handles called an emasculator, which used to make us cross our legs whenever Mrs. Strauss took it out to demonstrate.

Eventually I went looking for Thin Man. He was in the specimen room where they kept foetuses and other things in bottles.

"There's so much alcohol in here," he said. The specimen room stank even more than usual. Thin Man was smacking his lips.

"You're not drinking that," I said. "What if it's the kind of alcohol that sends you blind?"

"*Blind!* Oh, fuck! I can't see!" He started groping around until he grabbed hold of my nose. "Jesus, is that your dick? It's a midget."

"Did you really drink that stuff?" I asked.

"What stuff? I can't see anything."

Thin Man wore his hair short and parted on the side so that he looked like a teacher's pet. He was on detention for picking up his school bag at the wrong moment, before Mr. Bruce had given permission.

"Try it," he said, offering me a flask he'd found in the cupboard.

Flies were buzzing round. He shot out his hand and caught one between his thumb and forefinger in mid-air.

"I thought you were blind," I said.

"I have special skills. Go on, try some." He put the bottle up to my mouth.

"That's pretty strong," I said after I'd stopped coughing.

Miss Pink, our English teacher, came into the Prac Ag room, breaking off pieces of chocolate from a family-sized block and chewing them up. She looked like she was about to cry.

"What kind is it?" I asked.

"Old Jamaica," she said with her mouth full.

"Can I have some?"

"*Please.*"

"Please."

But after what I'd been drinking I couldn't even taste the rum-flavoured raisins.

"Where's Geoffrey?"

I told her that Thin Man was in the specimen room taking drugs.

"What kind of drugs?" she asked, looking puzzled.

"I don't know. Drugs drugs."

In class she could never tell when we were bullshitting. Occasionally she'd run down the hall screaming before the lesson was over. Then Slade would have to dress us all down.

"I wish I knew what was the matter," she said. She really was about to start crying. "Why doesn't he want to see me anymore?" She meant Slade. "He never wants to see me."

"Don't cry," I said. "Please."

Soon after Miss Pink had left, Slade came in. He'd been our English teacher the year before but now he was teaching us agriculture because we were short of teachers. He was hopeless.

"Jesus," he said, when he saw the emasculator. "You could do appalling damage with that thing."

I don't think he even knew what it was. I told him about Miss Pink. A few months ago he'd made her have an abortion. It was one of the things he'd explained to us in class. He used to start off each lesson with a sort of soliloquy. Originally it'd been stuff out of Shakespeare—*King Lear* and the like—but now he soliloquised about all his troubles at home and at work. That's how we knew about the abortion.

"What is that smell?" he asked.

"That's the alcohol," Thin Man said, entering the room. "Would you like some?"

"It smells positively ghastly," Slade said.

"That's only the foetuses, sir," Thin Man said. "You don't have to drink them."

After Slade had tasted the stuff in Thin Man's flask, he said, "That's not bad."

"There's buckets out there," Thin Man said.

"Why didn't you tell me this before?"

Right in the middle of *Romeo and Juliet,* just when Juliet says, "Wherefore art thou Romeo," a sixth-form boy had ignorantly called out, "In the garden, Love." Slade had accused me of doing it because I was always stirring in class. But I hadn't said a word. Before we went to see the movie, I'd had no idea that true love actually existed, and when it was over I was too confused by the discovery to deny Slade's accusation. That was how I ended up on detention.

In a while Miss Pink turned up again. Her makeup had dribbled down her cheeks.

"How about you two drongos get lost," Slade said.

I used a stick to lead Thin Man up to the greenhouse where Fist and Fat Man were supposed to be tidying up. They'd been wasting their time adding more beetles to Thin Man's jar of secret mixture and looking at pornography.

"Fucking don't come in!" they yelled.

I thought they didn't want me to see their pornography, but there was actually a snake above the entrance. It wasn't the harmless green one usually in there that we used to play with. It was a brown snake, one of the deadly sort, that must have crawled in from the apple orchard. When it flicked its tongue, I ran straight to the back of the greenhouse where the other two were huddling in terror. Thin Man was still pretending to be blind. He stepped inside the house and stood right underneath the snake like some kind of idiot.

"Fucking move!" we shouted.

Luckily he had his special skills. He got the snake by the neck, and it twisted itself up his skinny arm like a tattoo. Then he chased us round the greenhouse for a while, poking the snake's head at us.

After the others had left to catch their train, Thin Man and I decided that Miss Pink and Slade had probably finished arguing by now and we'd go back to the Prac Ag room to see if they'd let us off the rest of detention. Thin Man wanted to leave the snake in the greenhouse as a surprise for the next person who came in, but when he tried putting it down, the snake got angry and wouldn't let go. So he took it with him.

"Put that godforsaken thing back in its bottle," Slade said when he saw the snake. He must have thought it was a specimen. Miss Pink had gone.

"I can't," Thin Man said.

Slade put down the flask he was drinking from and tried to grab it. "Ouch!" he cried when the thing bit him. He tripped and fell, cracking his head loudly on the bench.

Thin Man pounced on the snake again. "Oh, shit," he said, realizing what he'd done.

"Sir?" I said, but Slade didn't seem to hear.

"I think he's drunk," Thin Man said. "He smells drunk."

We waited for a bit longer but Slade still didn't move. "I think he needs to see the doctor," I said.

By this time everyone else had left except for the prefects. They were in their room at the end of the Farm Mechanics Building wearing their cadet uniforms and cleaning their 303s.

"It's Romeo," they said when they saw me.

I told them about Slade, but they weren't interested. They just pointed their rifles at us through the window.

"Why don't we hunt them 'round the farm?" one of them suggested.

We returned to the specimen room, but Slade still hadn't come 'round so I frisked him for his car keys. He had an Austin 1800, a manual, which neither of us had ever driven, although we knew how to drive the tractor. We used to drive it down to the bottom paddocks to prune the fruit trees or check whether anyone had drowned in the dam.

We loaded Slade into his back seat and covered him with a blanket. Thin Man sat in the passenger's seat with the snake in one hand and his flask in the other, still claiming to be blind. After I'd bumped into a gum tree in the surgery car park, I walked over to the surgery and told the receptionist there was a man outside who needed help.

"What's the matter with him?" she asked. She was about twenty and the best-looking woman I'd ever seen.

"I think he's got snake bite."

Her uniform was so skimpy that when she hopped over to the window I saw her knickers.

"Where is he?" she asked. She waved me over next to her, which made me really nervous. "Did you see what kind of snake it was?"

"I think it was a trouser snake." I'd developed a habit of saying really moronic things whenever I was nervous, usually when I was talking to a girl. "I have to go. I've got to help end world hunger."

Thin Man had almost emptied the flask when I got back to Slade's car. "Is he still alive?" I asked.

"How do you know it's a he?" Thin Man said, feeling for the snake's hole.

"Not the snake—Slade."

I lifted the blanket and Slade seemed to be breathing.

"Did you get the doctor?" Thin Man asked.

"Yeah," I lied. "He's coming out when he finishes some operation."

"We can't wait," Thin Man said. "We're going to be late."

The two of us were supposed to be meeting Fat Man and Fist in town outside Wynyard railway station. We really were going to help end world hunger. People from everywhere were spending the night walking from Wynyard to Hornsby in order to raise money. You got sponsored so many cents per mile.

We locked Slade in his car and walked down the road to the little railway station. It had recently been rebuilt after being burnt down. The train was late and Thin Man and I polished off what was left in his flask while we waited. It took us another hour to get to Wynyard; once there, I decided to deposit my shoes in a locker. I was still wearing my school uniform and thought that bare feet would look more casual. Thin Man had on his cadet uniform.

"Jesus," Fist said when we met up with him at the top of the Wynyard ramp. "Why did you bring that fucking snake?"

"I can't put it down," Thin Man said. "It keeps wanting to bite someone."

"It bit Slade," I said.

"Good," Fist said. "I hate that prick."

By the time we all walked across George Street and did some more wandering around, we were late reporting to the area where the marshals were checking people's sponsorship cards. Thin Man and I had both forgotten to sign anyone up, but on the train we'd invented some joke sponsors, including the Pope and Mr. J. Goebbels. Nobody seemed to notice.

As we headed towards the harbour bridge, Fist and the others started taunting me.

"When are we meeting your girlfriend, Shitface?" they asked.

I'd been telling them about this girl I knew, Susan, the daughter of some old friends of my parents. After Miss Pink had taken us to *Romeo and Juliet,* Susan had sort of turned into my girlfriend. I hung around at her house and when her parents were out we'd sneak into their bedroom and do things on their double bed. That's what I'd told the other guys. It wasn't true. Her parents didn't even have a double bed and I hadn't done things with anybody. Now everyone wouldn't shut up about it.

Before we got to the bridge, Fat Man and Fist left off taunting and started chatting to a couple of girls who were stopping strangers so they could ask for a light. They looked even younger than we were. Fist lit their cigarettes and then Fat Man asked them what sort of songs they liked on the radio.

"Yeah," he said each time they picked one. "Yeah, I like that, too." They were stupid pop songs, like *Venus.*

"We really love that song," one of the girls said. "I always forget what group it is."

"Shocking Blue," Fat Man said. He knew all the groups.

"Yeah," one of the girls said. "Aren't they from Dutchland?"

Fat Man started singing, *"I'm your Venus."*

The girls sang along with him while they were smoking. *"I'm your Venus."*

"Penis," I said.

They stared at me.

"That's what they sing," I said. *"Penis."*

"You're insane," Fat Man said.

"You listen to it," I said. "They definitely say *Penis.*"

"I'm blind," Thin Man said.

Thin Man and I didn't see the others again. Across the bridge we started walking faster and faster. I kept treading on sharp things, and Thin Man's hand started to ache.

"It's already dark," he said. "Why doesn't this thing go to sleep?"

"It's a reptile. They don't sleep until it's winter."

"How can it be a reptile? It doesn't even have any legs."

"It's got plenty of legs. You're blind. You just can't see them."

"When are we supposed to be meeting this girlfriend of yours?"

Somewhere near Chatswood we stopped at a traffic light, and a woman who was waiting outside a bottle shop said hello to me. I thought I recognised her. She looked like the woman from the doctor's surgery, the beautiful one.

"Hey," she said. "Did you get blisters, too?"

She walked over and steadied herself on my shoulder so she could hold up her heel and show me. I had no idea what she was doing. She said hi to Thin Man and told him she liked his costume, meaning his cadet uniform.

"I'm blind," he said, waving his arm and stepping off the footpath. The woman pulled him back by his shirt just in time to stop him from being run over.

"Whooo!" she said. "Are you guys all on your own?"

I told her we were meeting a girl I knew.

"That's great. Where are you meeting?"

"I don't know. She's probably lost or something. She's sort of my girlfriend. But she can be pretty dumb."

"What's her name?" she asked.

"Susan."

The woman gave me a strange look. "Richard," she said. *"I'm* Susan."

"Susan?" I repeated, stupidly.

In my mind I had this picture of Susan as someone shorter and skinnier.

But since I'd last seen her, she'd obviously grown up. She had a woman's face now and a woman's figure. She'd recognised who I was straight away because I hadn't grown up at all.

Three guys and another girl came out of the bottle shop with a bottle of Mateus. The girl was Susan's friend, from her class at school. But the guys were older. One had a leather jacket and sunglasses like the guy in *Easy Rider*. Another one was smoking. The one with the leather jacket put his arm around Susan.

A few cars jammed on their brakes as I ran across the intersection, but I didn't look back to see who was calling after me.

"Was that your girlfriend?" Thin Man asked when he caught up. He couldn't run as fast because of the snake.

"Yeah. Hey, why are you limping?"

"I think the snake bit me."

"Where?"

"Through my pocket."

"What was it doing in your pocket?"

"I didn't want your girlfriend to see it."

As we walked up the highway, Thin Man started complaining that he didn't feel so hot. There was a police station at the entrance to a tunnel that went under the road. He walked into the tunnel and undid his fly. He had on daggy white underpants.

"Have a look. I think it bit me on the knob."

"I can't look at your knob."

"Well, I'm blind. I can't see it."

"Go to the police station," I said. "No, come back. I don't think that's a good idea."

"Shit. It's really throbbing." He waved the snake dangerously close to my face. "Does it feel swollen?"

I wasn't touching Thin Man's knob, even if he was waving a venomous snake.

"It's probably just the alcohol," I told him.

He started stroking my hair. "Your hair feels like a girl's." Then he started sobbing, or pretending to sob, I couldn't tell. "I think I'm turning queer."

"What are you talking about?"

"It's just as well," he said tearfully, "that I don't have much longer to live."

"Jesus, you better give that thing to me." I pinched the snake round the neck just above his fingers, and he loosened his grip so that it coiled around my arm. It actually felt nice and I started to worry that I was turning queer, too.

Thin Man pulled himself together, or pretended to pull himself together—I couldn't tell. But back on the highway he kept having to lie on people's fences and groan.

"We'll have to take a shortcut," he said.

We turned down a hill lined with huge, darkened houses where rich people seemed to be sleeping. There were no footpaths and we stumbled down ditches, and at the bottom Thin Man led me off into some bush that grew thicker and thicker until I told him we were lost and we'd have to turn back.

"We can't turn back," he said. "Think about world hunger."

Cobwebs tangled in my hair, my face was scratched, and the ends of my trousers got soaked walking through a creek. After about a thousand miles we emerged from the bush onto a moonlit meadow where there was a big, perfectly smooth circle that seemed to have been pressed flat by a huge weight dropping out of the sky. In the paleness it looked to me like the landing spot of an alien spacecraft. There was even a little flag in the centre, like the flag Neil Armstrong planted in the dust of the moon.

"Fore!" I heard Thin Man call.

Then I realised we were on a golf course. Under a shrub he'd found a golf ball that somebody had left behind like an abandoned egg. We crossed to the far side of the course and then through an electric fence that zapped us like a swarm of angry wasps until we were in a sort of park with a gravel road winding between elm trees. We came to a tall, stately building, then an indoor swimming pool where through the windows we could see little clouds of mist rising from the surface. Further on we came to a chapel with a balcony where a bunch of girls had gathered in their pyjamas. Thin Man and I watched from behind an elm as the girls flitted around. It was almost as if we were dreaming.

"Are they having an orgy?" Thin Man asked. He pronounced the "g" like in "organ."

"That's not an orgy. Listen. It's Shakespeare."

Each girl was taking a turn calling out lines from the play. "Romeo, Romeo, wherefore art thou Romeo?" one called. We waited and listened and when one of the girls came to the part where it says, "Romeo, doff thy name," I popped my head out from behind the tree trunk and called, "I take thee at thy word."

The pyjama girls looked out into the blackness until they saw me and then the one whose turn it was said, "What man art thou that, thus bescreen'd in night, So stumblest on my counsel?"

We must have been at a boarding school. The girls in pyjamas were reciting the lines from their textbook, but I'd copied them out so many times that I knew them by heart. After one of the girls finished the scene, she looked down at me and I looked back up at her and nobody said anything. Then Thin Man stood up, brandishing the snake.

"Serpent!" they all screamed.

It took us forever, but Thin Man and I finally reached the end of the walk at Hornsby and had our cards stamped at the car park to prove to our sponsors, including the Pope and Mr. J. Goebbels, that we hadn't cheated. We walked to Hornsby railway station where we found Miss Pink sitting on a bench. She'd been on the walk, too, but now she was crying again.

She and I sat together in the railway carriage, with Thin Man in front of us, and she fell asleep with her head on my shoulder as we travelled back to the station near school. She smelled of chocolate. Thin Man made rude signs about trains going into tunnels. I ignored him and finished copying *Romeo and Juliet.*

"I should have known he was lying," Miss Pink said when she woke up. "He was never going to come on the walk."

"Slade?" I said. "He couldn't. A snake bit him."

"That's just another one of his lies."

"Honest, it really did. We had to take him to the doctor. Look, we've still got the snake."

By now the snake was curled up inside Thin Man's cadet hat, having finally decided to behave itself. Miss Pink said it looked pretty and asked if she could stroke it.

"Did you have an abortion?" I asked.

"What? Oh, that. No, I actually didn't. I just said that to make Rex feel guilty."

"Well, at least I've worked something out," Thin Man said when we got off the train. "This snake's a she."

While it had been curled inside the crown of his upturned hat, it had laid about a dozen soft white eggs.

"I better get back to school and put these in the greenhouse," he said, heading up the road in the darkness, "or they'll never hatch."

I must have left Slade's headlights on when we parked his Austin because they were shining dimly in the surgery car park as if the battery was going to sleep. Slade was still under the blanket. He hadn't died or anything. Miss Pink tried to wake him up and I walked down the hill past the veterinarian's house, toward home. I should have given Miss Pink the exercise book with all the balcony scenes, but I'd left it on the train by accident. I'd also forgotten my shoes, which were still in the locker at Wynyard station.

"Did you have a good time ending world hunger?" my mother asked from the bedroom, softly, so that she wouldn't wake my father. I had my own key but I'd taken to climbing in the window since Miss Pink had organised for us to see *Romeo and Juliet*.

"It was OK."

That year for Christmas dinner my family ate bowls of brown rice and donated the turkey money to the starving people in Bangladesh or Biafra or somewhere. Slade recovered from his snake bite because Miss Pink drove him to the hospital after we found him in his car. They both left the school and we didn't see them again. For a few months I was dreading meeting Susan but when our families got together the next time, she had a new boyfriend and seemed to have forgotten all about my stupidity. As for the poor snake, it died a week after we'd taken it on the walk. Thin Man and I preserved its corpse in a jar in the specimen room. The eggs it'd laid in Thin Man's hat, which he'd carefully carried back to the greenhouse, hung around in a flowerpot under the bench, forgotten, until the beginning of spring when every one of them hatched into a tiny, venomous serpent.

Some Kinds of Reading in Childhood

BRENDA HILLMAN

Do you remember Picture Day?
    Then, when the packets came back—
  in each child's eyes:
        incomprehensible fire—;
  you were ordinary,
in the sense of: the endangered west;—
your mother wiped the windshield
with a shredded Kleenex
(that's why you deserved your oily treats)—

Inside the school, reading made sparks:
        peril, peril, peril-and-awe;
outside the school, acres of signs
        in cellophane noon,
under the school, termites take
  the tasty beams into their bodies—
  [*Incisitermes minor*] delicate hairless arms…
Save the volcanoes for later,
flame-folder. You did *such* a good job
with the maps!

The world has created a sickness
but the sickness is being
reversed . . . Consonants
can be reasoned with, but vowels
start fires—now! Breathing
twice: Now! Here come
the bandit occupiers:
silence & meaning—

Fair Science

JOSÉ RODRÍGUEZ

With books of Johnny Appleseed and Marie Curie
offering up their spines behind us,
we stood in the library next to our presentations
for the science fair. First

was the boy with the ant farm, all those legs
mining frantic roads that lead nowhere,
everything latticed, everything documented.

Next was the girl with the experiment
that proved the hunger of fire for oxygen,
a lighter in her hand, a candle posed
under glass in the table center.

Judges strolled by, smiled
without showing their teeth
at my drawing of a blue whale
on a gray sheet of construction paper,
its belly filled with bits of data:
100 tons, largest animal ever,
two to four tons of krill a day.

Every booth was supposed to display
domination, proof of knowing the form
beneath the surface,
as if everything worth knowing could be
chaptered into a bounded page.

It wasn't that I would lose,
but that the teacher had insisted
I enter the competition. It's just a drawing,
I'd thought. Something to do
after the math problems, something
to shore me from the playground of ruined homes
where children shouldered an anger
then hurled it at those
who'd learned to swallow it whole
and take the place of hunger.

So when she smiled, I began
inflating the belly of the whale—drawing,
erasing and redrawing—trying
to stuff more information into it, make it
worthy, until the paper frayed,
started flaking off. Little tearing sounds
like the sounds of the whale's
baleen brushing creatures against each other.

I learned then something could tear
and still look whole from a distance.

Take a Break for a Delicious Sno-Cone!

JUNE MELBY

How to make sno-cones:

First, don't kill anyone. Don't make them choke on small bits of plastic, which might happen if you push the ice chunks into the grinder with the plastic scoop—something everyone in my family does on a regular basis. The ice clogs when you dump it in; usually the chunks are too big. Also, the chute is metal—ice can stick like a wet tongue on a swing set. You're going to have to shove it a little, but not so hard that the plastic scoop gets mauled. The shaved ice is white and shiny. By some strange happenstance, the plastic is too. It's really hard to know if you've ground up the scoop or not. If you think you *might* have chewed plastic into the shaved ice, while the customer looks in eagerly through the front window of the Snack Shack, just calmly scoop out the snow from the plexi bin and dump it into the yellow bucket below. Say, "I want to start over; I didn't like that bunch," and put more ice chunks into the machine. The customer will not know of his proximity to death by choking, and in fact may actually be *flattered* that you took the time to chop more ice—better ice—for his long-awaited sno-cone. One truism about tourists: they like to feel important. A delay, when it's a delay *for* them and not a delay for someone *else*, can be interpreted as evidence of your personal interest and a wish to deliver them perfection.

Second, the grape flavor tastes watery. Don't push the grape.

Say, "Cherry, blue-raspberry, grape, or a combo?" The cherry is the best single flavor, and you will say so if asked, but generally you don't volunteer the information.

Mom says to give one squirt into the ice at the bottom of the cone, then two squirts into the dome on top. Do it slow so the ice doesn't dent. Add a straw.

The best ice is the cold ice, but customers rarely get that. We grind up ice for sno-cones one at a time because we don't get enough orders at the Snack Shack to shave up a mountain of ice and leave it to melt there all day. Plus, Dad would have a fit. Wasteful, wasteful. For one sno-cone, we chop one sno-cone's worth of ice. For four sno-cones, four sno-cones' worth. But the best ice comes after five or six sno-cones' worth. The whirling blades get good and cold. The ice chopped for the seventh or eighth will be so cold and fluffy that it may not even pack into a ball. If that happens, just dig into the mound with your scoop until you're at the bottom, then add some wet (bad) ice to your ball. People like their ice in a ball. It's how they imagine it should be. But we know better. We have become sno-cone snobs.

Mom and Dad let us have one free sno-cone a day. The first year at Tom Thumb we only got them on days when we worked, but now, three years later, we can have one every day. What days don't we work? Huh? But we all refuse to eat a sno-cone if it's made from wet ice. Even on the hottest day of July when we are dying. We wait until the blades are cold from serving up ice for other people, and only then add a few chunks for ourselves. The fluffy ice won't form into domes so it doesn't look picture-perfect, but it is the kind my sisters and I eat. The ice chopped last is like the snow that falls on your mitten in winter and you stare at it, so tiny, so cold, and so tight.

If the ice is wet, the cone may overflow before you get the third squirt on there. If so, stop. Hand the cone slowly to the customer. Say, "Be careful. This one is pretty full. You'd better take a sip right away." You know—and will never reveal—that if the cone is overflowing, it means the ice was not great. It will be gritty between the teeth and the flavor will taste dilute. But the customer always feels privileged that his cone is overflowing with syrup, which, he thinks, is like getting front-row seats in the world of sno-cones.

What the customer wants is what he imagines a sno-cone should look like. This is his vacation after all. Party, party, party. This is his week at the lake, and he has brought along his family, and they have played mini golf, and he is wearing his favorite red and orange shirt, and the kids have matching Brewer's baseball caps, and they are getting along better this year—none of them fussed when no one got a free game by hitting a ball in the clown's nose—and the sun is hanging low, and it's nearing time to head back, and this is the last day before the long drive home. And the little girl looks up at her father and, in her most delicate voice, asks, "Daddy, can we get sno-cones?"

He smiles and then he says to me, "Do you have rainbow?"

"Sure. I can do that." And I drape perfect stripes of brilliant color up and over the perfect dome of snow. I make their change, and I say "thank you." Then they stroll across the parking lot together, sipping cones and leaning toward each other.

If you see a bug inside the machine where the ice comes out, you can wipe it out with a paper towel even while the customer stares through the window at you from less than two feet away. They won't see that you are removing an insect.

After you have successfully made eight or more sno-cones, run into the yard to find one of your sisters. Hold up your left hand, spread your thumb away from your fingers, and say, "Look at my terrible rash!" Make the joke about probably dying from a terrible disease. Show off the tiny dots of cherry, blue, and grape that sprayed from the dispenser as you pushed down on the plunger—some of it always misses the cone and falls on your forefinger and thumb. The stains will stay for hours, even after washing with soap and water. You are not unusual if you think it's cool.

One day your dad will say, "I remember the time I chewed up a whole metal screw with a batch of ice—that time the screw came out of the blades."

"What did you do?"

"I just avoided that spot in the ice and scooped from the other side. I made only one sno-cone, fortunately. I don't know what I would have done if they had ordered a whole bunch."

The sno-cone machine rarely breaks down, maybe once every three or four years. This is something of a miracle. It was purchased when you were young enough not to question whether your parents understood the idea of food product safety and potential lawsuits. And the sno-cone machine has been working every day, Memorial Day to Labor Day. And nothing bad has ever happened. This, too, is a miracle. Sometimes, if people come early—it's before 10 a.m., but Mom and Dad let them buy snacks anyway—the sound of grinding ice is the first thing you hear in the morning. The roar of hungry blades wafts through the house and wakes you in your bed. It grinds and grinds and grinds.

On Incontinence:
Tim's Coming In and Out Party

MARY JANE LaVIGNE

I've got news for you. Original sin alone didn't get Adam and Eve to put on clothes. Undress can be downright inconvenient—no pockets, for one thing. No belt loops—where do you hook your fingers? Absent panties, boxers, or briefs, nothing covers your lower orifices when you sit in a chair. Wipe and bathe though you will, heads shed and so do the curly strands below. Clothes and continence are our seminal conformities.

Tim McNally and I are talking about nudity. We're watching naked men in the mud. Overhead, a rainbow throbs against the mountain's white haunch. The rain has settled the dust and moved east, leaving a smell like clean chalkboards. Through the lens of suspended droplets, the setting sun projects an arc of color, vivid and false as a Keebler cookie wrapper.

It's Monday afternoon at Burning Man. The festival's early arrivers have set up their desert homes and are out for their nascent revels. We're leaning against Tim's Honda, a late, model two-door. Tim has fitted it up with fins and painted it with swirls of color. Red tongues and black streaks of paint lick the rocker panels and form eddies of pigment on the hood. Our boots sink into the gray muck.

Allen Christian, *Rainbow*, 2010

"Would you strip?" he asks, nodding to the nudists. Although Tim and I don't know each other well, the Technicolor circumstances make the intimacy of the question somehow appropriate.

"Go naked, like them?" I picture my accordion belly, flaccid from age and carrying three kids. I look better dressed. "Nope."

Many Burning Man conversations start out being about nudity. One of the first things people think they know about Burning Man is that people are nude. One of the first things you'll discover when you get here is how very few buck-naked, birthday suit, bare-butt bodies there truly are.

"And you, Tim? Do you ever strip when you're here?"

"Me? No. I don't think anyone would want to see that."

"I wouldn't be so sure." Tim is leanly muscled with dark hair and a chiseled jaw. We watch the newest arrivals to the naked-mud-man rainbow party. "Look at that guy's paunch." I nudge his shoulder. "You're Adonis compared to him."

"I have an indwelling catheter," says Tim.

At our backs the sun moves a notch lower. The men's bodies glow as if spotlit. Viewing the male genitalia of strangers has never been my cup of tea. I grew up in a family of Catholic girls. We kept our clothes on. That's what God wanted. But often, something exquisite grips the edge of the forbidden.

"So what?" I say. "That could make it better."

In 1968, a little boy in my second-grade class ran up the rows between our desks, dropped to the floor, and slid on his knees like a rock star. He was a naughty little boy. He once bit me in the hand in the cloakroom and sassed our teacher, behavior that was both unusual and unacceptable at Randolph Heights Elementary in Saint Paul, Minnesota. But I really remember that knee-sliding move. It was beautiful and more than a little out of control. He was sent to the office. After he had left the room, our teacher told us his father was in Vietnam. Maybe his name was Bobby. He ended up leaving the school altogether. I hope he's doing OK.

Bobby's desk next to mine was empty for a few weeks until a girl with skinny blond pigtails and leg braces joined our class. She walked with crutches, the kind with bands around the forearms that you use if you've had crutches a really long time. She also had a urinary catheter.

In 1968, handicapped kids and regular kids weren't in classes together. It was considered unfair. We understood it this way: crippled kids would feel bad that they couldn't do stuff. Plus, they'd slow down the regular kids. Like so much else in the 1960s, those attitudes were changing. The pigtailed girl may have been part of that change. I do not remember her. I have thoroughly forgotten everything about her except her bag. I don't know how I found out what a urinary catheter was. Probably the teacher told me when the girl was out of the room. I remember glimpses of the white pouch, a loop of hollow tube, a plastic smell, and the odor of urine.

Tim McNally is from Upper Montclair, New Jersey. This is his fourth time at Burning Man, and he's returning after a four-year hiatus. He drove out solo, merging his multicolored, finned 2005 Civic onto I-80 in eastern New Jersey and exiting at Fernley, in western Nevada. You never get lonely in an art car. They attract too much attention. Passing motorists wave. Little kids in back seats crane their necks to watch. During fueling stops, someone is bound to ask about your eye-catching car. The questions are usually some form of "why?"

When Tim was a kid, he was a fan of Hanna-Barbera's cross-country car-race cartoon, *Wacky Races*. Dick Dastardly and his evil dog Muttley drive the Mean Machine, a rocket-shaped supercar. In episodes like "Ballpoint, Penn. or Bust!" the pair scheme to put the skids to the other ten cars.

Each vehicle had a theme, with fantastic shapes and special powers. Professor Pat Pending was an inventor. His car could fly. The Creepy Coupe sported a helpful dragon. Penelope Pitstop had a pink parasol. The lone female character, she'd reach at climactic moments for the stick of her sassy little racer and shift between lipstick and hairspray, prettiness being her special power.

Years later, Tim was browsing in a bookstore and came across *Wild Wheels*, a coffee-table book featuring photos and stories about art car artists and their remarkable rides. Wacky cars, Tim realized, were real. People actually built them. He decided to make one. Tim painted a 1985 Buick Skyhawk plaid. "I thought maybe people would be able to see I could paint," he says.

Tim wanted the New Jersey DMV to designate "plaid" as the official color on his Buick's registration papers. It took some doing but Tim got it done. Dig deeply enough into any artist's "why" story, and you'll hit a bedrock of inanity, the hardly explicable.

"The Plaidmobile became my persona," Tim says.

We're sitting around the long folding table, beneath the shade tarp in Art Car Camp. It's Tuesday, early afternoon, the time when people start to emerge for the day. At Burning Man, 12:30 p.m. is like 9 a.m. in the real world. Tim and I slouch in canvas chairs, watching our campmates putter. We're looking at pictures of yesterday's rainbow on Tim's digital camera. This starts the nudity talk again.

Later, Tim will say I suggested he take off his clothes, parade over to our friend Larry's camp, and have his portrait taken—indwelling catheter and all. I think the idea just came up. Around creative people, ideas pop like mushrooms on moist ground. For an art car artist like Tim, turning inside out becomes a habit, making himself noticed a way of life. I don't always understand it, but like little Bobby's rock-star knee slide, it has its own beauty.

Tim puts the camera aside and pulls his chair up to the table. With dark marker he draws block letters on two small squares of tagboard. One says "In." The other says "Out."

"Are you going to walk with me?" he asks.

All the girls used the bathroom at the same time in second grade. You had to wait until bathroom time, form two lines—a boys' and a girls', stand at the classroom door until everyone was settled, then walk slowly and quietly down the hall. It was an impressive bathroom. Granite stanchions formed the stalls, with panels of fumed oak and doors that had brass latches. It was a long row, at least a dozen toilets. Yet with those big, baby-boomer-era classes, sometimes you'd have to wait. For me this was excruciating. At seven, my bladder control was still somewhat tentative. I remember concentrating on that granite, trying to think thick, the opposite of liquid. Meanwhile, the *tinkle tinkle* sound of my classmates' peeing played tricks with my self-control.

One day, I just couldn't hold it. I probably could have kept it under control if I'd cupped my hand on my crotch, but my father caught me doing that once and so I knew it was shameful. I wet my panties a little while I was waiting and then again before I got them off. I sat on the toilet, trying to figure out how to keep it a secret. My eyes leaked a tear or two, whether from embarrassment at my wet state or relief that I could finally urinate, I don't know.

Between my bottom and the damp, flowered cotton of my underwear, I formed an arc of toilet paper. In secret humiliation, I waited in single file until all the girls were done, then walked down the hall, the mass between my legs awkward and obvious as a diaper. I took my seat next to the girl with leg braces, who always stayed in the classroom during bathroom breaks. The urine smell was overwhelming as our teacher explained long and short vowels. I've been a phonics dummy ever since. Somehow I blamed it on the pigtailed girl. Perhaps her name was Debbie.

How we reeked, the two of us. Now, a confession, more shameful even than being wet: I liked my smell, enjoyed each musky, feral sniff, mine alone.

It is Tim's choice to wear an indwelling catheter. At home he's been using an intermittent catheter, a catheter that does not stay in place. An intermittent catheter must be inserted hygienically and drained in a toilet at regular intervals. When Tim's on the road, that's tough for him to do. Out here in the Black Rock Desert, it would be impossible.

Burning Man has no plumbing. Port-a-potties are reliably clean only for a turn or two after the maintainer crew comes through. I picture Tim standing in a blue plastic booth, threading a tube up his urethra. He has the opposite of my second-grade problem: Tim cannot release his sphincter muscle. It may be the result of medication he took after they discovered his brain tumor. I think he said brain tumor. In truth, I'm squeamish about medical matters. I don't mind blood and like to think I stay cool in emergencies, but the particulars of illnesses make my knees weak.

Now is not the time for asking about the tumor. It's Tim's coming-out party. He's wearing a blue cap, sunglasses, a lanyard, and a clear plastic bag crosswise on his chest. The bag is full of water and labeled "in." It is slung tenderly, like a baby scooped in a blanket. Tim has labeled the urine "out" and strapped it to his left leg. A measure of crystalline yellow hangs in the bottom of this bag.

Tenderness in men turns me on, as does boldness. It is Tutu Tuesday and I am wearing red tulle. I've got red boots, a red wig, and a red parasol. Tim holds out his arm at a chivalrous angle. I tuck a gloved hand around his elbow, and we promenade down the road called Detroit, up the arterial route 5:30, toward Hanoi and the outer ring of the festival campground where my photographer friend is camped.

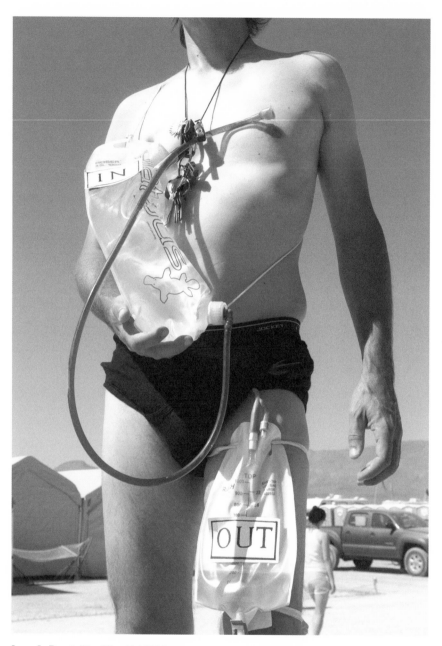

Larry LaBonté, *Tim (Close Up)*, 2010

It's late afternoon now, the hot, hot part of day. A fluff of ruffles bounces against my calves as I walk. The twirl of skirt and the boots make me feel like prancing. I feel swanky, like Penelope Pitstop, working the power of pretty. Tim is being noticed. Among the ballet-skirted men, assorted bare-chested, dread-locked damsels, and winged fairies of both genders, Tim attracts attention. I'm proud to be with him.

Many nod approval, a number cast quizzical looks, a buff, buxom beauty with a British accent presses her cheek against Tim's and gives him a kiss. We're walking behind a bank of port-a-potties when something odd happens.

A woman, solidly middle-aged, midriff tented by a loose T-shirt, stops suddenly in the street. Bikes twist around her and a small cloud of dust rises from her feet. Her eyes focus on Tim, the bags, the labels. "You should not be doing that," she says. "My sister has a colostomy. It's nothing to joke about."

"Why do you think I am joking?" Tim asks, just a hint of Jersey in his attitude.

"You make it weird for everybody." The woman turns away and shuffles off.

I imagine her as Debbie's sister. Perhaps she has spent a lifetime defending her sibling, deflecting attacks. Probably, she helps care for her sister. Probably, Burning Man is one time when she doesn't have to deal with it. I offer excuses for her as we walk on. It's not necessary. Tim's fine.

"I'm a freak among freaks," he says.

We come into the world naked, in a puddle of pee. We leave life shed of all artifice. In between, we clothe ourselves in personas, some chosen by us, others by fate. These may cover and contain. They may set us apart. What power did Penelope Pitstop have when she stopped being pretty? What power will I have then? Debbie was more than a girl with crutches. But what, I will never know. Tim painted a car plaid and joined the art car crowd. In the cross-country trek between birth and death, sometimes the most radical thing you can do is to strip bare.

Preparing Jeffers's "Vulture" Before Class

WENDY BARKER

I'm already predicting the reactions: *Who cares "how beautiful*
      he looked," that bird gliding "on those great sails,"
         this guy is freaking weird
if he wants to be shredded like that. So I'm wondering if I should
      mention what happened a year ago when
         I turned from a booth on
wind power at our neighborhood's GreenFest to face a Eurasian
      Eagle Owl on a man's gloved arm. Stared right
         into me. I don't know
how long I froze, swept into that centered gaze. I guess tonight
      I could propose that maybe death Jeffers' way
         wouldn't be worse than
the doctors slipping a gastric feeding tube into my father's
      stomach, puncturing his lung, then jamming
         a ventilating tube down
his throat, after which he never talked again. "Iatrogenic mishaps,"
      such things are called, the complications, side
         effects of common medical
procedures, like the euphemism "therapies" for the chiseling
      through bone, the screws in my mother's knees,
         the implanted defibrillator
that shocked her heart back to its familiar thud after it had
      wrenched to a stop. Finally she gave up eating,
         and then, even water. She'd
never read the Dylan Thomas poem, never raged against
      the dying of the light. I know what Goethe
         said, but is it really light

that leaves? I've read accounts of mystics who talk of luminosity,
    radiance that beckons, leads them to die in utter
        calm. That Eagle Owl, its clean
ferocity—a moment nothing short of rapture. No wonder people
    say those birds connect us with the universe
        beyond. As if to scoff
at all our needles, tubes, the tinkerings and machinery we submit
    to, hoping we'll delay what has to come. But
        the vulture, Jeffers knew,
feeds only on flesh no longer living, and, even then, a social
    bird, it calls to neighboring flocks to join
        in cleaning up the land, this
bird that, for the Pueblo people, signaled purification. The Parsi
    Zoroastrians exposed their dead on "towers
        of silence," a final act
of charity, providing the birds with food that otherwise would
    go to waste. *Cathartes Aura:* "Golden
        Purifier"—in Buddhism,
compassion. Which is spacious, patient, allowing for existing
    things to change. I remember reading
        that once a toddler was
found on a mountain peak beside a vulture. He'd been missing
    for three days, but was smiling, utterly
        unhurt, though on his
grimy shirt were pierced two sets of talon marks, a rip
    from a hooked beak. "What an
        enskyment," says
Jeffers. What a way to begin a life, or, I'm thinking, end.

Waking Up at Four A.M.

DAVID ALLEN EVANS

I reach back and grab a cool metal bar
at the head of the bed—the way any

primate grabs a limb to steady itself—
and there they are again, in my head,

near the end of their fight: the tiger,
and the once-frisky young bull on

that dusty arena floor years ago
in Guilin, China . . . all the people

yelling, the bull—no longer able to
elude the inexorable claws and teeth,

and gradually winding down—the tiger—
aiming its precise bites again and again

at the same raw spot on the right
foreleg—easily ducking the sluggish,

predictable horns—the bull finally
breaking down, collapsing . . . the scene

plays out until something gives way in
my mind's merciful dust, loosening

my grip on the bar, yielding to
the softer claws of sleep.

How Myths Begin

PHILIP S. BRYANT

Last evening toward the very end of twilight, the sky took the shape of a deep turquoise bowl, the outer rim highlighted with bright orange and red of the distant horizon. I saw two pheasants running the length of a football field, across the plowed furrows. At first they looked like two small coyotes: I'd recently heard coyotes laughing late at night. They moved fast, two brown and golden blurs racing across the tilled earth. All of a sudden, when I was absolutely certain they were coyotes, they took flight and arced high into the air over the highest treetops. That's when I knew they weren't coyotes at all, but two pheasants. Could they have been coyotes somehow changed into pheasants? Is this how myths begin? *No way,* I thought. But late that night, right after I turned off my light. I lay in bed and through the open window I could feel the cool wind blowing in, like wings gently flapping. From out in the dark fields came the faint sound of coyotes laughing.

Ayeeyo

NIMO H. FARAH

Wind parches the morning dew.
I hear muezzins and roosters call through brick walls.
Ayeeyo lights the charcoal, fans until it catches
to blaze with the breeze.
She grinds cardamon, ginger, and cinnamon.

The same routines carry each day. The tea stays brewing.
Spices lift her spirit. In prayer
her wrinkled lips whisper praise. Whisper gratitude.
Arthritic fingers gently move tusbah beads.
Ayeeyo asks for mercy.

Sitting with Ayeeyo, I remember her stories.
She was three when, sitting under the shade of a tree,
a serpent sang to her.
Thorns of that same prickly acacia pierced her ears
before gold dangled from them.

She marked that old tree. Dawn was her witness.
She marked the tree with her blood
after she pulled her first tooth.
Ayeeyo dug a place under the root
and buried a wish for this tree to remember her.

Now she sits beside me moving her beads
as she moves her tongue: sixty-six for compassion,

ninety-nine for forgiveness.
Subhanna Allah, Alhamdullilah, Istaqfurrulah, Allahu Akbar.
Subhanna Allah, Alhamdullilah, Istaqfurrulah, Allahu Akbar.

If I could summon the wind to remind her, I would
appeal for a breeze to carry her back
to the tree where she whispered her secrets, dreamt
about her dowry, saw camels in the distance
with humps the size of her wishes.

Hooyo

NIMO H. FARAH

she worries about time
I worry about distance
her tongue is tired
keep talking
my ears are lazy
keep listening
she guides me
to be
an emissary
I sacrifice
the afternoon
to drive her in this city
after a journey
she names things
we can't see
she named me
after a heaven
my home
since my beginning
mostly
we're each other's happiness
which is the meaning of
my name
happiness
her daughter

Whittling

KATHLEEN WEIHE

(after reading poems about Mary Magdalene)

I forgot to pray this entire year.
Thus I never left my body.
Broken leg, torn ligament, what did God
have to do with them?
So I'm camped inside this woody shelter,
getting softer by the moment.

As a small girl—some of you might not
believe this, thinking of logs and stones
as a boy's purview—I carved chunks
of rotten logs into canoes my porcelain
menagerie could float in, down the Rum
River and into the mighty Miss.

And what does God have to do with this?
Who else could convince me
that whatever I created would hold
together long enough for the
journey to still feel like home?

Or, no. I am off the subject.
This year. Fifty years ago.
Trees don't know, and neither do I.
Prayer has shrunken to a hard, woody
knot within the body I call all mine.
But look at how much further the world extends.

This is what we've always known:
Prayer is to hold the cottonwood tufts
in a bag; prayer is to be better than boys,
or at least as good; prayer is to whittle the boat
and believe it is a masterpiece. One no one else
needs to see. Just between God and me.

Test Group Four:
Womanhood and Other Failures
SJ SINDU

My love affair with women started when I learned about the female suicide bombers in Sri Lanka. I was five. It blew my mind that women—the make-upped, dark-eyed beauty queens of the Indian Bollywood movies—could be dangerous enough to strap on explosives beneath the folds of their sarees.

My lover's scar is crocheted across his chest with baby pink yarn by someone who was just learning. The scar runs through like a tiny mountain range, stretching from armpit to armpit along the line of his pectoral muscles but never syncing with the contours of his body. When the surgeon scooped out the breast tissue, he left my lover's chest flat.

The scar is pink like his nipples, soft and spongy where it bubbled up from the stitches and healed around them. Sometimes he's afraid he'll catch his nipples on something and rip them off. He has nightmares in which he is nipple-less.

There is a dark spot where his nipples used to be, a sunset gradation of color into the scar. Dark hairs sprout, tall and curly, around the scar line. They weren't there before the testosterone. They grow a forest over his chest and down his stomach.

The outer edges of his scar bulge out in dog ears, a side effect of having had large breasts.

His lovers, the ones before me, wouldn't look at his chest. They would turn away, mumble into their coffee, tuck their hair behind their ears. They wouldn't touch him there, their fingers cringing from the ridges of the scar, their bodies shivering at the absence. He can't feel his chest anymore. Numbness reaches up from his scar, a vacancy of nerves, hollow when he pushes on the skin. His lungs underneath can discern the pressure, but the message of touch is lost between the skin and his insides.

My mother keeps a leather-bound album of my baby pictures tucked away in the recesses of her closet. These pictures are few, and it took years—decades—to collect them in one volume. Most were lost to late-night flights from our family home in Sri Lanka, where we always kept bags packed. The bags had to be light enough to carry for days, spare enough to unpack and repack at the army checkpoints. Photo albums were treasured but bulky, and my baby pictures won out over my parents' wedding album. We were ready to leave as soon as we heard that the battle line was nearing our town.

Now the pictures sleep peacefully in my mother's closet. I've stolen a few photos of my own. I need to remember.

It's tempting to retell my childhood veiled in virginity, a chaste Hindu girl's strict upbringing. But it's a little boy who stands in these pictures, one who was given too much freedom and adored to the point of exhaustion by extended family before they remembered that he would bleed every month.

I had short curly hair and wore boy's clothes. In beach pictures I wear only my panties. I mourn the loss of that flat chest that allowed me to be rambunctious. Wild.

At six years of age my best friend and I pretended to be Americans on vacation at a beach. We walked around in our panties inside locked rooms, windows shut for modesty. We played at being American women—smoking, drinking, kissing—unconstrained by sarees and rules.

To Emily Dickinson: I once met you—but you were dead—

To the middle-aged white lady who pretended to be Emily Dickinson at the library, whom I believed and loved until I told my friends and they made fun of me for not knowing that Emily Dickinson was dead and this lady was a fake: You were too pretty to play this part of lonely writer. I should've known. Even the Americans like their smart women ugly.

The dusty blue linoleum feels warm even though it snows outside. The tip of my nose is cold from the air. I lie against the warm floor, and the heat seeps in through the frilly cotton pajamas my mother made for me. My little brother laughs in the living room; his toddler voice hiccups around the walls as my dad plays with him. My mother types her thesis at the computer.

I am drawing. Today I'm practicing lips, diligently consulting a three-ring binder of tutorials I have printed out from the Internet. I fill my papers with lips like the ones the tutorials demonstrate, the round curves of women's lips that bite down on secrets and the flat plains of men's lips that don't smile.

I am in love with a man who doesn't believe in God but believes that English majors and hippies are the fussy frou-frou in an otherwise functioning society. He teaches me how to catch and throw a softball, and buys me fountain pens and leather-bound journals. He tries to train our cat, and when he can't, he maintains that our cat overgeneralizes. He lets me run my hands and lips along his chest scar, asks me to give him testosterone shots. I take pictures of the hairs that explode slowly on his jaw. Together we celebrate the dissolving curves of his body, my insides squirming at the woman slowly dying.

To my lover: Do you know, *kanna*, I learned about life from the female soldiers that patrolled my hometown. And about love, too. Those women had things figured out, their wisdoms wrapped away in the tight braids of their hair.

I see my best friend when I visit Sri Lanka after high school. We have seen eighteen from two different oceans. I wear makeup and short skirts in the Sri Lankan heat. She has hair braided down her back and makes tea for everyone. I wonder why she won't look me in the eye. I wonder if she remembers the pretend cigarettes and booze.

She doesn't talk. I talk too much.

When I bled for the first time on New Year's Day of 1999, my parents threw a party. We drove from Boston to Canada and rented a reception hall that specialized in Hindu celebrations. *Manjal neerattu vizha* loses its poetry when it spells "puberty ceremony" in English.

My parents hired a makeup lady who pulled and tugged my unruly hair into a bun, added extensions so that my flowered braid hung down to my butt. My chubby body wrestled into a saree. The blouse was tight and I could barely breathe. The makeup lady pinned jewelry to my head and brushed powder on my face, and when she was done, someone pretty looked back at me from the mirror. As a last touch she pressed a jeweled, fake nose ring into my septum. It dangled in front of my mouth. All day long I suppressed violent urges to sneeze.

I watch my mother kill mice. I kneel on an office chair, pumped up to its full height so I can see the frigid steel of the lab table from my fourth-grade height. The mice are a white that matches my mother's lab coat. She pulls them one by one out of their cage labeled "Test Group Four." They have to die, she says, because they are sick.

She presses a black Sharpie to their necks, and they are dead, just like that, *tuk*.

Five Syllables

KATHLEEN COSKRAN

She drank yesterday's coffee. He complained. That's how it started. Small things. She left the cupboard doors ajar, drawers open, the dishwasher gaping. He hated the way she brushed her teeth, the splatters on the mirror, the snake of her floss in the trash can.

At night, in bed, she breathed audibly—too low to be called a snore—but he could never forget she was there. It was more than the hump of her body, her heat, the curl of her back, the tug of the sheet balled in her fist.

She suggested marriage counseling. Her idea like everything else, so he was rehearsing his part, making a list. He couldn't rattle on mindlessly as she could, laying down a stream of words in no particular order, thought leap-frogging thought, so that when she finally stopped with that brilliant smile, he had no idea what she'd just said.

He wrote down: "That smile." Top of the list. How to explain? That smile pulled him in the first day, lassoed him, made him pause at her table in the library, bend his head to her book where she was pointing at a phrase: *The ineluctability of being*, smiling and saying, in the voice of a siren—another complaint, the subversive rhythm of her voice—she was saying, "How do you say that and what does it mean?"

"Ineluctability," he had said. "Seven syllables. You must say each one to get it right." He pronounced the word again and she stared at his lips, absorbing every movement, her hazel eyes almost touching him with their luminescence.

Should he add the disturbing eyes to his list?

No. Maybe that was the one thing she couldn't change.

In-e-luc-ta-bil-i-ty. Her lips—oh, those lips—write it down. Her lips tasted every syllable, slowly, with his, and then again, a little faster, then in a rush—*ineluctability*—*ineluctability*—twice, fast—and then that laugh again, the laugh of delight. He was being fair. Her delight had delighted him, but it still felt like a trick, one of her tricks.

He wrote down *trick*.

"But what does it mean—ineluctability?"

"It's something that can't be avoided or resisted," he had said. "Something inevitable."

"Ah, I see," she said. The laugh again. The eyes. The smile. "I perceive," she had said, "the ineluctability of coffee with you."

"Now?"

He crumpled the list. What was the use? They were together. Ineluctably. Five syllables.

Meridel Le Sueur Essay

The Work of Art

LIDIA YUKNAVITCH

> *The worker can unionize, go out on strike; mothers are divided from each other in homes, tied to their children by compassionate bonds; our wildcat strikes have most often taken the form of physical or mental breakdown . . . . The repossession by women of our bodies will bring far more essential change to human society than the seizing of the means of production of workers.*
>
> Adrienne Rich

One: Origins

How did it happen that my hands came to carry words? When did it begin? Was it when I was still a girlfish tucked inside the fleshwater world of mother—before limbs fully formed—long before speech—when sound was still liquid, everything filling my eyes and ears and holding my very skin—the dynamic and unrepresentable poetic dimension of language—its rhymes, rhythms, intonations, alliterations, melody—the music of bloodflow and oxygen—when the heart's beating of a woman carrying me gave my body, my still forming bones, my breath form enough to enter the world?

I was born via Cesarean section. What grew in the moment that sterilized, gloved hands reached in to pry me loose from my corporeal lodgings? What was the first sound in the outerworld? The first image, when they carried me as far away from a motherbody as they could, to bathe me clean, to swaddle me, to place me in an incubator like a word into a new sentence so that they might stitch the woman's gaping belly gash closed? Did it matter that I missed the birth canal, that I escaped prematurely, that I entered the world as if already taken and lifted toward light without moving through dark?

Was there blood?

Artistic forms exist that resonate like songs by and through the bodies of women. The body is an epistemological site—a site where meanings are generated and negated—not just biologically, but theoretically and formally. The maternal body is exemplary: Wave. Cycle. Gestation. Lactation. Reflection. Rhythm and sound found internally, before they are met symbolically. Birth, requiring vast and epic death as sperm and egg forgo their very lives so that the third thing might live.

But when I speak of the maternal body, I do not mean essentially. I mean corporeally—the body of possibilities yet unbounded, the recreating and decreating realm as vital to being and knowing as all our legitimized and sanctified knowledges. How to open the mouth of that?

What I want to write is this: bloodscream fleshsong. A tearing open of the symbolic. Teethcunt gushing. But who would let me?

Forgive me for beginning with birth and the bodies of mothers.

But how else to speak to you about being a woman writer?

Labor.

How else to speak the secret: there is a place inside language that is yet corporeal. Timeless. Sanguine fluid song. Hidden beneath the order of things. A sentence: corporeal.

Certain facts about how I became a writer trump logic. Trump the form of an essay. I am the mother of a beautiful alive son. I am the mother of a daughter who died in the belly of me the day she was born.

From her birthdeath I became a writer.

What form should that take?

Two: Eating Paper

I don't remember coming to writing. I mean I do, I remember coming to the white of the page, but not as *writing*. I drew and painted pictures as a child. Even on walls and streets and tabletops. I couldn't stop. I was frequently made to wash the color from walls.

My sister, who was eight years older than I and thus already blooming imagination, understood that I was trying to say things before I had enough language. And so she began to put pieces of paper with words on them onto objects in the house: Chair. Door. Table. Television. Window. Refrigerator. Ashtray.

Signs.

Under my skin I shivered when I'd find one of her words. My ears became red and hot. When I ran from room to room hunting for the next word, wet happened between my legs. Sweat or the heat of a girl's skin, speaking. Running and running through the house. Two girls alone now and then.

Once, when we were running around the house playing the paper word game, my father the architect came home early from work. I remember being out of breath from chasing my sister from room to room, the pieces of word paper fluttering around the house like butterflies. I remember her laughing, her eyes squinting closed and her long mane of auburn hair trailing in waves after her and how we fell to the floor holding our stomachs when we got to Toilet. Underwear.

But when the architect entered the house, he backhanded my sister, leaving a wrong rose blooming on her cheek. Clean this mess up. He stepped toward me, but I was as small as a word, and so he turned away, and I picked up pieces of paper.

Carpet.

Silverwear.

Sink.

Skin.

Sister.

Then I hid in the closet in my room with stuffed animals and shoes and dust bunnies and, one by one, ate the small pieces of paper. My face too hot. My skin itching. My chest feeling like it held in a deranged bird. I remember being glad there was no piece of paper with his word on it. I thought if I ate the word of him, I might die.

I remember the sound of the faucet behind the closed door of the sister bathroom.

Pica is an eating disorder, usually found in children and sometimes pregnant women, in which the subject eats non-nutritive things. Like dirt. Rocks. Bark. Paper. All of which I ate as a child. It is medically considered to spring from cravings based on mineral deficiencies, though more recent studies have located the behavior on an obsessive-compulsive spectrum as well as in autism cases.

I don't know how many words I ate that year. I was four. I could spell *architect* before anyone else my age. A dark, dark house, father.

Later, I drew on and painted one entire wall of my bedroom. Mostly it was a hundred shades of red—intense, large, out-of-whack spirals with black scratches and scrawls in the center.

How powerful the imagination of a child. Eating paper in a cave, living beyond signs, painting walls bigger than her body—a girl making in the face of the world.

Three: To Be Haunted

When I was fourteen, Mary Shelley visited me in a dream.

When I say that, you have to picture something besides a dream. It was not "dreamlike." Though she was dressed in a period costume, and her hair matched that mise-en-scène, and she folded her slight hands in her lap across the moss green of her skirt spreading out and down like a lush waterfall, she was more real to me than anything that was happening around me at that time. I sat up in bed. I crossed my arms over my almost breasts. I pulled my knees up to my chest and rested my cheek on my arms.

She told me the story of how she came to write *Frankenstein*, which I had already read but didn't understand. She told me about being a girl in the company of her lover, Percy Shelley, in the villa of Lord Byron at the Villa Diodati by Lake Geneva in Switzerland. When she said Shelley and Byron, I pictured men with white, billowing shirts and unruly hair, their faces and eyes ablaze with something ungodly. When she said villa and Switzerland, I saw a kind of castle with cultured grounds against a black forest and haunted by Alps.

She told me how they would drink wine and smoke opium and how their faces would change. Their voices. She told me what each of their handwriting looked like.

Her eyes were large.

Her hands so delicate.

She told me the discussion had turned to galvanism and raising the dead electrically—lightning still seemed magical then, she said. She said they sat near a fire and read each other ghost stories, and I pictured her body there on the floor with charismatic and possibly crazy men. Poetry frightened me at fourteen. It made my ears pound blood and the top of my head and my thighs itch.

Then she stopped talking and touched my hair and tilted her head to the side. My room was quiet and I could feel the night, the warmth of blood in her skin and my biceps flexing and unflexing, my toes curling and uncurling. She opened her mouth.

"You must remember this. Motherhood is not monsterhood."

Since I was fourteen, I had no idea what she meant. I pictured my own mother and the jugs of vodka and wine she had piled in the bathroom closet. I pictured my sister, who had long since fled our Oedipal household for intellectual pursuits out in the world. What I did not picture, what I could not picture, was my body, nor the life and death that would be carried there, nor the body of my writing.

I woke up the next morning in a lake by a villa. No, it was sweat. I awoke drenched in my own waters.

When I was sixteen, I read *Frankenstein* over again. It was as if the entire book had been rewritten. Or I had. The words didn't say what they had before. The story didn't go where it had before. Under the words I saw a woman's hand—not the grand male brilliance of invention or epic hallucination—but this: Bodyvoice. Word given back to a body. Abject. Sublime. The living dead.

Percy Shelley drowned, and Mary was a single mother supporting a son for the rest of her adult life. She died of a brain tumor. She was eighteen when she wrote *Frankenstein*. She said it was the moment when she "stepped out of childhood into life."

Four: There Is No Map for Grief

Trauma brought me to the page. It is that simple.

When my daughter died in the belly world of me, I became a writer—so that all the words that cannot name grief, all the words threatening to erupt from my belly and uterus did not explode up and through my skull and face and shatter the very world and sky.

Oceans of other people's compassions have washed over me, but those of us who have lost children—we are a living dead tribe. We smile and nod and thank people for their concerns and efforts. The labor of our lives is actually quite simple: stay alive. So that others might go on.

Wounds make artists. I wrote a book from the body of my dead girl.

There is no map for grief, but there are bridges to others.

When I was thirty and finishing a dissertation on war and narrative, a box arrived via UPS to the door of my home. The sender was my aunt, my father's sister, a woman I had become estranged from over the years for her ill treatment and unkind words toward me, my sister, and my mother. The box was about the size of a small television. I removed the brown paper and tape carefully, then wondered why I had been careful. The cardboard box under the brown paper had a red lid. Why? I wondered. When I opened the red lid, a hundred photos and yellowed papers and documents spread before me like hands. Nothing from my aunt—there was no explanation for what was inside the box.

Deep mistrust spread through me even as I put my hand down into the photos and pieces of paper. Something, a tiny electrical charge, moved up the crouch of my fingers and up my forearms and into my biceps and shoulders. I tilted my head to the side.

Then I took the photos out one at a time and looked at them.

I had never been to Lithuania, the land of my paternal lineage. But I am the only one on either side of my parents' families who has blonde hair. I have the square jaw and small, blue eyes of a Baltic woman. I know because I looked at the photos and they . . . looked back. Myself. I saw selves who looked like me for the first time in my life. Even their bodies were of the shape and tune of mine—broad-shouldered and small-waisted, muscled arms and long necks and spines and Slavic noses.

I felt . . . secretly amongst people, when all my life I'd felt isolated.

But the photos were not alone.

Also inside the box were cut-out articles and Xeroxed copies of a story repeated over and over again.

The stories were about a photographer in Lithuania during the Russian occupation. This photographer managed to document a secret massacre at a hospital in a small, rural town in Lithuania. With his small, black box and second sight he had captured Russian soldiers shooting doctors point blank, the doctors' and nurses' dingy white scrubs speckled and blooming with blood caught in frames. Patients, some already on operating tables or in beds shot in the heads and hearts, their mouths forever opened into "O" or "why." Horrific imagery of mindless slaughter. Men. Women. Children. The uniforms and rifles of soldiers.

The photographer was my great-uncle, I learned later.

He was then sent to a Siberian gulag for eighteen years for taking the photos. But the Russian soldiers only found one camera, one roll; he'd secreted away the first camera and its secrets under a floorboard of the hospital, knowing his art was a death's head held carefully between his hands. From what I'm told, this is what "saved" his life. Otherwise, he'd have been shot on site.

My great-aunt hid the photos behind the wall boards in her home in

Lithuania at the head of her bed, in the long wait waiting for her husband and his beautiful hands to return to her.

My grandmother hid the photos in her attic in Cleveland, Ohio, even as there were no more reasons to hide them, I suppose.

My aunt discovered them when my grandmother died, and sent them, I found out later, because she knew I had an interest in—that my studies in graduate work were in—"war and art."

After receiving the photos, I made a ritual. Every night I would walk to a writing shed to the side of our house. I would light a wood stove and bury my torso in a blanket waiting for the room to heat up. I would watch spiders that had spun new worlds in the corners or across the windows overnight. Occasionally I'd see a mouse going outside coming inside going outside. I'd hear crickets and frogs and a creek's water making lines next to me. My husband and son safe and well in the house, the amber, internal light of home making them glow from afar, the black and blue light of external night light taking me away from wife and mother and toward the body where I make art.

Every night I followed this pattern. This corporeal pull. A novel was coming from my body in images and rhythms I hadn't known were even alive in me—or perhaps they were coming from the dead histories living in us all. A novel that came from the box of photos.

For seven years.

Five: Foreign Name

People ask me about my name.

They go, "Yuknavitch." What's that? "Lithuanian," I say. But they just look at me blankly, picturing something like Russia. Or vast, cold wastelands. It's not Russia in that word. It's my great-uncle taking a photo of Russian soldiers massacring doctors and patients and goats at a tiny hospital in Panaveyzes during occupation. Even the horses got shot. If you've not lived through war, you haven't thought it through your imagination until you've studied the dead horses, their entrails splayed in the foreground, the hint of human death in the background, clad in medicinal white. Blood mixed with snow and dirt and animal. It's the seventeen years he spent in a gulag for taking the photo, his crime bearing witness, his wife writing letters she could not send, hiding them instead behind the loose board at the head of their bed, hoping for the day he returned to whisper, "I have loved you in absence" in a language you'd mistake for child's gibberish. What is an unread letter but the country of Lithuania to an American? The word "war" is not something we bring to the word "Lithuania." The word "oppression" does not signify amidst larger, more historic namings. And yet I tell you. People who look like me. They died for making art. When I look at black-and-white photos—when I hold them in my hand—the faces of the people in the village where my last name last lived before it was hacked to pieces in translation—they are the only faces I will ever look like.

"Juknevicius" was a word, once.

Six: Labor

You are a woman writer so you make room for your work you make room for your thoughts you make room for your imagination you make room for your desires you make room for your fears you make room for grocery shopping you make room for housecleaning you make room for sex you make room for exercise you make room for pleasure you feel pretty good about that until the night you wake up at 3:00 a.m. and realize Jesus fucking Christ, I have too much unfinished writing lying around like arms and legs strewn across floors and is it really true that what I'm good at after all is making rooms?

You are a woman writer so you follow the script life of mother of lover of wife of partner of breadwinner of well dressed of good hygiene of good citizenship of comb your hair of put deodorant on of shave your hairy man-hating legs and armpits of wear the same shoes on each foot of don't succumb to large grandma underwear of shit pluck those face hairs and how the hell did my pubis grow a forest how is it possible even my rib cage has rolls of aging?

You are a woman writer you go to your teaching job since that's one of the only jobs you can get as a woman writer that is not humiliating degrading upsetting service-oriented though you are still service-oriented even though you have degrees and letters behind your name some little turd student can still go to "rate my professor.com" and NOT give you any hot peppers because you are not hot you are old to him and then he can comment any way he wants and the world is left open to interpret what "Dude. She sucks" means.

You are a woman writer and every morning you wake up but your children were awake before you staring at your sleep-crusted eyes and drool mouth and bad hair and bad breath and sagging tits and drooped over to the side belly going

MOMMY WAKE UP and MOMMY I'M HUNGRY and MOMMY I'M
BORED and what what what do you have to say and do for them because really,
that's all they care about because really, children are NEED INCARNATE so
why are you still in bed you sorry-ass excuse of a mother? You cook breakfast
you feed them you bathe them you dress them you thank god even if you don't
at all believe in god they are old enough to go to school you drive them to school
you come home you dress yourself you feed yourself you bathe yourself you avoid
mirrors. Avoid mirrors. There is no way you want to look at your sagging flesh
and dark bruised cups under your eyes and yep they are still there: unshaved
legs and underarms and ever thinning hair and ever slumping posture and tits
moving closer and closer to your thighs and anyway every morning of your life
you wake up and go WHAT THE FUCK IS THAT in your own underwear
or a new weird thing on your skin or a new weird feeling in your abdomen or
shooting rubber band pinches on your leg skin that come from nowhere or night
sweats or chills or headaches from Hades or can't someone just let me sleep in
for ten days straight without wanting anything? Can't someone cook for ten days
straight or clean for ten days straight or answer the children's want for ten days
straight or have sex with my lover or husband for ten days straight or just can't
someone let. You. Be? So you can write for ten fucking minutes?

You are a woman writer and worse: you are an American woman writer and
you are tired. You are more tired than you have ever been in your entire life. But
there is no space or time or definition for this kind of tired in America. You live
in the place of Superpower. Privilege. Wealth. Stars.

Suck it up.

Seven: The Work of Art

I know a woman named Menas who is a painter in Lithuania. Though she
travels to Vilnius monthly for food, to perhaps see an old friend, for supplies, she lives
in a rural area with very few people, a great many trees and streams, and regular
visits from animals and the elements.

When I say Menas is a painter, you may wonder where she "shows" her work.
What gallery. Have you seen her paintings? Is she on the Internet? Can we
"friend" her on Facebook? But these are not the right questions.

When I ask Menas about painting, she laughs and says, "Painting is the
labor of dream." There is nothing wrong with her English.

Menas lives alone on a falling-apart farm. In the past, the farm was a Soviet

Russia work farm. In the present, the farm simply houses her as both she and the buildings do what women's bodies do—move away from children and family and scripted desires as the aches and pains and changes in bending and blood and bone toughen and wrinkle flesh, and hair—like wood—grays and weathers and thins.

Her paintings live in a barn that was used in the past for horses and cows and chickens and goats and machinery. They rest stacked against one another in great monuments to her dream labor, but haphazardly—nothing like an American painter's studio—more like history gone from the order of power to the chaos of ordinary wildflowers and moths and rodents. The paintings smell like hay and dirt and wood more than turpentine and linseed and oil pigments. Sometimes the dirt and refuse and perhaps even rodent or insect shit and probably even a spider or two get into the paint before the canvas dries, and so her work wears an extra texture of . . . place. History.

The content of her work is difficult to describe. The colors, composition, and imagery are abstract rather than representational, but that seems idiotic to say. I have now known her for twenty years, and so to speak to you in Art in America terms not only seems foolish, it seems worse. Like a terrible lie. Or injustice. To speak to you of her paintings I have to talk about bodies.

The body of her work is not an "oeuvre." It is not the end product or output of her artistic production.

Her body of work—her labor—is corporeal.

When I stand in front of one of her larger works, say one that is 6 feet by 10 feet, I feel "inside" a river, the river rocks rumbling under the soles of my feet, the ice of the water traveling up the bones in my shins to my ribs and shoulders and skull. Or I feel "moved" by wind in leaves, my body raising its hair and flesh toward the sky, and before I know it, I see that I've extended both of my arms out to the side of my body and closed my eyes and rocked my head back, as if to say, yes. Or I feel "turned" by the colors of fall leaves and that moment before the deep hues of gold and red and brown and purple decrease into winter's dead detritus. In these paintings I feel the land not "out there," but in my body.

There are other paintings. Larger than life and a little intimidating. It's hard to step up close to them, and yet it is impossible to stay away. I always end up touching them or leaning into them. Which one cannot do in any gallery that I know of. But in a barn, you can put your body against a painting. In the painting I am speaking of now, I feel . . . like there is an inside out. I feel a corporeal reversal. Like blood and flesh and the heart's beating and corpuscular surge have broken through the membrane we hold so dear, called skin. The reds are more than red. The whites and blue whites and grays are nothing else but bone colored, and they are cracked where they should be bold and hold. There are indications of vertebrae, but they shatter the line of a spine. The blues are raging and bright lines that reach maplike and course and spread almost violently. Sometimes a more black than black rage scratches from near the center and scrapes toward the viewer— looking almost as if it is trying to become a word, language.

There are no faces or bodies, and yet I feel more embodied than seems humanly possible when I am with these paintings.

When I ask her about the deep internal of these paintings, Menas laughs and says, "It is not in words. It is body. Why words?" There is nothing wrong with her English.

When people ask me about Menas, I say I know a woman artist in Lithuania who fed her children on dirt and roots and potatoes and weeds and the milk from a cow and rain water for years.

Still they grew.

I say she loved her husband so much she carved his name on her own belly with a knife, and with the pulp and juice of wild raspberries, dyed it skin true.

She had no money in the past. At different times she was owned as a laborer by the state. Her hands have touched many kinds of work. She has next to no money in the present, though she survives through excellent barter systems and trade with people who are still alive over time and history.

There is no story of this woman, of what happened to her, of how she came to be a painter, an artist.

There is no "news" that carries her name like a sensationalized trial on TV.

I can't point to something that will show you how important the work of her art is.

Is a painter a painter if no gallery or critic writes her name, carries her? Is a painter a painter if no one will ever know how art came alive in her hands, how painting day after day is a labor no one owns but her? Why should anyone care how grief birthed her art?

What is the work of art? Do we toil differently, me with my domestic and capitalistic trials and tribulations, and Menas with her chickens laying eggs, or the ones that try to lay eggs but hatch deformed things, the residual effects of

Chernobyl something you can hold in the palm of your hand, her farm gone to seed, her family like a supernova flash that is an unrepresentable image?

We trade across time and lives.

Menas trades me paintings for stories.

She tells me in a letter, "Many thanks for your stories! They keep me! I am alive of them . . . " There is nothing wrong with her English.

Lithuanians, Latvians, and Estonians were primarily a rural people for centuries, their largest cities inhabited by other ethnic groups. The lyrics of their folk songs ring and rise with forests, mushrooms, animals, and azure shimmering lakes.

Most Americans don't know how to picture the city dwellers in Vilnius— stuffed as they are with their big-boned and thick-muscled bodies in concrete apartment blocks as the heat turns their apartments into ovens in the summer and cold cells in the winter. We only know Vilnius from war stories and poets.

Most Americans can't see in their mind's eye the way the land pulls away from cities and urban dwellings and stretches out and away as if it could escape. Perhaps they realize the Baltic Sea licks the shores of the country, but isn't it freezing and inhospitable? Isn't Lithuania without mountains? Wasn't it dotted by Soviet farms and laborers? Most Americans have no idea what the new freedoms are for people who have been owned and traded and made into state property.

Menas tells me about saunas. A Lithuanian sauna is a mixture of Russian traditions and a kind of Finnish comfort. The bathhouses are usually two-story wooden houses with a sauna cabin on the first floor, rooms on the second, and a pond to jump in right after the sweat. Winter. Spring. Fall. Summer.

Menas tells me how to fill a day with fishing in lakes so cold and blue you can see the underworld of waterlife. How to ride horses across land knuckled with rounded hills and through birch and pine forests. How to spend long afternoons filling baskets with mushrooms or berries.

And in evenings, over e-mail or in letters—the only letters I receive any more since in America no one pains herself to commit to the old labor of letter writing—Menas tells me over and over again how her entire family was blown to bits—husband, son, daughter, in front of her eyes—while she held a basket of kindling for the fire, her hair blowing back away from her face and the skin around her eyes and mouth pinching with heat.

Each time she tells it, it is as if it is the first time. Each time (with a glass of pear wine or brandy at the end of a day—I know because she has shared the smallness of the ritual—I can see the tiny glass going to her lips), when night falls and I am in the writing shed next to my beautiful family, my beautiful home, my appliances and computers and bills and cars and shoes and food and wine and cutlery that is "worth" more than her entire farm, she tells it to me.

There are plain ways to say it. When the Soviet Union fell, her rage and despair and grief took shelter in a falling-apart farmhouse. Alone in the labor of a life.

I met her accidentally because of my research. For an American degree. An American Book. An American Woman's Life.

Menas says, "I become painter, to live."

But I think maybe it is simpler, her becoming. I think it is a choice to face not staying alive, with expression and labor and body. She is out there. Making new corporeal forms. With or without any of us.

Years ago, when Menas learned that my daughter died in the belly of me, she said, "Then you are down at bottom of water now. But see? You can walk the deep. That is why you here. Can see me?"

Possibly the most perfect sentences anyone anywhere has ever said to me.

In this way Menas became an invented girl in the novel I wrote. In my novel, the girl haunts the lives of American Artists, but also feeds their content. She is beautiful and terrible all at once.

I'm looking at a photo of one of her paintings right now. It is black and blue and as big as the wall of a house. Maybe it's the bottom of the water. Maybe Menas's lost family is there, floating or walking the depths, and maybe, too, my beautiful dead daughter, maybe even Mary Shelley. The image is arresting. I must remember from her to push on the sentences until they break open and reveal all our otherness. I must remember to be a body that generates new ways of seeing and saying—the labor, the work of art.

A woman's body. Without apology.

This language.

My daughter's name was Lily.

This annual essay, inspired by the work of Meridel Le Sueur, was funded by the generous contribution of Margaret Wurtele.

How Pale the First Moon of the Year

ALAMGIR HASHMI

How pale the first moon of the year.
Your words, damp air of the unspoken,
or perhaps that same treacherous
ground beneath our feet
sliding in sheets of rain; this last killer landslide.

You say, weeks of mud; I agree.
Let someone else notice the coming numbness.

The cabin, sheltering the lost here,
now a pile of sticks or straws,
souls out of place, nowhere to fall.
At least the sky no longer sieves
through the roof.

Bird wings flapping somewhere,
within hearing distance,
a shriek pierces the dark snows.
Weren't we warned of the drifts,
passing touch of bodies, disturbed sleep?

Tracer lightning still rummages in the dark:
it's only a goat track winding through the hills,
going round and round. And then

an uneasy stop to rush through,
as only a leafless elm fends for itself.

How the naked roots clutch at the edge of a crag
in here, and here, and here.
It's not the roots; shortness of breath
sets off a riff
down the tremulous valley.

The Café of Our Departure

PRISCILLA ATKINS

> *We don't know how to say goodbye—*
> Anna Akhmatova

Near the *sous-sol* of our lives, where nothing sacred
escapes, there is a room where no one goes

of their own accord.
Yet, eventually, a crowd gathers.

One by one, we descend from terrace tables
in search of our dearest friend

who unbuttoned his shirt, laid out
the wild daisy of his life.

The cancer so slow no chemo would touch it;
so rare.

Now, in the *sous-sol* of our grief, we do not weep.
And then we weep.

Days dreamt in scrim of terrace clatter. Forkfuls
of lemon cake, while one street away

stroll silent silhouettes; flowers gray
and no rain catches. Gravity turns, and turns us.

How will we do this?
Life is the one house where someone knew us.

From Five Poems about an Apple Tree

SARAH FOX

> *after George Oppen*

> *The question is, how does one hold an apple / who likes apples*
> George Oppen, Five Poems About Poetry

> *From the Great Above she opened her ear to the Great Below*
> The Descent of Inanna

1. *The Gesture*

The question is: how does one hold fetal components
who "held" baby

and how does one, who was graveyard, plant
the salvaged tissue—what form of life?—
under the rootball of an apple sapling?

How does one hold in the mind a form
—which one intended to clutch, feed—
that is said to have existed
inside the body

which evades completion, holds
variously only in the mind

like a shade? The form imprints
on myth: singing god,
full-bodied and magically endowed,
perennial tree in my ear.

The question is:
when will there be a tree
clutching its own discrete and mineral form—
life in time—not mistaken
for a baby

boy reaching branch-armed, abandoned,
for a mother body?

2. *The Little Hole*

The little hole in the ground
for the little tree, little bowl

for baby yolk,
cold dirt's nerves exposed
to air, root

synapse: statuary—monument—
Stands the tree, its firm place.

Little surgical vacuum,
cervical dial. Hades
hole between looking and looking
back.

Doppler static, motionless
radiographic heart hollow,

babyshape's eye/nose
shadow basins. The world's on the other side

of a hole. Home, the senses.

Look at it: the tree is.
The baby: transplanted,

space to space, vein-entangled.

4. *Parousia*
    Impossible not to doubt what can't be seen: his dimensional body,
    his death moment inside me (irrevocable).

    (For two weeks I hosted his death.)

    His birthing (I do not believe he was born. I did not give birth).
    Scraped and suctioned while I slept in lethal darkness.
    Masked men circled me with their indifferent knives.

    The "baby": "removed."

    No air ever touched him.

    Not that he will come again—
            That he is
    now
                still

somewhere distinct
in the world, the future—
Arms outspread, feet bound in roots—his image, existing.

Clutch

MARY WHARFF

It's the unborn again, those yet-to-be blessings. Mark says sometimes you have to draw the line. He says babies born in shells are optional. He *humphs* like I'm tree-hugging dandelions when I say death is death.

Meanwhile he hoses out the birdbath. "Did you see the nest?" he asks and points with his head toward the redbud tree.

I push up off my knees and throw tangles of creeping charlie into the weed pile. The redbud is crowded with blooms, but I see the nest right away, close to the top. A breasty robin hops around the edge with a fat earthworm dangling from her beak, and the earthworm flips around and curls up on the ends. But there's no hope. Not for that worm. The robin's chicks grab at it with those chick beaks that always seem too big and heavy for the chick's toothpick throats. Not exactly cute, either. Like homely babies. The ones you lie about to the mother, how adorable! The ones the mothers love whether you lie or not—beauty being a beholder thing, blood being non-negotiable.

"Too bad geese don't shit like robins," Mark says.

He goes on: all the goose shit—on the sidewalks, up the drive, in the yard. Every spring it's the same: wild geese everywhere. Every spring they pick our lawn, our pond, our limestone paths, and red brick patios. Goose shit everywhere. Turds as long as his index finger.

"Why us?" Mark asks and aims the hose at a turd on the stone path.

Mark thinks the geese pick our yard for the same reasons his customers do— it's lush and colorful and full of beautiful roosts. The tall grass around the lily-pad pond is especially attractive for geese. But the geese don't understand that Mark's photography business depends on the grass and the pond and our yard. The yard keeps us in organic food and hybrid cars and an Arts & Crafts bungalow with hundred-year-old oaks. The prairie flowers are blue and yellow and pink at this time of year and attract the newly graduated and newly joined and newly born and the forever bound by the ties that bind. Mark's customers say they feel more natural in nature. And it's true. Our backyard makes any family look happy.

"Old women die when they break their hips." His voice is tight, too high, begging. "They'll slip. I'll be sued. We'll go broke."

This could be mere supposition, but I hear a dig. My freelance reviews and essays don't bring in much. "A penny for your thoughts," he likes to tease. It's really a dollar a word, but I'm not that wordy. I like a tight premise, a crisp sentence. Even for topics like arts and culture. Especially. Life is ambiguous and art is more. People suffer, I think. People want to get it.

"Shhh," Mark says when I start to argue. He points as something orange and fast flies by.

"Oriole," he says, though we both already know that. The oriole lets out a string of whistles that ends with a drunk-sounding *blurt*. Mark grins. I've seen him grin at geese *ongks*, too. That *ongk, ongk, ongk* of a high-flying V. But only out on the highway. Out there, he'll slow down and we'll watch like we've watched a thousand times and he'll say, "look at the way they draft off each other," like he's said a thousand times, and I won't mind the repetition like I haven't minded a thousand times. Bird lectures tipped my love for him. My Nikon Premier LX 8x32 binoculars tipped his for me.

Mark hoses down the rest of the walks and tells me he can't keep doing this. It's too many hours out of too many days. He says he can't care what I think or he thinks or the Wildlife Federation thinks.

I stop thinning out a patch of black-eyed Susan sprouts. Mark gives me a dog-eyed look, hopeful but intent.

"The geese have to go. There's only one thing that works." He's called a guy who can do it.

My tongue presses the back of my teeth.

Mark's *one thing* is this: his guy shakes the eggs to kill the goslings. His guy then returns the eggs to the nest. Mark and I will watch while the goose and gander keep the eggs warm and, they think, safe. We'll watch until eventually, but not right away, they figure out the eggs aren't going to hatch. They'll decide something is wrong with their babies, disease, maybe malformation. They'll understand that those things happen.

Then we'll watch them leave. And never come back. Because this spot didn't work out for their family. Geese know when to move on. Geese remember.

"So the geese will have bad memories of our pond," I say.

"Geese don't have memories. They have instincts."

"So they'll instinct that our pond is bad news."

"Something like that."

"So we'll have to watch them fly over us."

"Right!" he says as though we have finally agreed.

I pick a crocus and toss it on the pond. It's too delicate to make even the tiniest ripple. Mark puts his hand on my shoulder.

"When?" I ask.

Mark says tomorrow morning because this afternoon he's got a shoot with a huge family. The Zuerchers. Thirty-seven relatives, five generations, Great-Great-Grandma on down.

"There's one more thing." His hand moves down my back and stops at my waist and closes in to hold me tight.

"The Zuerchers have twins. Girls. Twin girls." His tone is too quiet and too earnest, that tone that makes truth sound false and false sound wrong, like you are wrong or the lost ones are wrong, because losing is wrong and the lost lost and you lost the lost and are lost.

"I'll be fine," I say. It's been a long time. Long enough.

"I bet they'll be darling," I say and let go of his hand. "Got to write that review for the paper."

On the way back to the house, I kick a turd out of the grass and onto the limestone path.

My hands stall above the keyboard. This review has troubled me. On the upside, the local arts center was noisy and cramped the night the exhibit opened.

And the exhibit was creative, dozens of masks made with discarded objects—plastic grocery sacks, smashed pop cans, buttons, broken glass and tile, screws and nuts, and so on. The variety was interesting, the connection of face to waste was clear. Still, something didn't work for me.

I can see Mark through the window by my desk. Great-Great-Grandma Zuercher is blushed pink in a way that lets me know he's told her she's "brewed such a fine brood," he'll have to give her the throne.

I thought Mark would bring me down to earth as gently as he's leading Great-Great-Grandmother to the garden bench by the pond. Mark's very ability to rationalize was one of the reasons I said yes when he asked me to marry him. Balance being a good thing for a couple. I didn't expect contradiction—enthusiast one day, exterminator the next.

I keep spying as Mark moves the Zuerchers around, tallest in the middle, shortest on the sides, four long rows. He puts a lanky girl with orange hair on the end of the second row and an older man wearing a red shirt on the other end. Apparently the man didn't read Mark's instructions about wearing beige or brown clothing so the yard colors pop. The lanky girl assumes a pose with her hand on her hip, the long orange hair flowing lava-style over one shoulder and her breast and waist, all the way to her hip-hugging belt. The older man twists the top button of his shirt while he looks down at the grass to one side of his feet, then the other, as if his spot isn't quite right.

I think I would have put them together, right in front. Bull's-eye. But Mark places the twins in the center. Matching cream dresses. Lacey hems. Golden bangs cropped in a straight line across each forehead. Skinny legs and lacey anklets and white shiny patent leather shoes. The only distinction is a flesh-colored Band-Aid on one of the four knees.

Our twins were fraternal: one boy, one girl. Naturally distinct. Even at five months, you could see the boy would be bigger, bulkier. A heavy-set kid. The doctor joked with us, "Your boy must be starving his sister."

Mark somehow gets every Zuercher to smile at the same time, again and again and again. And I decide to go easy on the exhibit because the arts center is all about encouragement and it was the artist's first show. I write: *This exhibit inspires me to think about the faces I see every day.*

Later, chemicals stir up a sour odor in the darkroom.

"Did you know," I say to Mark, "it takes a goose a whole day to push out just one egg? Did you know that?"

Of course he knows, but I continue.

"So she pushes out five eggs, maybe six, sometimes as many as twelve eggs, one by one, one day at a time."

He is silent in his usual *I'm-in-the-middle-of-developing* silence.

I wonder out loud why the eggs are called a clutch. Clutching the eggs would not be good for the babies.

A timer dings. Mark flips on a light and holds up the negatives of the Zuercher clan.

"Damn," he says. That orange hair. He sees a clash, the carrot too harsh for a powdery spring sky.

I see summer, an early tomato, a heat wave. I see a flare in the family.

At my computer again, I write: *Despite the solid craftsmanship, I'd like more to hold onto.*

As it turned out, my placenta detached too early. Our son and daughter both starved. The doctor said our twins were lost. I screamed, "Well, find them!"

Mark shows me his favorite proof of the Zuerchers. The twins are holding hands, but that's not what he likes. What he likes is Great-Great-Grandma. "Look," he says, and he's right. That little bent woman appears straight and broad and her face glows and though I know it's daffodils making that light, that deep, yellow, encouraging light, it doesn't look that way. It looks like the light is coming from her. And the old man's red shirt, that girl's lava hair, they're not so much muted as mixed in. The color of dawn. And sunset for that matter.

Tears make my cheeks sticky and Mark leaves me alone with the photo. I'm sure he thinks it's the twins. I can't seem to tell him I think it's the old, happy mother.

Mark asked the doctor if I would be able to get pregnant again. The doctor nodded and Mark asked, "When?"

He said to me, "Do you hear that, Emily? You're OK. We can try again soon."

At my desk, I write: *I'd like to experience something new. Not so much the face as mask, false and impenetrable, but face as gateway, face as true.*

"The gander will be on the lookout. He'll honk at your guy," I say to Mark that night in our bed.

"He'll fight for his babies," I say, and roll in his direction. "You would have fought, right?"

He looks at me. It's an unfair question. He's right. There was no one to fight.

"Emily." His breath comes out tired on my face. "Do you have a better solution? We have to do something."

I close my eyes. After a few minutes, there's more breath on my face, but this time it's the breath of the man who has promised to love me. His fingers trace my cheekbone. "Babe."

I open my eyes and we look for each other. His brown eyes, my brown eyes. We'll never know if the twins would have had gold flecks like his or gray rims like mine. Their eyes will always be that newborn blue. I will always see blue.

I blink. "It'll be OK," Mark says.

I try not to blink again because I want him to see. I'm the one who did it. I'm the one who let go.

Early the next morning, I edit the last sentence of the review, from this: *after all, it is not so easy to read a face.* To this: *after all, it is not so easy to face a face.* Then I go out to the pond and stand near the winged sentinel. Soon the truck will arrive, steel-toed shoes, large hands.

The gander *ongks* at me, then he *ongks* toward the tall grass hiding his goose and their clutch.

"I know," I say and cross my arms.

Meditation on Hunger at 2 A.M.

TODD DAVIS

Night is the black earth in the garden, a peach
held to the sky as the moon writes the history

of its shadow on the bedroom floor. Awake,
I remember cherries in a white bowl and think

of the faces of those I have loved
rising to the surface of the pond

where I fish with my sons. The flesh fades
if not fed; this is the business of living.

In his dying my father taught me language
fails. Thus, his love for the turnip's sting,

even when soaked in butter and cream,
or the sweet on sweet of honey drizzled

over baked apples, makes an elegy
of autumn olive as it takes over this field.

How could it be otherwise, and what choice
do we have? Like him I give thanks

for the neighbor's draft horse, asleep
and dreaming in its stall, enormous teeth

moving over oats that still sit in a scoop,
waiting for a hand to offer them.

In Which the Persona Confesses to Boxing the Blue Horses

LISA GRALEY

This long night I have heard you breathe
and felt your breath upon my shoulder,
close as we've come to trading secrets.
This night I have dreamed the blue horses
in their droop-eyed sleep and long lashes,
standing in the meadow, and looked
for sleep in you of the kind dammed hearts
will fight and finally give in to.
I have dreamed you, pursued and pursuing.
I have heard you whisper in an unknown tongue.

What bread I've broken you've tasted
and know without looking the contents
of the burlap sack, nothing noble
or inspiring there. We carry
our wounds and murders with us,
odd bags of bones and maps
where we meant to be this time next year
divining rods and withered seedlings,
lodestone and flint, leftover charcoal,
whatever leather we used to use
petrified now and crumbling.

What I haven't said, you've heard;
what I haven't opened
you've weighed in hand.
The figure not revealed,
you've calculated and chosen.
Maybe truth would wear
a different color
did you not press so steady
your lambent gaze.
across the open grate.

Listen, it was I who boxed
and shunned the blue horses
with the same heat
I once desired and loved them.
For you must know, I did once
desire and love them.

Fine the line, it's been said,
between taming and crippling.

Maytag Washer, 1939

NORMA TILDEN

> The Alliance of Art and Industry: Toledo Designs for a Modern America *opened*
> *last month. The focus is on the 1930s and '40s, when the Ohio city emerged as a hotbed of*
> *product design . . . A 1939 Maytag washing machine was so smoothly rounded and*
> *practical that its design remained unchanged for 40 years.*
>
> *The Washington Post*, April 6, 2002

Maytag, you crafty girl, you got your picture in the papers. You got them to look at you, coolly appraising your rounded, "practical" curves, your tapered legs and porcelain skin. Maytag—ingenious, lovely thing—you worked your way out of the basement.

In "Nineteen Hundred and Nineteen," writing in the wake of what was then regarded as surely the last Great War, poet William Butler Yeats mourned the passing of "many ingenious, lovely things," delicate old masterworks of art and intellect that now lay buried under the brute rubble of history. These were ornamental things that once had seemed "sheer miracle to the multitude"— polished ivory statues, beribboned dancers, bronzed peacock feathers—refined and precious monuments to a view of civilization that should have been "protected" from the routine violence that "pitches common things about." Or so the poet thought.

By the beginning of the next war, the multitudes were turning to the more practical miracles of "common things," mass-produced and easily replaced. Already in 1934, Philip Johnson had gathered hundreds of ingenious, lovely things for a show of masterworks of design at the Museum of Modern Art. He called these

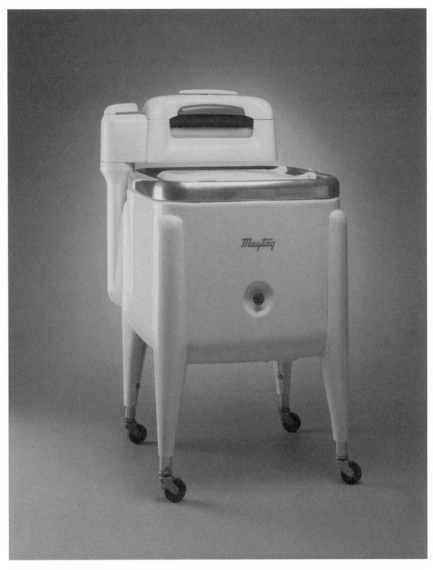

Harold Van Doren & Associates with Thomas R. Smith (engineer), *Washer Model E,* patented 1939,
The Maytag Company, metal, enamel, plastic, and rubber, 44.25x38.75x26 in.

democratized treasures "Machine Art"—industrial bolts and screws, household tools, electrical coils, incandescent bulbs, bronze bearings, tire treads—all of them showcased as organic forms, at once functional and beautiful. Except that by the 1930s Yankee ingenuity had managed to collapse the distinction: these things were beautiful in use.

It was Yeats again who, early in the century, had invented a "beautiful, mild woman" to speak for him on the beauties of industry: "To be born woman is to know / Although they do not talk of it at school– / That we must labour to be beautiful." Yeats called this labor "Adam's Curse," and spoke of it as the fine and difficult work of poets and women.

You knew about Adam's curse, Maytag, ingenious and lovely thing, rocking in rhythmic labor in the steamy basements of Ohio—that 1930s "hotbed" of industrial design. And in your presence, clustered around you with our mothers, their faces blushed with steam, we would learn what it meant to be born a woman: the intricate mechanics of beauty and use. In those days, to find a mother— usually any mother would do—we raised the heavy trapdoor to the cellar, making our way through the canopy of dripping clothes suspended over a delicate cat's-cradle of waxy rope. The clotheslines were themselves ingenious webs, crossing over and under each other in that cramped space, lowered to receive the dripping weight of the laundry, then hoisted toward the basement ceiling on flimsy, notched poles. Although they had not learned of it at school, our mothers understood this levered counterpoise of heft and height: lifting the newly laundered sheets above the floor on sagging stilts, then lowering them dry and almost weightless. Briskly, they would pinch off the colored plastic clothespins, folding the sweetened base- ment air into the sheets as they wrapped them loosely into themselves, then nestled them, like bunting, in the wicker laundry baskets.

Any Monday, we could follow the sounds of the Maytag down through the veils of linens and delicately patterned housedresses, the stiff, dark cotton of uniforms and "work clothes," the soft muslin diapers and summer-printed sunsuits. We followed the rhythmic humming and the heavy smells of potions until, some- where below that damp canopy, we found our mothers gathered—Pauline, Yolanda, Josephine, Nelda, Connie—with the Maytag wringer washer, rocking as it worked, all of them beautiful in use.

The mothers were busy mixing lotions and powders with modern, chemical names, their faces reddened in the warm fog of perfumed salts: "Oxydol" for heavy-duty cleaning, its name a potent blend of chemistry and girlish play; "Fels Naptha," to be scrubbed with wiry brushes over grass stains and the greasy knees of work-pants. For whiter whites, there was the mystery of "Rinso Blue," which came in two forms: a thick, cobalt-stained syrup or a tidy wafer, like a poker chip, dissolving in a whirlpool of molten blue when dropped into the churning cauldron of the Maytag.

The gentle washing of fine things required a box of "Ivory Snow," which, even before we peeled back the cover, seemed buoyant, a cache of paper thin, luminescent flakes. Each of us begged to be the helper chosen to drift the flakes in a simulated blizzard over the tub. There they would quickly melt into a layer of yellowed suds, swirling back and forth in the repeated, half-circular motion of the Maytag's busy agitator. Delicate garments were tagged "Ivory Washable, 99 and 44/100% pure." But Ivory was not just for lingerie. For a few weeks back in 1940, 800 people a day had visited the "Ivory Washable House" at Radio City in New York. Garishly colored ads in *House Beautiful* touted "the famous house that could be washed from front door to back," but only with Ivory Soap, 99 and 44/100% pure. Those lucky New Yorkers who toured the house must have left Radio City with a deep appreciation of Adam's curse. "As practical as it is decorative," the ads proclaimed. Like other miracles of machine art, the Ivory House promised to be beautiful in use.

My mother and I worried that impurities might lurk in the remaining 56/100 of 1 percent. For us, then, there was a dangerous white jug of "Clorox Bleach," surely 100 percent pure. Clorox represented the epitome of better-living-through-chemistry, so powerfully clean that they called it "Ox"—or so I thought. My mother stirred it into the washtub with a sawed-off section of broomstick, scrubbed to the color of raw oak by its weekly plunge into the rinse water.

When the Maytag's churning action stopped, our mothers used the broomstick to fish the sodden fabrics from the sudsy mix and move them to the rinse, lines of blueing running up their arms toward the caplet sleeves of their housedresses. Then, one piece at a time, they fed the dripping laundry through the hard, rubber lips of the wringer. Behind it, one of us was stationed to catch the flattened garment, pull it through in a ropey twist, and layer it like ribbon in the basket, ready for the clothespins and a space on the line.

Fels Naptha for work clothes . . . Rinso for whites . . . a heady mix of chemical smells, dampened voices, and steady, industrial sounds that I remember, still, fifty years later, as both sweet and strong. In the cellar, as they scooped and measured potions, even their language seemed to be processed through the pursed lips of the Maytag: "That bitch Marie—she put my brother through the wringer. And now, mark my words, she'll take him to the cleaners, too." Tide for colors . . . Dreft for baby things. "'Hazel,' I told her, 'don't you let that man soft-soap you.'" Giggles bubbled up through the mass of steamy ringlets bobbing over the tub. Someone replied, "Listen to me, honey. You need to put some of that starch in *your* undies." The vaned agitator, metal before the war but now a rugged plastic, forced water through the clothes. These were the luxurious, sloshing sounds of your labor, Maytag. Always you seemed overfull.

Pictured here in the morning paper, you are still lovely, though no longer in use. The stuff of your labors is hidden now, injector hoses coiled behind the tub, agitator finally at rest in the gray, freckled cavity beneath the porcelain lid. "Well-rounded design, then and now: A 1939 Maytag Washer." With a mild shock, I realize that I am looking at a crude, metallic rendering of a woman, solid and big-bellied. Her slim legs barely support her swaying girth. She stands on exhibit at the Toledo Museum of Art, turning slightly to the side, a pregnant woman, at once proud and bashful. Her shapely legs, smooth and white, thicken into thighs where they extend up the side of the tub. These are legs "that go all the way up to her ears," the manly compliment I overheard from my uncles, laughing on the porch stoop where they huddled after work. Four legs, not two; this design was an improvement on nature: two legs to support the heavy belly, two to hold up the wide hips at the back. From the base of the tub, they taper to slim ankles banded in chrome bracelets, then slip into tiny, round-toed shoes on black castor heels. Against the stark backdrop of her museum perch, the Maytag poses hieratically, like an Egyptian wall princess, all four small feet fixed at the same sharp angle perpendicular to the body, as if to prevent her from slipping away. Circling the top of the tub, a girdle of bright chrome holds the enormous, bulging cavity in place. Squarely in its center is a protruding black navel—a plug of some sort—for filling and emptying the tub.

And there, above the enormous belly, is the small head of the Maytag, its mouth a wide, black hole hooded by a red metal lipstick smear. Just visible inside that chasm are the tight, rolling lips of the wringer. At once prim and merciless, those lips could pull you in, then send you out stiff and one-dimensional. A single arm holds the head in place. Above it, instead of an ear, rests the tiny mind of the clutch. The Maytag's head can be moved aside for easier access to her trunk. The only other flash of color is a word in neat, feminine script, written in lipstick cursive across the tub: "Maytag," your name, a game for girls in spring.

When the wash was done, the fierce agitation finally quiet, the clothes, still heavy with sweet-smelling water, sagging just above the cement floor, my mother would rinse the Maytag with Clorox and polish it dry. She would leave it, cool and empty, prepared for tomorrow. Immaculate metal—you could see yourself in it.

Upon Examining the Bar Code

JONATHAN GREENHAUSE

The bar code's the most romantic symbol in modern human language.
Thick, thin, thick, thin, thin, thick, thin, thick, thick, thin.
On and on, black bars run in an eternal prison of incomprehension,
        an innumerable array of trees traipsing their ways
toward other silhouetted trees.

The bar code's influential marks make for interesting conversations
        among absolute strangers
in barrooms, cafés, airport hangars, and changing rooms.
There's a mystery in its mixture of solitary figures
        fixed in a seemingly random vertical order.

There's repressed memory in the manner of its recognized configurations.
Black, black black, black. Black, black, black. Black black, black, black.
        In these undecipherable lines,
there's poetry leading to commercial endeavors,
a leaning toward and propulsion into the pleasing purchase,
        a sweet exchange of taste and tender.

Bar codes bring about change, both real and transformative.
Scanned by lasers they raise their veil of secrecy,
        revealing the underpinnings of their practical generation,
the icons they've attached to transferred to foreign hands.
Possession's passed on.

But with bar codes, the obligatory exchange is cautionary,
        most often kept at a single serving.
Once the object's been rung up,
it's rarely released again within the magic sphere of the marketplace.
Its run of value's relinquished, its thick and thin black bars
        reverting once more into a solitary prison,
into a code of silence.

It's an Age, We've a Planet (a Fragment)

MATT MAUCH

We can't see his heart in his thumb,
the thumb anxiously rubbing his trigger finger
fingerprintless, smooth. We can't see the idea of a daisy
and centuries of daisy and other petal symbology
in her pocket among the nickels, pennies, dimes.
They can't see that we can see them.
We don't know who the hell is seeing us.
Seeing is only a kind of touching, yeah,
but it's the saddest kind. Touching each other directly
with so many of us leering would be too
televised, too third planet from the sun.
One look at, and we know that touching
is the last thing we'll ever do. One look away from
says, Man, it's the first thing we probably should.

Maybe Minorly

DOBBY GIBSON

The ghosts are everywhere here,
in the extra place setting the waiter whisks away
and in the voices in books you surround yourself with.
In the weird things we whisper to ourselves
about the weather and what it means,
like what to do when the lanterns freeze,
or when sailors should take warning.
We say someone is *spirited*
when they hold the ghost,
because we know we can't pass
through the snow without thinking of them
and feeling at least a hint
of the sound of a plow
scraping the boulevard
and then the silence that follows
and is as fleeting as forgiveness.
When the cattle suddenly lie down.
When the sparrows vanish.
In the moment the coroner is forced to decide
between *accident* and *undetermined.*
And as the worst of the storm finally arrives—
which is also the best of the storm—
night falls.
We can barely see strangers' headlights
beautiful through the snow,
and then we can just barely see the snow.

Orphans in the Terrorist World

RIGOBERTO GONZÁLEZ

S eptember 12. The date comes around each year, wearing the ugliest window on the calendar. As of 2001, it brings its equally grotesque older
sibling, September 11. The two dates grate on me like subway trains
shrieking to a halt on both sides of the platform. I'm forced to reckon with two
days of remembrance back to back—9/11 and my mother's death.

I still don't have the courage to talk openly about 9/11, or even write much
about it. And for a year or two after the event it irritated me to no end to be asked
by non–New Yorkers if I had been in the city during the terrorist attacks. The
question's usually posed so nonchalantly, as if the answer could be given with
the same casual tone. No, I was not in New York City on that fateful day, but in
Seattle, calling or e-mailing everyone I knew in Manhattan, everyone I had left
behind when I moved out of the city only six months before. And everyone I
e-mailed eventually responded, dusty but unharmed. My only personal connection
with the Twin Towers was that I went to browse the clothing boutiques in the
underground mall once in a while, when I passed through. Because I was a middle
manager for an after-school program in Brooklyn at the time, I had to attend
meetings at the city-wide coalition headquarters in the Wall Street district each

month. But that personal connection became overshadowed by the patriotic agenda that exploited and manipulated a communal grief. There was very little room for "Me" when there was now a "We." I felt excluded every anniversary after that, so now I simply refuse to participate, making sure I hide out from the false sentimentality of the American media.

This method of coping came easily for me, since by that time I had been practicing that self-exile for many years. On September 12 I try to avoid any contact with family and friends. By now they have grown accustomed to my need for privacy and don't bother me about my reclusive behavior. I descend into solitude for a day, and ascend the next morning somehow refreshed, cleansed of a darkness that first took hold of me when I was twelve years old. But each year, it comes back, this overwhelming clobbering of my spirit. And each year, I survive it.

In September of 2002, after taking a year off to travel and heal after my last significant relationship ended, I was back living in Brooklyn, sharing a railroad apartment in Williamsburg with a musician whose middle name was Windchild, a good friend of my former boss (who was somewhat of a hippie herself) at the after-school program, though I was now a visiting assistant professor at The New School in the Village. I didn't particularly care for my new neighborhood, which was young, bohemian, and very white, but the arrangement was temporary while I kept my eye out for an apartment in Manhattan, in Upper East Side specifically, because I liked how peaceful and clean it was—a far cry from the lively side-walks of Williamsburg, where the loud energy distracted me from my work. I found solace in an unexpected invitation to a party on September 11 at a loft near the local bank, where young people gathered to watch the New York City sky-line light up across the East River.

I had every intention of ensconcing myself for two days, but the hook of the party was: "Anything but 9/11," in response to the media overkill and political posturing that would be surrounding the first anniversary of the event. And true to the theme, the conversations at the gathering were about anything but 9/11. Someone brought a large cooked fish, perhaps a salmon, which sat in the middle of the buffet table, getting picked to the bones as people, mostly artsy types, circulated through the room talking painting, poetry, film, and fashion. All the while, the highballs and martinis completed the air of sophistication the hosts were aiming for. I gravitated toward the intimate clique of queers generating the most witty banter and laughter. *(She asked me what I thought about her outfit. I told her it was out all right; now we just had to hope for a fit!)* It was a very multiethnic group, but mostly Asian, so I had no reservations about moving seamlessly into the conversation, and the group responded positively, if not politely, to my presence since I was also one of two Latinos at the party. Meanwhile, the industrial-sized martini shaker rattled in the background. Perhaps in anticipation of the following day, I drank myself stupid and stayed in bed weathering my hangover through most of September 12.

That particular year was a milestone for me. I had officially outlived my mother's age at the time of her demise. She had been thirty-one, I had turned thirty-two. In July of that year I wandered the city alone, trying to find a reason why I should live longer than my mother. I was not suicidal exactly, just unsure about what the stars expected of me. I had come this far, from Zacapu, Michoacán, to New York City, trying to elbow my way through the overcrowded halls of struggling artists. Would it pay off at the end, this sacrifice of living so far from home? Would it matter, this chosen profession: writing?

The next day, I walked through the streets of Manhattan. Facing the high-rise buildings was like facing the ocean, recognizing something grander than the small self. As I crossed paths with hundreds of other lives, I became comforted that there was no spotlight on me to scrutinize my actions. I was not the center of the world. I didn't have to make the right decisions, just the ones I could live with. That was the key phrase: "live with." The key word: "live." I had to live. That's all.

That evening, after hours of stepping on the concrete sidewalks and not leaving behind a single footprint, I didn't want to go directly to my Brooklyn apartment, where I knew my roommate would be playing his keyboard and chasing his two Siamese cats, so I decided to check out the riverbank view from the ground.

I got off the L train at Bedford and walked toward the East River. People were headed in that direction but I didn't see any opening, just an abandoned shed. An older white-haired man with two dogs in tow was nearby so I simply asked how to get to the water.

"I'm going there, too," he said in a thick accent. "Follow me."

He was Polish, like many older folk in the neighborhood who were being displaced by the hipster population. My landlady was Polish, as were the women at the Laundromat, and the workers at the deli. There were still signs on the windows in Polish, and occasionally I heard it being hurled out from one side of the street to the other.

We got to the bank via that elusive hole in the fence and came upon other trespassers who were already comfortably seated on cement blocks that resembled benches facing the Manhattan skyline. I smelled pot, but didn't think anything of it. This was, after all, the college-age crowd, the dreadlock-wearing white kids with trust funds and debit cards.

"It's beautiful," I declared, and became thankful for my luck. This was the most appropriate birthday gift—a view of the city I had fallen in love with from the moment I first arrived in 1998. From this angle it was postcard perfect, palpable because it was breathing back at me.

The old man stuck around, keeping an eye on his pets, and he struck up a conversation. I welcomed it, inspired into friendliness by the view. He told me he had arrived in New York in the '50s, that he was later joined by his sister, with whom he still lived. He said it had been so difficult to fit in and to find a job at first because of his limited English, but that by some good fortune he was approached by a man who helped him out because he was also from the motherland.

The old man added: "So I asked him, 'How you know I'm Polish?' And he said to me, pointing down, 'The shoes! The shoes!'"

We both laughed, though I was unclear about how the shoes were the telltale sign of his nationality. In that moment, perhaps rendered vulnerable by my sense of gratitude, I even imagined that this might be my first friend in Williamsburg, aside from my roommate, of course. So I didn't think anything of it when he turned to me and said, "You know you are a very handsome man."

I smiled, accepting the compliment, and that's when he leaned over and stuck his tongue in my mouth.

For a brief second I slipped into denial. I was no stranger to the kamikaze kiss, but the setting was usually a bar with men my age, well-groomed and balancing a cosmo in one hand. This man was as old as my grandfather and we were standing in mud while some deadbeats puffed on their joints nearby. I wanted to tell him how sorry I was that he had sullied this night for me. It was my thirty-second birthday and today I was older than my dead mother. Reaching this age was like receiving permission to move on and live longer. In my twenties I was convinced I wouldn't make it, and more than once I planned my exit to the sharpest detail—a razor blade across my right wrist. I went as far as testing the path of the cut, a stupid exercise that left scars on my flesh. I wanted to accuse him of giving us queers a bad name, of betraying my trust and offending me when all I wanted was his guidance, his friendship, even.

I stared him down. By the way he took a step back, he seemed to understand that I had not been flirting with him this entire time. He looked afraid suddenly, and fragile. So I simply smiled apologetically and thanked him for showing me to the bank. And as I walked away I had to laugh at how silly the whole exchange had been. Once I got to the street, I laughed out loud and realized then that this awkward pass from an old man was going to keep me from plummeting into depression that night.

I slept well and peacefully.

I finally left Williamsburg in the spring of 2003 and moved into a one-bedroom Manhattan apartment on East 88th Street and York, on the opposite side of the East River. This was also my first encounter with the dreaded Housing Board process, even though I was renting the place from my accountant. Still, it was worth the trouble and the countless paperwork, including three reference letters, a letter from my previous landlord, which I forged, a copy of my job contract with salary statement, and a notarized letter from my bank, revealing information about my personal accounts.

This was the first time I was living in New York without a roommate, which meant that the hardwood floors and the view of gardens and greenhouses were going to cost me dearly, but for a year I pulled it off. The other benefit was that my favorite gay bar, the O.W. (as in Oscar Wilde), was just a short cab ride away on 58th. For months I collected cab receipts that were oddly around the same amount because I traveled those same thirty blocks many times after last call.

The Upper East Side, which every New Yorker who doesn't live there calls boring, has a quaint neighborhood feel east of Lexington Avenue. After a few short months I earned the right to be remembered by the people who saw me often at the cleaners, the deli, Gristedes, the post office, and Maz Mezcal, the Mexican restaurant on 86th that served the best *mole poblano* in Manhattan. The subway line was so removed from where I lived that foot traffic was never dense, so I was able to adopt a new exercise routine: walking down 1st Avenue all the way to Murray Hill, sometimes farther south, and then back up again. Thus, my days went like this: mornings at the New School, middays at the computer, afternoons on the concrete treadmill, and evenings at the bar.

When September rolled around, I knew what I wanted to do on the eleventh: hide out at the Town House, the gay bar across the street from the O.W. When

I felt like being left alone, I went to this bar because it's frequented by older gay men, most of whom are classy and respectful. They've been around and have seen most of it, so they can spot a guy who's looking for action but also one who's simply walking in for a relaxing happy hour cocktail. That was me on September 11.

I detected a conversation about 9/11 at the bar upstairs. A white gentleman kept declaring in his broken English that he "could not believe it, the buildings, they fall!" The bartender was wearing a tight-fitted shirt with the American flag covering the entire front side in colorful sequins. I quickly made my way to the downstairs lounge. It was quieter, the light more subdued, and not very populated at the moment. I pressed myself into the corner and ordered a dirty Absolut martini. I appreciated that the bartender wasn't chatty or even anxious for an audience to tell his testimony about where he was or what he was doing the hour the Towers collapsed. I had seen those unforgettable images on the television back in Seattle, where I was visiting my cousin. I had no television at my apartment so I rushed over to his house to keep abreast of the situation. Shortly before the collapse, cameras had inadvertently recorded the sight of bodies falling—jumpers who had succumbed to hopelessness. I was sitting on the couch when I heard my cousin talking. His voice had startled me back to consciousness. I had fainted.

It wasn't watching the footage that had caused it—it was remembering suddenly that days after I moved to New York City in 1998, I saw a woman jump from an apartment on Madison Avenue. My then partner had recommended that I walk around the neighborhood at 62nd Street between Lexington and 3rd Avenue to get to know the place. I had been timid about exploring, awestruck by the sheer size of the buildings around me, by the numbers of people on the sidewalks. I had never lived in a city before.

Eventually I took his advice. I wandered the streets in the area, always heading west because going to Central Park gave me a purpose: I wanted to sit on a bench and read. I was already a little apprehensive about spending my first winter in the city, so I was not deceived by how mild the weather was that day, December 8, to be exact. With a coat, a hat, and a pair of gloves in my bag, I was ready for anything, I thought. On my way back from the park, I was meandering along Madison when all of a sudden a mass of something dropped from the sky. Since I had seen restaurant workers toss large bags of garbage onto the sidewalks, I thought that's what it was. It wasn't.

A woman had jumped. I zoomed in on her yellow socks, soiled at the heels. Pedestrians all around me stopped and stared. Chauffeurs leaning against their town cars spoke into their cell phones. I turned around, headed straight for home, and waited until I locked the door behind me to cry, though I wasn't sure what I was crying about. I felt a sadness I didn't understand. What kind of place had I just moved to? I imagined that once the body was removed and the sidewalk cleaned, the flow of foot and vehicle traffic would continue unaffected by the soul that had caused little more than a pause in the system. I cried into my partner's arms when he got home after work, and I told him I never wanted to speak of it again, though it took me months to recover. When the 9/11 footage appeared on the screen three years later, making me black out for a minute, I realized I had only repressed that memory.

The bartender downstairs at the O.W. was more preoccupied with his new cell phone than with giving any patron much attention. On any other night I might have been indignant, but not on that one. I appreciated my invisibility. But as I sipped my drink, letting the olives tumble up the side of the glass toward my lips, I felt I was being watched. Behind me, a white guy about my age, but bald and with a hairy chest, walked past, and then walked past again, as if sizing me up from different angles. I turned around and watched him sit at one of the small vinyl seats in the corner of the room. He was attractive, with a shadow of a beard on his face that has always been a weakness for me. He smiled. In an instant I left the bar to join him. *What the hell?* I thought.

We struck up a superficial conversation about this and that, made jokes, and flirted.

"Yes, I'm a professor at The New School."

"Oh, really, I went to NYU."

"It's kind of quiet tonight, isn't it?"

"Well, it *is* the day it is."

He reached over to touch my cheek; I reached over to feel his hand. The chemistry was unmistakable, I convinced myself. I didn't even flinch when he made the odd request to look at my socks. I lifted the cuffs of my pants, and he reached down to pull them up.

"I have a thing for dress socks," he said. *Whatever floats your boat, buddy,* I thought.

"What are you thinking?" he asked.

I knew the answer to this question, which was clearly an invitation for me to make the first move, so I said boldly, "I'm thinking: Why aren't we in a cab on our way to my place?"

"Actually," he said, "I was hoping to circulate a little more this evening."

The rejection hit me like a sucker punch. He must have seen my eyes widen, my pride drop to the ground, taking my face with it, because he quickly added, "It's not what you think. Look, I can't explain it to you now, but I want to. Can I call you tomorrow? What time do you usually get up?"

"Sure. I'm up by nine."

I appreciated his pity, so I wrote down my number on a napkin and gave it to him, expecting never to hear from him again. I said my quick goodbye and a few minutes later I was in the back seat of a taxi. What a surprise to actually get a call from him at nine o'clock the next morning.

"I'd like to see you tonight," he said. "I'll give you a call at noon."

He called right on time, letting me know he would call me again at three. He did, and we made plans to meet at my place at six. I didn't ask him about his frequent phone calls, partly because I was distracted by my own sense of disorientation since it was September 12, the anniversary of my mother's death. I thought it particularly tacky to have a boyfriend over on that day—something I've never done before—but I had been left dissatisfied the night before and spent all day warding off a depression about my mother with the anticipation of my new beau's arrival. I distracted myself from the anxiety of his pending arrival by sitting at my desk and working on an essay about my mother.

While I typed, I kept looking at the altar I'd set up for my mother: a sepia photograph of Avelina Alcalá at nineteen, a rosary draped over it, a few lighted candles, and a Day of the Dead skull. These objects were set up to trigger my inspiration, but I made it a point to hide them away before the boyfriend arrived. I didn't want to have to explain them or the fact that I was hooking up on such a significant day.

He arrived on time, at exactly six o'clock. I buzzed him in and as he made his way up to the second floor I took one quick glance around to make sure everything was perfect. A bottle of wine. Check. Condoms in the drawer. Check. A sheet to spread on the futon couch in the living room. Check. He knocked, I let him in, and within minutes we were snuggling on the couch.

"Take it easy," he said, pushing me politely away.

I shook my head. "I don't get it. I thought this was why you came over."

"It is, but can we take it a little slow?"

I had to admit that was a new one—a phrase I had never heard from another man. But I complied. "Okay." I got up to pour some wine, then handed him a glass. "What would you like to talk about?"

"I don't know. Well, what did you do all day?"

"I wrote. I'm working on an essay."

"What about?"

"Oh, my mother," I admitted, and immediately felt a knot in my throat.

"Is she still alive?"

I was disarmed by the question. I took a sip of wine. "No."

"I'm sorry. When did she pass?"

At this point something in me crumbled. Whatever libido had me humoring this guy's strange courtship habits fell apart and I felt naked, but not in a sexy way. I turned to him. "Can I be perfectly honest with you?"

"Of course."

We had now agreed to be so open with each other that I could see the child this man once was in the expression on his face. "Today is the anniversary of my mother's death. She died twenty-one years ago. The reason I was at the Town House last night is that I prefer to be alone during this time of year. Then I met you and I figured I might as well get laid while I was out there drowning my sorrow in a martini glass. Now I feel like an idiot because this is the most disrespectful thing I could have done in memory of my mother."

Suddenly his eyes bulged. He put down the glass to rub his hands against his temples.

"What's the matter?" I said.

"You're not going to believe this," he said. "Yesterday I got a call from my father in Florida. My mother died, and I couldn't get a flight until tomorrow, so I went off to the Town House last night to distract myself, and all day today I had friends keeping me company in three-hour shifts, which is why I kept calling you back—you're my six o'clock—since I just met you I wanted to make sure you didn't back out. And now I'm here and your mother is dead and my mother is dead and it's freaking me out. What do you think this all means?"

I put my glass down as well and held his hand. "Maybe it just means that our mothers are watching out for us. Knowing you were coming by this evening got me through the saddest day of my year, and I'm here to show you that it's possible to be without a mother for twenty-one years."

"Maybe," he said. And we left it at that.

We chatted for another hour like a pair of cousins and then he was on his way to meet his nine o'clock appointment. We kissed goodbye and promised to be in touch once he returned from Florida, but we never did. It was as if this day was all we were going to have, all that we were meant to have, we two gay men, orphans in the terrorist world, who would roam the rest of our days without our mothers.

My appointment at The New School came to an end in the summer of 2004. Without a job in the city, there was no way for me to afford the Upper East Side apartment, so I decided to leave New York for a spell. I accepted a one-year university appointment in Ohio and in August I moved to Toledo, where I expected nothing more exciting than the winter that was going to come my way. After a brief tour of the campus and town, I knew I was right. Since I had no car, I had to walk everywhere, and occasionally a Good Samaritan would pull over and offer me a ride. Twice this happened while I was out on a power walk, as if watching someone exercise on the street were an unusual sight.

There were a few gay bars but none within walking distance, and though people were polite, there was something impenetrable about these Midwesterners, as if they could detect my many levels of foreignness: Chicano, New Yorker, gay. That didn't stop me, though, from appreciating the pretty corn-fed college boys at the local coffee shop, where I sat for hours grading papers or reading, and then glancing up at the more attractive men who came in to order their vanilla lattés to go.

In early September, I was sitting at a table reading and ogling, when I noticed a husky brown-haired man sit a few tables down. When he smiled, I smiled back and didn't mistake it for flirting since I thought that such an explicit activity would probably never happen in a place where people were proudly Catholic or Christian. This was an election year and already the propaganda was furious with declarations of loyalty to a certain political party that was running on a religious platform. Ohio, the powerful swing state that year, was already receiving much attention.

But all the political dramas would come later. In the meantime, I sat there reading and sipping my coffee. When I looked up next, I noticed that the guy had moved one table closer to me. He smiled again. *How odd,* I thought. *And ballsy.* I figured this would probably be the closest I ever got to action in this state so I decided to pursue it. I smiled back. He motioned to ask permission to come over to my table and I nodded, thrilled at how easy this was becoming.

"Howdy," he said.

"Howdy."

"You're not from around here."

"No."

"Just visiting?"

"Sort of. For the year."

"I'm from here, but I'm visiting also," he said. "Visiting my parents. They still live here."

I'm not sure if it was the Midwestern method, but the chitchat lasted a good hour or so before we got into anything remotely resembling a flirtation. But we got there, and an hour after that we were romping around on my futon couch. I'm also not sure if this too was the Midwestern method, but he was loud and the walls in that building were thin, and I knew that if there had been any speculation about my sexuality, it was now confirmed.

We had a good time, but that was all. He told me he loved Florida and had a boyfriend back there waiting for him, but that they had an understanding about these things. I didn't judge; I benefited from the arrangement.

"Can I come back?" he asked.

I laughed. "Anytime."

"How about this Saturday?"

A chill ran down my spine. Saturday was September 12. I had kept from cheapening that day last year. Would I ruin it on this one?

"Sure." I couldn't resist. And a few days later there he was in my apartment. We had sex, we drank wine, and he snored all night. I didn't feel guilty at all that this was happening on the anniversary of my mother's death, though I kept thinking about it.

The next morning we said our goodbyes. My lover was off to Florida and to his boyfriend, and I was staying behind to teach Latino literature and twentieth-century American poetry to a group of college kids who were mostly attending the university to become schoolteachers. I didn't expect to hear from him again but I got a call a few days later.

"Hey," he said.

"Hey. Are you calling from Florida?"

"No," he said, sounding sad.

"What's the matter?"

"I had to postpone my return a few days. Plus, there's some hurricane hitting the area so I may end up staying longer. I'd like to see you again."

"Sure," I said. "Anytime."

"You know, I just want to let you know that I really like you. Seeing you again doesn't make this seem dirty, not like a one-night stand or something. And you've heard me snore, for Christ's sake, so it's more like intimacy what we've got going on."

I had to roll my eyes at that, thinking that this guy was just trying to keep from feeling guilty that he was cheating on his significant other. But I played along.

"So when are you coming by?" I asked.

"I'm parked out front, actually."

I rushed to the window. Indeed he was parked outside. "You weirdo. What the hell's the matter with you?"

"I needed some time to think. Can I come up now?"

"Come on up," I said.

We snuggled on the couch. He seemed distracted and since I was his surrogate boyfriend while he was away from Florida, I felt compelled to own up to the responsibility.

"So talk to me," I said. "What's going on?"

I was completely unprepared for the tears, which he wiped off quickly.

"What?" I asked, genuine concern in my voice this time.

"I haven't told you the reason I'm here. I actually came down here to bury my mom." My face flushed. "She was in bad shape and slipping away, so I made it down here in time to watch her die. She finally passed when I saw her at the hospital the night after I left here. I was at the foot of the bed. My sister and my dad were on either side of her. When she finally died, her body jerked up and I felt her go through me. It was the most intense feeling I've ever felt and I realized that it was a gift, or a blessing, to let me know she thought it was OK that I was gay and living with another man in Florida, that she loved me no matter what."

I thought it impossible that this was happening again. Was I to be the provider of solace to gay men who were about to step into the uncertain, motherless world I had inhabited for so many years? Or maybe I was misreading some message, perhaps from my mother? Was she telling me to stop picking up strangers? Or was she telling me it was OK that I was engaged in this lifestyle, that she loved me no matter what?

I decided not to reveal any of this to Mr. Florida. What he told me had been beautiful and it was his moment of bliss, so I left it at that. We didn't have sex that evening, but he did spend the night. I set the alarm while he called his father to let him know he was staying with a friend, that he needed some privacy and that he'd be there bright and early, in time for the services. He pressed his body against mine and I held him. When he broke down in tears, I cried with him.

The next morning he said he would be back to Toledo sometime in the near future, and that he would give me a call. He told me that there was something quite special about me. "I mean it," he said. "That's not just a line."

I smiled and let him leave me there, certain that I would never see him again. Whatever he needed from me he had already taken. Whatever he had to give me had already been offered up. I closed the door to the apartment and proceeded to put up the altar for my mother. I had become so distracted that week that I had neglected to set it up in time. Somehow I knew my mother was fine with that.

Gray Horses in a Green Landscape

ELEANOR LERMAN

After the rain, on a rural road,
in an hour that has never come before—
That is how the dream always begins
And if the dreamer is a young girl
(meaning, the girl that we remember,
the dark-eyed one, always alone),
if she can make it past the abandoned houses
that have collapsed, like human faces dismantled
in last year's nightmare, then this will be her reward:
to see gray horses waiting in a green landscape
Two of them, the color of clouds
Immediately, the girl will recognize them
as the precursor to next year's spells
and all those that will follow afterwards
in the next year and the next

But women, women, surely we will recognize
that there is only so long all this can go on
What has been dismantled remains in pieces
and even desire, as it dissembles, begins
to sink its teeth into something more mysterious,
whispers that now, it aches for no one's body;
now, it has no need to sleep. All it wants
is to watch as the horses live and die and
live again. To learn what their real names are
and what sustains them as the landscape
changes into a shining river. And later, when
the wind picks up, what they hear it say

Mysterious Interventions

ELEANOR LERMAN

If we are going to meditate
on the purpose of existence,
which, like it or not, after
a certain age is all we are going
to do, then we might as well start
with Life As We Know It, into which
we were born confused. Or in which,
at the moment, we are being beaten,
raped, babied, burned, or bribed
Thus, the list of certainties is short

The train schedule, yes. And we
have mastered "how to make a purchase"
Sex was mostly automatic: if a cat
could do it, then we could, too
But go one level up, as in, "The sex
was fine but why am I here?" and
no one knows the answer, excluding,
of course, the people who do, and
each and every one of them is wrong
Believe me. *Page not found*

And yet, the compulsion does not
diminish—to wake up in the
middle of the night, awash in infinity,
and ask yourself, ask yourself,
because there is no one else
Because the nature of God,
as some suspect, is not to care

That is, unless something can be
gleaned from the occasional clue, as in
the kiss you will always remember
The night of a thousand falling stars
The mysterious intervention that
changed what you think of as your life
but may be something else. And if
so, that is where the real work begins

Worming Through Old Books

From Amidst a Sea of Sodden Tractates by Sanctimonious Divines, The Crystalline Wisdom of Law's Serious Call Deserves Reader Rescue

A BOOKWORM

Wililliam Law, an independent-minded English cleric of the eighteenth century, possessed an ideal name for the writing of theology. He did not waste that advantage, producing—during a lifetime of writing too often devoted to petty doctrinal disputes and attacks upon the immorality of the London stage productions of his day—one firmly agreed upon, if today largely unread, classic in the canon of Christian devotional works. Its title is as solid and forceful as its author's name—*A Serious Call to a Devout and Holy Life*. Its prose style is marked by a directness of voice enhanced by a baroque beauty of syntax, with theme and variations of the ideas under discussion played out with the intricate order of a harpsichord suite. While the tone is calm and reasoned, the passion underlying the mere words is intense—for Law is stating the case for a life of happiness that he fully expects will seem miserably unhappy to the bulk of his readers at the outset of the book, and it is only with an effort of mind that Law can speak to us of what is true without shouting at us to open our eyes. But shout he does not, and the book brims with engaged awareness throughout, due, I think, to that first fundamental decision of restraint.

In the years just after its publication in 1728, when Law was forty-two, the book exercised an acknowledged influence upon John Wesley and other leaders of the Evangelical revival of the time, which, contrary to the current usage of "Evangelical" in the United States, was devoted to social reform and piety as lived emphatically through deeds. Samuel Johnson read the book while a student; his frankness as to how he approached Law's text makes the praise Johnson offers the book all the more striking:

"I became a sort of lax talker against religion, for I did not think much against it; and this lasted until I went to Oxford, where it would not be suffered. When at Oxford, I took up Law's *Serious Call*, expecting to find it a dull book (as such books generally are), and perhaps to laugh at it. But I found Law quite an overmatch for me; and this was the first occasion of my thinking in earnest of religion after I became capable of rational inquiry."

Johnson became a devout Anglican in his mature years, though it should not be thought that Law's influence was inevitably so decisive. Edward Gibbon, author of the venerated *Decline and Fall of the Roman Empire,* came to know Law, who had served as private tutor to Gibbon's father and remained a household presence when Gibbon was a boy. In Gibbon's historical masterwork, Christianity is fiercely taken to task for its depradations of classical culture and its bloody persecutions once it rose to power within the Roman Empire. Gibbon, like his friend, the philosopher David Hume, regarded religion as a wish-fulfillment at best, a delusion at worst, and in no case a guide to what rational men might call truth. But even Gibbon paid Law knowing respect as a gifted adversary: "If Mr. Law finds a spark of piety in a reader's mind, he will soon kindle it into a flame."

Gibbon was not such a reader, we may infer, and he was not alone among Law's readers, nor even among Law's religious readers, in quite simply finding the *Serious Call* too serious. The tendency to austerity both inward and outward grew ever stronger in Law, even after the publication of the book by which he is remembered. In the latter years of his life—he died in 1761—Law became devoted to the teachings of the seventeenth-century German mystic Jacob Boehme, translating the entirety of Boehme's works into English, a remarkable undertaking given their length and their difficulty, imbued as they are both with highly charged personal accounts of Boehme's illuminations and with a thicket-like, theoretical terminology that draws from Rosicrucianism and alchemy. This later mystical bent of Law, by way of Boehme, was not shared by John Wesley and his fellow Evangelical reformers, whose vision of Christian worship was populist to the core and alloted no time for metaphysics. But the Bookworm will testify that he sees in the style of *A Serious Call* the testimony of a mystic who was not yet quite aware that he was one, or would be styled as one, by the outside world— a mystic whose mysticism was no more and no less than delight in the service of the Lord and certainty of that Lord's grace and care and redemptive power. But that delight would brook no mere formalities of worship. Law and Boehme as well (who was censored by Lutheran clergy in his native land for advocating the importance both of faith and of works) were mystics of an active conviction.

As Law wrote of prayer: "Bended knees, whilst you are clothed with pride; heavenly petitions, whilst you are hoarding up treasures upon earth; holy devotions, whilst you live in the follies of the world; prayers of meekness and charity, whilst your heart is the seat of pride and resentment; hours of prayer, whilst you give up days and years to idle diversions, impertinent visits, and foolish pleasures; are as absurd, unacceptable services to God, as forms of thanksgiving from a person who lives in repinings and discontent. So that, unless the common course of our lives be according to the common spirit of our prayers, our prayers are so far from being a real or sufficient degree of devotion, that they become an empty lip-labour, or, what is worse, a notorious hypocrisy."

A metaphoric phrase such as "empty lip-labour"—there are many more such throughout the book—is one of the rewards of reading Law, and not the least of those rewards. His language is relentlessly unhurried, taking the time to be vivid, and so he holds the attention of the reader by offering pleasure as well as instruction. As for the instruction, there are within it assumptions that cannot be shared by readers—the Bookworm included—who do not share Law's belief in the uniquely divine revelation of the Gospels or the appropriate role of fear of eternal hellfire in shaping one's religious convictions. But the art of reading old books is necessarily that of finding nourishment and joy in them without burdening oneself by expecting to agree with the author on all things.

If one ignores Law's theological underpinnings and focuses instead on the way of life he proposes—to live always according to the best of oneself, guided by spiritual wisdom and not by material gain—one discovers that Law may well be the most astute portraitist in the English language of the practical realities and consequences of the "devout and holy life." He shows the reader what it means to take spiritual truths seriously, not only in terms of public worship and family life, but also in one's choice of employment, use of free time, choice of foods and quantity of consumption at mealtime, treatment of the poor in the streets, hours allotted for sleeping, manner of dress, control of lustful desires, and willingness to sing at prayer time even though one's voice is wretched.

Even if the reader is as unreligious as the Bookworm, there is the dawning, as one reads, that one might well share Law's convictions at least so far as to regard every moment of existence as a statement of one's love (or lack thereof) for the world and everyone in it. Everything matters, every decision is prayer of a kind—to what or to whom is for us to say. This is the underlying drama of Law's book, which makes it, for me, a page-turner.

Declarative

STAN SANVEL RUBIN

Here and Now
by Stephen Dunn
W.W. Norton & Co., 2011
103 pp., $23.95, paper

Double Shadow
by Carl Phillips
Farrar Straus Giroux, 2011
55 pp., $23, cloth

Flies
by Michael Dickman
Copper Canyon Press, 2011
78 pp., $16, paper

Blinking Ephemeral Valentine
by Joni Wallace
Four Ways Books, 2011
58 pp., $15.95 paper

Nietzsche struck what would prove to be a persistent note in an early essay by calling the making of metaphor a "fundamental drive of man" which "cannot be written off even for a moment, since one would thereby be writing off man himself . . . . " It is art, he says, that tears apart the rigid web of concepts we take for Reality by "arranging new figurations, metaphors, metonymies, constantly exhibiting the desire to make and remake the existing world of waking man as colorful, irregular, inconsequential, incoherent, charming, and eternally new . . . . " (*On Truth and Untruth: Selected Writings*, HarperCollins, 2010, 42). Appalled at the conflation of metaphor with the real, various philosophers set themselves the task of making philosophy "Modern" by attempting to reduce language to an empirical, logical basis, cleansing it of the metaphoric and metaphysical. At roughly the same period, the great Modernists were experimenting with the use of figurative language, creating a new poetry often too obscure for average readers to appreciate. Its verbal complexity became a sign of its value. The Romantic ideal of organic form (itself a metaphor) morphed into a notion of the poem as autonomous object, a made thing as complex and inexhaustible as nature itself, as in William Carlos Williams's famous formulation, "a small (or large) machine made of words" (*Selected Essays*, 256). The generational sense of dissatisfaction with an impoverished reality was never better expressed than in Wallace Stevens's "The Motive for Metaphor":

> The obscure moon lighting an obscure world
> Of things that would never be quite expressed,
> Where you yourself were not quite yourself,
> And did not want nor have to be,
>
> Desiring the exhilarations of changes:
> The motive for metaphor, shrinking from
> The weight of primary noon,
> The A B C of being,
>
> The ruddy temper, the hammer
> Of red and blue, the hard sound—
> Steel against intimation—the sharp flash,
> The vital, arrogant, fatal, dominant X.

Stevens's motive for metaphor echoes Nietzsche's. But are there intrinsic limits to "the desire to make and remake the existing world of waking man as colorful, irregular, inconsequential, incoherent, charming, and eternally new," even in art? Must X win in the end?

Some of the most hard-headed and provocative work on metaphor in recent years has been done by Mark Turner, in concert with linguist George Lakoff. As if recasting Nietzsche in the light of contemporary cognitive science, the two authors argue that "[m]etaphorical understanding is not a matter of mere word play; it is endemically conceptual in nature. It is indispensible to comprehending and reasoning about concepts like life, death, and time" (*More Than Cool Reason: A Field Guide to Poetic Metaphor*, University of Chicago Press, 1989, 50). Just when postmodernists seem to have blown apart the notion of truth in favor of a wholesale relativism, Turner in turn demolishes the relativistic underpinning of postmodernism, arguing that "though a text may result in various readings, all of these readings are constrained by our modes of cognition. So deconstructive criticism, like most literary criticism, is in the dangerous position of potentially pinning its analyses on potentially mistaken presuppositions about thought, knowledge, and language" (*Death Is the Mother of Beauty: Mind, Metaphor, Criticism*, Cybereditions, 2000, 12).

In *More Than Cool Reason: A Field Guide to Poetic Metaphor*, Turner and Lakoff urge us to distinguish between "basic conceptual metaphors, which are cognitive in nature, and particular linguistic expressions of these conceptual metaphors" (50). Thus, the Romantic search for a metaphoric truth in Nature and the passionately contrived originality of the Modernist are alike expressions of the same basic patterns of human cognition. Their seeming differences melt into matters of style and culture. Fortunately, Turner doesn't intend to do away with the critic, whose job, he acknowledges, is "to hold worthwhile conversations about literature" (*Death*, 12), but he does challenge us to be more informed, more "responsible" about what it is we're talking about.

Cognitive science has not yet displaced literary theory in the contemporary curriculum, nor subjectivity of taste among poetry reviewers, and fortunately seems unlikely to do so anytime soon. However, it may provide a way to reflect on the contemporary poetry scene as a field of verbal performance situated in a history of such performances. We might conclude that, in our own moment, Stevens's "X" is dominant; nothing seems to characterize contemporary American poetry more than its tendency to disown or disrupt the "poetic." It's as if, after Magritte, the poet wants to declare first of all, "This is not a poem."

Stratagems differ, but, in addition to the more or less disappearance of metaphor as a poet's means to truth, I would cite the following contemporary poetic practices (admittedly, I'm lumping a lot together here): not simply the blending and crossing of genres, but the near total loss of genre as a compositional element, the shying away from music, the inattention to line, the denial of a unitary "I." These may be signs of more than the style of a generation; they may indicate a loss of faith in the power of poetry to matter unless it is positioned as something other and more significant in the world. On the other hand, there are moves that seem intended to reclaim some lost importance for poetry. These might include the prominence of story, or at least anecdote (often presented in blocks of prose); the return of surrealism in a playful, exhibitionistic form (the original Surrealism was intended as a path to truth); the embracing of the social and political; and perhaps most tellingly, the valorization of theory, as if the poet wants to say, "I'm smarter than the poem and you are, too."

My point is not that these practices are wrong. I am simply questioning what they tell us about the relationship of poetry to itself, its self-definition in our time. One answer is that they reflect a loss of faith that the poet's voice can transcend or transform the reality in which it speaks. They speak to a now familiar sense that all the grand claims for poetry (as opposed to the celebrity Poet figure) have been made and discarded. What is increasingly apparent is what I might call *declarative poetry:* a poetry that by and large abjures metaphor and decoration. It builds lyric effects primarily on the basis of carefully deployed phrases and statements. It's a poetry of cunning transparency.

Two masters in this vein are Stephen Dunn and Carl Phillips. Their new books demonstrate their very different methods. Stephen Dunn's *Here and Now* has a telling title. In his previous work, Dunn has perfected the poetry of contemporary middle-class life, with its entirely unheroic, quiet desperation. His favored persona has been a participant observer of the daily hypocrisies, small yearnings, and occasional moments of grace associated with such a life. Dunn's sentences, noteworthy for their absence of flourish and contrivance, do not call attention to themselves either as language or music, but force us to consider the unnamed speaker who utters them. This speaker has been blessed, or cursed, with enough self-awareness to understand his own complicity in his world, the limitedness of his ability to transform it, let alone himself. All he can do is settle for honesty.

There's a philosophical purpose here as well as an aesthetic one. Dunn's essays on poetry, collected in *Walking Light* (BOA, 2001), a book every student of poetry should read, reveal how smart a thinker he is, how seriously he takes the responsibility of his task. In one essay Dunn writes, "The writer's burden is somehow to keep alive and vital amid all that's deadening and dangerous in the world" ("The Poet as Teacher: Vices and Virtues," 141). This is no small burden. To be adequate to it, Dunn eschews the transcendent, the metaphoric, and the comforting, all of which might obscure his unrelenting view of what is and get in the way of the rigorous self-knowledge that seems his ultimate goal. That the result of such discipline is a necessarily limited, partial, and finally unsatisfying form of truth is what keeps him writing and us reading.

Dunn's representative speaker has tended to be anonymous, a sort of suburban *l'homme moyen sensual*. *Here and Now* tilts more to the personal, drawing on the circumstances of the poet's own life with a new directness:

> Our good friends are with us, Jack and Jen,
> old lefties with whom we now and then share
> what we don't call our wealth.
>
> ("Evenings Like This")

> My wife is working in her room,
> writing, and I've come in three times
> with idle chatter, some not-new news.
> The fourth time she identifies me
> as what I am, a man lost
> in late afternoon
>
> ("Bad")

> Most of my students have forsaken home,
> or are planning to. They don't want
> to have dinner with anybody.
> They've mastered the boredom
> they think conceals them.
> . . .
> But there, isolated among them, is that boy,
> my Rimbaudian, all testosterone and refusal,
> the one I always teach to . . . .
>
> ("Shatterings")

Here and Now constitutes a stocktaking of the poet's roles as husband, teacher, neighbor, friend, poet. It's a gentle inventory, to be sure, deceptively easy on the reader. The defining wit is there, and the defining circumspection, but the latter is lessened, like a fence edged back a few yards. But the poet is not so easy on himself.

The subdued confessional that runs throughout Dunn's work is foregrounded in the opening poem, with its title redolent of judgment and consequence, "The Puritan and the World":

> The world thought
> I didn't understand it,
> but I did, knew that to parse
> was to narrow
> and to narrow was to live
> one good way.
> Awash with desire
> I also knew a little was plenty
> and more than I deserved.

When memory enters, it is particular and personal ("those cloud berries I picked / last summer in Nova Scotia"), and it casts an unrelenting light on his motivations:

> They were bitter, truly awful,
> and ever since,
> something in me
> wanted their beautiful name
> repudiated, the world
> held accountable.

Dunn holds himself to account. He has fashioned, book by book, an art of remarkable virtuosity, like a jazz musician who loves his instrument and perfects his playing of it within an intentionally limited range, so that his playing comes to encompass ever richer subtleties of nuance and tone. To appreciate such art requires more than enjoying the performance; it involves attentive listening with mind as well as ear. Where a Dunn reader might expect to feel as if s/he is overhearing an interior monologue, in this volume there's a more candid invitation to the reader. The note of self-reflective honesty is unmistakable, as in "Stone Seeking Warmth" (the only metaphor is the title):

> Look, it's usually not a good idea
> to think seriously about me.
> I've been known to give others
> a hard time. I've had wives and lovers—
> trust that I know a little about trying

to remain whole while living
a divided life.

While the wry twist may be what we came for, the invitation is one we can't
and shouldn't ignore:

But if you are not dissuaded by now,
well, my door is ajar.

Carl Phillips's eleventh book, *Double Shadow*, has a simple title which begs
to be read complexly; in this it is like previous titles, such as *The Rest of Love*
(2005) and *Speak Low* (2010). Phillips's art is made of partial statements, lacunae,
broken thoughts, sentences that start in one direction and end somewhere else,
if they end at all. His is the precision of incompletion—not of the syntactical
units, which are well punctuated, but of the incomplete lives and unfulfilled yearnings
they evoke:

I love you, he said. He was
    shaking. He said:
I love you. There's an art
to everything. What I've
done with this life,

what I'd meant not to do,
    or would have meant, maybe, had I
understood, though I have
    no regrets.
                                    ("Civilization")

Unlike Dunn's speakers, so carefully situated in a specific milieu, Phillips's
are suspended between insubstantial worlds or in a world of their own, identifiable
only by their longing. They grope for, but never achieve, a state of wholeness. Phillips
refuses the promised transcendence and rhetorical unity of metaphor. His poems
might themselves be thought of as metaphors for a state of being, one which is
always lost or never attained. Phillips's work is notable for its absence of ordinary
poetic devices. It's as if he's not making poetry as we know it, but a way of speaking; in Williams's terms, a Phillips poem is not "a machine made of words," but
a generator of existential language. The vocabulary is simple, the complicating

declaratives transformative and strange. They trap the speaker in the moment of speaking, evoking the rootlessness and poignancy of being, a condition almost beyond words.

The poems in *Double Shadow* play out as if against the fleeting backdrop of a myth, a fragmented drama only dimly glimpsed, concerning kingdoms, warfare, and torture—forgotten voyages, all suggesting a realm of ritual and fable:

> . . . And how the stars
> swelled the dark, guiding the man whose whip
> made the mules go faster, though they would have
> run, I think, even had there been no whip, being mules, and
> broken long ago, and with no more belief than disbelief in rescue.
> ("Ransom")

Phillips reinvents the intimate language of the lyricist with extraordinary originality, nuance, and power, even if it is the power of negation:

> the world—that had seemed before so vast—,
> and canyoned—the world as body, and the body
> beneath us, small, masterable, singing *I've been
> unto myself a model for all darkness and all light,
> singing I have given as a mirror gives, giving back
> the night–*
>
> But it's morning, now. The blues
> are various. The blacks are. The deaths are random.
> ("Night")

The openings alternate between declaratives: "There's a man asking to be worshipped only" ("Next Stop, Arcadia"); "It had the heft of old armor" ("Almost Tenderly"); "For the longest time, he said nothing" ("Master and Slave"); and fragments: "Like any other kingdom built of wickedness and joy" ("First Night at Sea"); "How he was carried in a ramshackle cart alongside the sea" ("Ransom"); but they lead equally to incompletion:

> Now that the festival of Saint Wish for It and It
> Shall Be Yours is at last over, dying slowly
> behind me, I've come down to the shore. Black
> waves, silver on black . . . This time, I'll accept
> what I'm given. I'll say I deserve it. Who

knows? Couldn't I
                    mean that, eventually?
                            ("Dark Angel")

There is pain in isolation and pain in connectedness, in love. There is also pain in thinking, remembering, and wanting. This is the condition Phillips registers like a seismograph. But he has created a means to describe what remains otherwise indescribable. *Double Shadow* may be most satisfying to those who already admire this unique poet. It's a remarkably beautiful collection; many of the poems are as unforgettable as they are ineffable. Since they are also nearly impossible to memorize, the reader who seeks to understand them in that way must resort to the pleasure of reading them again.

The danger in the poetry of statement is not that it lacks the cultural signs associated with poetry as an art. These, after all, have varied in time; formalism, for example, has been seen in recent years coming and going and coming again. The risk is that such poetry may become merely gestural, an indication that the poet is hip to the prevalent idea that no meaning can really be made, only pointed to in the world, or played with in the materiality of language, or in the spectacle of performance. Then it is a poetry of lack, defined by gestures that show what it isn't.

Michael Dickman (not to be confused with his twin brother, Matthew, also a prize-winning poet) takes the risk. Still in his thirties, Dickman has acquired a fierce reputation for cutting-edge sensibility. *Flies* received the James Laughlin Award for best second book, among many accolades. Unlike Dunn and Phillips, who can be read in the light of a body of work, Dickman is in the process of proving himself.

The poems in *Flies* contain recurring images, notably hands and face, which point to the struggle of identity and individualism within family. They seem to drag a weight of past anguish which is never explained. In the long title poem, the poet says: "It's time to drag the family out / so I'll know I'm alive."

One poem that demonstrates Dickman's method of dealing with his material is "Shaving Your Father's Face." The poem opens with an offhandedly surrealistic gesture that offers about the minimum we can expect from metaphor, yet registers a tone that runs through the book:

First I get a father
from some city
of fathers

One with a neck

bright
red

It's clear that "your" of the title really refers to "my," and this plus the touch
of surrealism in the opening is typical of the way Dickman evades and confronts
at once, as if to half-step around emotion is to avoid being banal. It's also a way
to dance around the true import, whatever that might be. One of the moves
Dickman likes to make is the suddenly longer line:

And with all the bird bones in my fingers carefully tip his chin back
into the light like love
so I can see
so I can smell

I tell a dirty joke and drag the steel across the universe

There is a lot going on here: visual patterning to surprise the eye, a touch of
metaphor ("bird bones") and then a statement that displaces the potential bathos
of the "light like love" simile:

There's nothing better
than shaving your father's face
except maybe
shaving your mother's legs

Dickman's is a poetry of small units under tight control, lest one get away,
taking the poet's and our emotions with it. In this disarticulation of the sentence
into its constituent phrases, potentially "hot" meaning is skirted in a cool way.
The implied emotion shifts from violence to love to a perhaps mocking irony. But
there are no cues to response; the voice remains a surface somehow uninfected by
what lies beneath it. Neither the story that contextualizes the Freudian drama
implied in the lines quoted, nor the import of the violent imagery is elaborated
or explored. They pack the punch, but are not the point—not, anyway, to be
recognized as mattering beyond the shock value.

Most of the poems in the book have multiple unnumbered sections, each taking up more or less a page. "Shaving Your Father's Face" has two more sections of roughly similar length; each performs as much a permutation of the first section as a continuation of it. The second part begins, "In the evening / his face attracts moths and daughters" and particularizes the razor blade the speaker is purportedly using:

> I like to use Merkur Super
> platinum-coated
> stainless
> steel
> You can write on water with it
> Rust free
> Rostfrei
>
> Made in Germany
> so it
> will last and last

"Rust free / Rostfrei" is a rare instance of the poet attending to something like music.

The third and final section opens with another triplet, paralleling the first, but now the second-person pronoun of the title is owned by the speaker: "Shaving my father's face / I'm not shaving / my face // I'm shaving my brain." Like the first, the third section breaks into a long line followed by three short lines stacked one over the another, this time composed of simple articles instead of verbals:

> Stuffing toilet paper into all the new holes I cut so it looks like a
>   field of red flags
>   paper tulips
>   love notes

The ending again combines intimacy (almost tender here) with a further hint of violence:

> You could bounce a dime off Dad's skin
> My hand
> on your face can you
> feel it

There's no punctuation and no conclusion. The pronoun shift from "your" to "I" to "my" seems as significant as the poem's lurid imagery.

This is a poetry of smooth surfaces and implied depths, with a somber sense of losses. The result is a peculiar tension that keeps a reader reading while it challenges the expectations of transcendence or transformation which are the Western tradition's metaphoric inheritance. Dickman's relentless lack of enthusiasm can grow tiresome, and his strategies seem, after a while, repetitive. At times he tries too hard *not* to show effort, and shows only attitude, as in the opening of "Emily Dickinson to the Rescue":

> Standing in her house today all I could think of was whether she
> took a shit every morning
> or ever fucked anybody
> or ever fucked
> herself

Yet the third and last section of the same poem achieves an unsettling lyricism:

> I used to think we were bread
> gentle work and water
> We're not
>
> But we're still beautiful
>
> Killing each other as much as we can
> beneath the
> pines
>
> The pines
> that are somebody's
> masterpiece

Here all that is not said fills the empty spaces.

"Stations," the most ambitious poem in the collection and also the longest, is a clipped meditation on religious belief. Neither a mystic quest nor capable of affirmation, the fourteen Roman numbered sections (it is the only numbered poem) play a series of changes based on the antinomy of "the world of shit" versus "the little cross." The poem shows Dickman working to orchestrate a larger structure with larger resonance. In this, it is genuinely exciting. The ending achieves a terse and effective eloquence:

> We are the loneliest murderers ever invented
> I lie down on the grass

Hammered into love
You will not be able to mistake it
Like cancer in children
You will hear music

The poems in *Flies* are rarely as satisfying as their best moments, but the moments are worth reading for. In them, we can hear a distinctive voice attempting a distinctive method. Whether this is a new poetry or only a new set of mannerisms is for Dickman's future work to show.

The title of Joni Wallace's first book, *Blinking Ephemeral Valentine,* signals the brazen, dynamic and unconventional style of her work. Wallace's book, winner of the Larry Levis Award, offers high-voltage, nonstop verbal excitement. She's a poet of abrupt phrases who doesn't worry much about explaining herself; her poems start where they start and go where they will:

Pox on the living.
Movie prize of some long
ago actress, not me,
and she shall witness
our breaths fly out
in a minor scene,
waxwine of stiletto heels,
fur voltage, radiant,
ringlets ringed in smoke,
do you have a light?

          ("Reel-to-Reel")

Crescent train, a.m., heads west,
little *o* for a headlight, little robber's
gashed glare

          ("Star-Spangled Valentine Shagged in Drab")

Indelible horses.
From your lips a whorl,
a vellum soliloquy of stops
and sirens bowl down.
Princess Hold Out,
around your neck
a string of caterpillars

          ("Zoetrope, Small Horses and Animals")

There's no way to read these poems without responding to their dazzle. The moods are brash, voracious, mercurial. Voice and language are alive, elusive, allusive, too, stirring the subject, stirring the reader. Wallace's declaratives are like thrown bombs. They can make us respond almost viscerally because of how much they pack into small spaces. Here's the entirety of "Valentine with Girl Falling and Music":

> Once upon a time a skeleton girl who fell to earth singing.
> Below her a lake, dazzling fish, elongated fins. Then
> glass slippers, a scorpion luminescing link-to-link.
> *I'll raise an ocean a phosphorescent tide, an ice-colored kite sunk*
> *into ice-colored heavens,* says she. Gravity, our forecast, our
> lovely-engine-slightly-gunned, miss you, kiss you.

Wallace celebrates color, image, and yes, metaphor at the velocity of a first-person speaker who doesn't burden us with autobiography:

> Miles from here we are palimpsest ghosts
> on a throne of chrome, a vacancy half lit in the ruby wattage
>   of tail lights
>   ("Poem for This Speed")

The poems' claim on us is in the way they fill the moment; the words collide like crash cars, like lovers suddenly meeting, twisting individual meanings in new directions, creating new constellations of an instant's duration:

> *Body electric,* he mouths, then *abacus beads, quicksilver on wire.*
>   ("Twenty-First Century Best Boy")

> *you and I.*
>   *handkerchief/tourniquet*
>   ("Valentine Behind Door Number One")

> *Be* beauty, blinks the mirror-mirror, a treble winging over me.
>   ("Self-Portrait with Weather")

Wallace's declarative phrases collapse into each other in a rush rather than accumulate sequentially toward a larger meaning. Although Wallace holds an M.F.A., this is the sort of stuff that can't really be taught.

Blinking Ephemeral Valentine has four titled sections, with at least one "valentine" in each. But it doesn't feel like a trajectory. What narrative there is is hinted at in the playfully Gnostic or Zen-like epigraphs appended to each, starting with:

One
> You are here,
>> map says,
>>> big toy world

The effect is more like palimpsest.

An aftermath of spoiled romance and the vocabulary of an on-location film shoot, both seemingly enacted in the American West, thread these verbal montages loosely together. A character named "Jack" appears in a few choice titles.

Off and on, there's a flash of Plathean darkness:

Come into the sable night,
thing-witch with your strap
of knives, a blue-black bat
shadowboxing your hand.
>> ("Still Life with Jack")

What we're drawn to is proof enough:
these pills, other acts of disappearance.
I've written a song about a girl who swallowed the blue planets:
Kevlar, Caroline, O Beautiful Bomb.
>> ("Red and Blue Planets")

But such echoes are overwhelmed by the headlong, pulsing energy of these wonderfully skittish poems that wear their alluring titles like jaunty hats. The wounds will not triumph here; they set the stage for further transformations:

Talk me down if you can.
I'll come back in a canary yellow taxi,
my arms filled with flowers, my butterfly bandages
right as the cold and iridescent drizzle
>> ("Everywhere Like Paris")

How much of this style would be too much? In a culture of polemical fervor and sometimes apocalyptic despair, in which the authenticity of personal experience is under scrutiny from all sides, Wallace reminds us that a poet lives in the fecundity and abandon of language, its ability to gorge on and reconfigure experience. She injects the almost forbidden notion of pleasure back into poetry. That's something we need.

The poetry of declaration can portray an unromantic honesty or constitute a flamboyant practice of its own, achieving a theatricality of presentation that risks insincerity. At its strongest, it can be a poetry that offers a convincing expression of being that is appropriate to a time of noisy uncertainty, when poetry itself has become Frost's "diminished thing."

Book Review

A Summa for Our Times: The Biographical Impulse and New Nonfiction Form
MARY CAPPELLO

The Emperor of All Maladies: A Biography of Cancer

by Siddhartha Mukherjee

Scribner, 2010, 571 pp., $30, cloth

How to Live, Or a Life of Montaigne in One Question

and Twenty Attempts at an Answer

by Sarah Bakewell

Other Press, 2010, 389 pp., $25, cloth

I.

I have seen no more evident monstrosity and miracle in the world than myself. We become habituated to anything strange by use and time; but the more I frequent myself and know myself, the more my deformity astonishes me, and the less I understand myself.

Michel de Montaigne, quoted in *How to Live*

This year yielded an astonishing number of compelling biographical works as major contributors to nonfiction form, and there are many that I expect to dive into this summer: Susan Cheever on *Louisa May Alcott*, R. Tripp Evans on *Grant Wood*, Manning Marable on *Malcolm X*, Wendy Moffat on *E. M. Forster*, to name a few. But in this year's quest for a state-of-the-art of creative nonfiction, I wanted to find books that were *biographically inflected* without adhering to strict biographical rules, or, edging into the territory of literary nonfiction, biographies that did not take for granted life-writing as a form.

Siddhartha Mukherjee's biography of a disease (cancer) and Sarah Bakewell's life in one question and twenty answers (Montaigne's and her own) enticed me with their experimental-seeming subtitles: here were turns of the biographical screw that I hoped would be more than marketing ploys. Was Mukherjee's title hoping unconsciously to invoke Jumpha Lahiri's *The Interpreter of Maladies* (but why?); was Bakewell's reminiscent of any number of self-help books it intended to gloss? Both books are brisk and breezy page-turners whose felicity belies the labor involved in their making. Both recall biography as the place where thinking like a fiction writer bears upon nonfiction. Narrative, well-paced and well-placed; dramatic intensities; and suspense-filled interludes make the journeys through these books more of a ride and less of a fight, and the books' carefully graded climbs leave the reader with a feeling that s/he's accomplished something.

From the outset, Mukherjee sets his readers up for a tantalizing literary hybrid, explaining that *Emperor* is "also a personal journey of my coming-of-age as an oncologist," in effect, an autobiography. But his rationale for calling the book a biography introduces flimsily formulated ground:

> This book is a 'biography' in the truest sense of the word—an attempt to enter the *mind* of this immortal illness, to understand its personality, to demystify its behavior. But my ultimate aim is to raise a question beyond biography: Is cancer's end conceivable in the future?

So long as cancer is understood as "having a life," it can be met by biographical form; to conceive of its end would require a different form. This sheds interesting light on life-writing's conditions and terms. By invoking biography's "truest sense," Mukherjee introduces un-theorized trouble into the mix. While biography's "truest sense" need not match its definitional sense (literally, "life writing"), one wonders where Mukherjee gets his impression that psychology, or "mind," is at the heart of the genre. History may be closer to what Mukherjee is up to in this book (and he does call *Emperor* a "history" and "chronicle"). What's telling about his definition, though, is a significantly frustrating conundrum that the writer perhaps hoped "biography" could clarify, if not save him from: how does one *write* cancer without playing to its cultural mythos—i.e., its personification or its capacity for metaphor as detailed by Susan Sontag? Is what makes cancer an emperor, with or without clothes, the fact that the disease resists representation?

If the only thing Mukherjee had written was a riveting chapter titled "A City of Strings," *Emperor* would still be remarkable. Here, he pieces together the scientific drama and the economic and activist forces that brought the drug "Herceptin" to people with breast cancer who tested positive for a "her2neu" protein. The puzzle of starts, stops, accidents, inquiries, wills to live, and wills to know show the drug's "discovery" to be anything but an even or singular path. *Emperor* blows the typical cancer suite of emotions—faith, hope, and charity—out of the water, replacing cancer, the illness laden with sentiment, with the idea of cancer, in the U.S. at least, as a big business, a political machine, and an advertising campaign (even though it's not always clear if Mukherjee aims to critique the history he recounts or rest easy with a journalistic presentation of the "facts").

Sidney Farber, the "father of modern chemotherapy," turns out to be a "conceited and inflexible" figure whom few people could stand, and the picture of Farber creating a playground of Disney World uplift for the sick and dying children he experimented on competes for ghoulishness with the history of in-stitutionalized denial that for nearly a century endorsed Halsted's "heroically" disfiguring radical mastectomies. Farber's work with Mary Lasker to make cancer the target of not just a battle but a full-scale war in need of federal funding, leading in time to the American Cancer Society, forms one of the larger-than-life centers of Mukherjee's ambitious cancer saga. The war is shot through, so to speak, with mind-bending discoveries, like the fact that a chemical meant to kill (mustard gas) was called upon to cure, and that scientists were forced to reconstruct the foundational paradigm of molecular biology with the identification of a "retro-virus."

This same biographical imperative to mine for knowledge while revising an historical record is what moves a reader through the pages of *How to Live*. Thus, we learn wonderful details of Montaigne's life (if we didn't already know them), like the fact that, made into the subject of a pedagogic experiment, Montaigne was "brought up as a native speaker of Latin" and was six years old before he understood French; that he was lured out of bed with a lute each morning; that he couldn't keep a journal; and that he preferred to read biographies and his-tories over poetry (a favorite being Plutarch's *Lives*). That Stefan Zweig chose to write a long essay on Montaigne while in enforced exile during World War II forms a fascinating section on the reception of Montaigne through the ages, while the book as paean to Montaigne's invented form confirms every essayist's counter-intuition that it's better to take what one doesn't know or fails to know as a starting point than to follow the grammar-school dictum "write what you know": "one must imagine ['I don't know'] appended, in spirit, to almost everything [Montaigne] ever wrote," explains Bakewell. The extraordinary rendering of Montaigne's unrivaled friendship and love for Étienne de LaBoétie is beautifully stirring and potentially revisionist since Bakewell leaves us with the sense that the essays were written to La Boétie as monuments to his memory (he died at age thirty-three) much in the way that some literary historians understand Emily Dickinson's poems to have been written to her sister-in-law, Susan, and that the poetry was born of that passionate exchange.

My own predilection is for nonfiction's affinities with poetry, so I was drawn to associative, cacophonous, mellifluous, and strangely telling lists as they figured in each book even though these were few. I wanted to dwell with Mukherjee's list of remedies for cancer through the ages rather than keep pace with the book's journalese, which is all too well-suited for a flight across the country (the moment the book appeared, it was on sale in airport bookstores everywhere):

> . . . tincture of lead, extracts of arsenic, boar's tooth, fox lungs, rasped ivory, hulled castor, ground white-coral, ipecac, senna, and a smattering of purgatives and laxatives . . . . In the 17th century, a paste of crab's eyes, at five shillings a pound . . . goat's dung, crow's feet, dog fennel, tortoise liver, the laying of hands, blessed waters, or the compression of the tumor with lead plates.

Lists of "wildly divergent customs from all over the world, marveling at their randomness and strangeness" were one of Montaigne's favorite devices, Sarah Bakewell reminds us, so, in "Of Custom" and "Of Ancient Customs," he writes of:

> . . . countries where women piss standing and men squatting, where children are nursed for up to twelve years, where it is considered fatal to nurse a baby in its first day, where hair grows on the right side of the body but is shaved completely off the left side, where one is supposed to kill one's father at a certain age, where people wipe their rears with a sponge on a stick, and where hair is worn long in front and short behind instead of the other way around.

The arrangement of *How to Live* might reflect Montaigne's writing itself— "a self-portrait in constant motion," or a "book with a wild and eccentric plan." Indebted to Montaignian felicity of form, the book is bound to make readers want to enjoy a summer of nothing but Montaigne in the same way that people pretend they have spent whole summers of their lives with the pleasing demands of a multivolumed Proust. Yet, *How to Live,* when it comes down to it, is neither wild nor eccentric, and when the book plays to Montaigne as a kind of hero, or capitulates to hagiography in a manner typical of biography with a capital "B," it remakes the *Essais* into the brick that it physically is rather than invite us to frolic inside its estuaries and streams. Impatient with philosophers who depart from the version of Montaigne the book endorses, Bakewell seems intent on dismissing Descartes and Pascal, for example, with the assumption that they misread or failed properly to appreciate the great master. A commonplace assumption about Montaigne is that he created a version of an everyman in his essays: he produced a familiarly inviting voice that readers and writers centuries later turn to for solace and identification and that leads him to be dubbed the "most human of writers" by Bakewell (and others). Here there is a wish, if not a tendency, to de-historicize Montaigne—to laud the Montaignian voice for being human (all too human) and therefore transcendent of his time and place—rather than to read him (alongside Descartes and Pascal, for example) as a contributor to the history of the *idea* of the human.

It's hard, if not impossible, however, to write biography without constructing monoliths. One might wish for the shape-shifting and multifarious list to serve as an allegory for *The Emperor of All Maladies,* especially given Mukherjee's critical assertion that the orienting obsession, fundamental error, and essential problem of cancer research and cancer treatment in this country has been the search for a "common cure" for a disease understood as a "single, monolithic entity," or the need for a grand narrative that is an effect of the discourse of a targeted war against "the" disease. To imagine cancer differently would require us to write it differently, which in turn might enable us to treat it differently. "The hierarchical practice of medicine," Mukherjee writes, "its internal culture, its rituals of practice, were ideally arranged to resist change and to perpetuate orthodoxy."

The history he tells, however, doesn't resist that practice but constitutes it. *Emperor* transmutes a complex and intricate history into a single-minded drive to conquer a single-minded disease—which might suggest that cancer as heterogeneous entity resists imagining, and it resists biography, too. *The Emperor of All Maladies* has nothing to say about the history of alternative cures, prevention initiatives, or, for that matter, non-Western conceptions of the disease: it's a book about an empire passing as a book about an emperor. The literal place of colonialism in the history and production of cancer is something Mukherjee announces and skirts at various points inside the book. *Emperor* is just as inconsistent in its promising to demystify cancer, in the tradition of Susan Sontag's *Illness as Metaphor*, all the while remystifying it, most especially in its nearly operatic closing chapters, where cancer is understood as an illness that personifies the human urge for immortality. In bracingly lucid passages, Mukherjee explains that cancer is a "clonally evolving disease" because it follows a "mirthless relentless cycle of mutation, selection, and overgrowth." Generating cells that "are more and more adapted to survival and growth," cancer "exploits the fundamental logic of evolution unlike any other illness": "every generation of cancer cells creates a small number of cells that is genetically different from its parents." Cancer is prone to constant regeneration, resistance to attack, and morphological fortitude: all that it knows is that it wants to live forever, and it will do anything to ensure its immortality. Or, cancer is a life force that necessitates the death of its host.

There is no question that a person who has undergone treatment for cancer will read this book differently from a reader who suspects she is immune. It would be terrible to suggest that a book could cause cancer, and yet, at moments, I felt as though a cell might begin reforming within me while I was reading, so powerful was Mukherjee's picture of cancer's mutating drive. Anyone, for that matter, who has been required to remake him or herself in light of an illness, endure the indignities of being ill, or live a life athwart illness as an identifying narrative may have a distinct response to the way that actual persons figure in this history of the disease writ large. (In a consumer world drenched in pink accoutrements, breast cancer patients especially are the readiest to comply with group-think about their disease or to comply with the order to wear their disease as a badge, making it all the more difficult *to be* in light of it.)

One of *Emperor*'s thinnest threads is its opening with Carla, a thirty-year-old woman diagnosed with leukemia who is the young oncologist's earliest cancer patient. One worries that an editor advised the writer to include a few stories of patients in the nearly 600-page book in order to humanize his biography of a disease. (In this way, the book joins a cadre of nonfiction books by physician-writers of the past twenty years bent on convincing a lay public of their doctor-authors' capacity for feeling.) It's hard to understand why Mukherjee felt the need to develop the characters of patients *other than* Carla (unless it's simply a journalistic tic) since they only serve as exemplifying statistics. On the other hand, where I wished patients to be more present, they were absent. "These were all deep, audacious, and meaningful victories borne on the backs of deep and meaningful labors," Mukherjee writes of treatment breakthroughs. He neglects to say on the backs of *patients*. Tamoxifen is described as a drug with "barely any significant side effects," but patient-readers will know that it can cause blood clots and uterine cancer.

Most unfortunate are Mukherjee's energetic equations of cancer with a person's identity, and his implicit assumption that people with cancer identify entirely as such: *I have cancer, therefore I am.* The book that has primarily featured a history of ruthless and heroic male researchers and physicians ends with another female patient's tale as bookend to Carla's. This patient, however, does not survive. Coming to the end of her "battle," Mukherjee imagines that "[s]he had stared into the vault of her resourcefulness and found it empty" in this "game that had taken over her life." In describing her this way, he thus commits the cardinal sin of wellness: the exertion of an epistemological advantage over the Other about whom one always knows more than she can ever know about herself.

Which is also a fundamental challenge, and problem, of biography.

II.

Of a hundred members and faces that each thing has, I take one, sometimes only to lick it, sometimes to brush the surface, sometimes to pinch it to the bone. I give it a stab, not as wide but as deep as I know how. And most often I like to take them from some unaccustomed point of view.

Michel de Montaigne, quoted in *How to Live*

What can be said of Montaigne can also be said about cancer: both, it turns out, are ready sites of projection, which makes their being the subjects of biographies—a genre that is Other-directed on the face of it—an interestingly complex undertaking. Siddhartha Mukherjee dubbed *Emperor* a biography because, as he continued to write, "it felt, inescapably, as if [he] were writing not about some*thing* but about some*one*: [his] subject daily morphed into something that resembled an individual—an enigmatic, if somewhat deranged, image in a mirror." This "feeling" of the presence of a ghostly double, we later surmise, derives from a way of imagining cancer in terms of "malignant growth and normal growth . . . so genetically intertwined that unbraiding the two might be one of the most significant scientific challenges faced by our species." Metaphorically speaking, and projectively, Mukherjee starts to experience cancer as an evil twin, an image that he allows silently to govern *Emperor* without exploring it. Maybe, like Montaigne, he'd have gotten closer to his subjects' multiply conflicting truths if he'd been willing to produce a "grotesque" literary form, to quote Bakewell on the great essayist's collocation of "monstrous bodies . . . without definite shape, having no order, sequence, or proportion other than accidental."

Literary form is neither arbitrary nor neutral, as Bakewell's book makes clear, but in its wild willfulness, it can have the power to teach us not only "how to live," but more subtly how to hear, how to listen, how to conceive, how to move, how not to tame, and therefore, how to imagine and thereafter, act—all this, *without* being prescriptive, dogmatic, didactic, or representative, but wily and seductive, unsure, humble, and unmoored.

I pull a volume from a shelf as I am wont to, and if it is the *Oxford English Dictionary,* I enjoy it for its heft, for language weighs—I don't wish to forget this—and I weigh: both it, and I, are heir to gravity, and to dust. I can't think "biography" without this image of the book as brick, doorstop, Bible, or diction-ary, but somehow the body gets lost in the equation. Biographies as analogs to reference books, conveyors of information, *summa?* In an age of informational crisis (some call it overload, or TMI) in which the major representational medium is the screen and its free-floating nets (never snares), how do I know? What do I know? How do I know what I know, and how do I tell one thing from another? In this age of infomercialism, a writer of literary nonfiction who wishes to compose a biography may find himself instead writing an extended Wikipedia article. I consider this a problem.

A biography is *not* a *summa,* those massive Medieval compendia that summarized the theological or philosophical knowledge of their day. Biographies only look like *summae.* The *summa* is much more interesting because summists charted contradiction, whereas biographers make the mess of life cohere. Summists were also known as "sententiaries," and their summae, "sentences," as in Peter Helias's *Book of Sentences.* I should like to be a maker of sentences, and a reader of sentences, and I like the challenge of wondering if any of us were asked to produce a *summa* for our times, what form it would take. If the life is in the language, how has language, in the form of sentences—their shape, grace, pittedness, or edge; their rip-rap, rustle, explosiveness, or sledge; their exogamy, vituperativeness, insanity, or dredge; their mellifluous uncanniness, their twitchiness, their breathy sign of life, or urgency, or death—fallen out of the biographical equation?

Non-narrative biography might seem a contradiction in terms, but it's worth courting: writing the life as a form of what we could call "shard work," in which coherence is not the aim so much as distillation is, or as a series of what Roland Barthes in *Sade/Fourier/Loyola* calls "biographemes," defined thus:

> . . . were I a writer, and dead, how I would love it if my life, through the pains of some friendly and detached biographer, were to reduce itself to a few details, a few preferences, a few inflections, let us say: to 'biographemes' whose distinction and mobility might go beyond any fate and come to touch, like Epicurean atoms, some future body, destined to the same dispersion . . .

Of Barthes's mother, for example, "she felt comfortable in somewhat tangled gardens, etc."; of Sade, a "white muff"; of Loyola, "flowerpots"; of Ignatius, "Spanish eyes." To pare the life down and assemble its discontinuous pieces; to admit the shape of dream into the life: one color advances while another bleeds about the edges—a single letter thrums in the silence of a half-forgotten room—a key turns into a rose, and so on; to restore the dream to the dreamer-subject in a language that doesn't merely describe but gives life to what it more than names: biography as a tympanic bell concert.

Journalist DT Max recently told *The Guardian* that his biography of David Foster Wallace, due out next year, won't be "a conventional 500-page type thing, one of those big, thick biographies. They are terrific, but I didn't think it was the right way to tackle David Foster Wallace—it's a little paradoxical because he wrote such big books himself." Instead, he said, his book would be more "in the form of an argument." The tome-like nature of biography has a tendency to cut the book off from what surrounds it; thus, if biographical writing is going to reach into the more variegated terrain of creative or literary nonfiction, it might need to be read alongside books unlike itself on similar subjects. Can a Montaignian gulf be breached, for example, by pairing *How to Live* with a literary, theoretical meditation on Emerson that appeared this year, *On Leaving: A Reading on Emerson* by Branka Ansic (Harvard University Press, 2010) that starts with the Emersonian question, "Who is alive?" Or, what if we were to read conventional life-writing alongside a book that comes at Joseph Beuys by way of his materials, *felt*, whose chapters are tuned to the pitch of text as textile, Chris Thompson's *Felt: Fluxus, Joseph Beuys, and the Dalai Lama* (University of Minnesota Press, 2011):

Felt is a nonwoven fabric, a body without axes, created through the multiple, random inter-lockings of spiral strands. The material owes its structural integrity to the chance bindings among its irregular spiral fibers. Felt is arrived at through the leaving-to-chance—even if it is a methodical and meticulous leaving-to-chance—of the combination of the spiral fibers, textures, and interstices of wool.

Biographies are more often written about the dead than the living; like the outmoded sense of memoir as memoirS—a coda to the life, the thing that needs to get written when there is nothing left to write, no more left to say, but whose status in the world makes the life noteworthy: always it's a backward glance. At worst, it's a CliffsNotes guide to something greater than itself. Rarely if, ever, is biography a form of felt.

Theoretical books, however, are no picnic: their insular insiderness can be exasperating, deadly dull, and just as dutiful as church. Needless to say, strictly academic writers have a great deal to learn as well from biographical stylists, but coffee-table books might serve as antidotes to both. I happened upon Jessica Kerwin Jenkins's *Encyclopedia of the Exquisite: An Anecdotal History of Elegant Delights* (New York: Nan A. Talese/Doubleday, 2010) when I was looking for large-scale books on royal weddings and the history of British monarchy for my brother's fiancée, who fancied such. I bought this book instead, and ended up keeping it, for here was a biography of a theme—in this case, the exquisite—and an autobiography made up of choices. Here, too, was an archive that the writer could call her own, and that I could carry, as if to say here's something that matters in an info-glutted age, a hand-hewn assemblage of nectar and ambrosia, silence and string, white paint, dark towers, and cumulonimbus.

How to Live seems to assume that the self Montaigne invented in his essays, and indulged, is the same one we experience when we blog, but I'm afraid this is a pipe dream. There's a difference between a Montaignian mirror (or Renaissance tain) and a screen, or, for that matter, the screening devices that govern our senses of ourselves (she says, as she hallucinates the chiming of her cell phone). The six-teenth-century person's inner life, or lack thereof, is not the same as our inner life (or lack thereof), and the self heralded by the Internet seems more often than not the same for all, sprung from a tower of opinion polling in place of thought.

Biographers as writers of literary nonfiction have their work cut out for them (and then some): we are not simply conveyors of information or trans-mitters of knowledge. In the "information age," I'd love to access each writer's collections—the creation of an uncommon archive in the form that is a book. Most of all, if the genre is going to evolve, we might need to bring incompatible modes and knowledges (yes, plural) into the same space so as to quell a poverty of too-sequestered readers, each to her own tastes, monads and monoliths, pop consumers and disciplinary elites. I want a reader who can tell one thing from another (we could call such readers discerning minds), at the same time that he reads across, within, and at the intersections of various types of nonfiction prose, never singly or alone, no longer convinced by a book's fixed borders or bounds.

Which brings me back to cancer and its infiltrations. Let's return to the retrovirus: Rous sarcoma virus possessed a property "unprecedented in any other living organism." It could convert RNA back into DNA when the central dogma of molecular biology forbade such a transition: such molecular transcription had only ever been imagined as a one-way street—DNA yields RNA, not the other way around. Literary form is neither fanciful nor decorative nor a trick, as is so often hinted at in *How to Live*, though tricksterism should not be underestimated for its radicality or political aplomb, and if tricking were more often a part of nonfiction prose, at least eros would be restored to it. Newly to imagine the shape that the transcription of a life can take in writing (but, no, it's transformation, not transcription that we want) is not so different from reimagining the face of a disease, the nature of its course, its origin and demise, what and how it responds to or resists. To be able to imagine new forms of thought (literary genres) is also to be able to imagine new forms of life: not how to live, but how to make life living. Sarah Bakewell reminds us that Montaigne produced a beautifully formed, malformed writing in an attempt to look his own deformity in the eye: "I'm full of cracks and leak out on all sides," he wrote. I look forward to the new de-formed and gangly biographies twenty-first century writers need to find the courage to produce.

Contributors' Notes

Priscilla Atkins, originally from Illinois, has lived in many places, including Massachusetts, California, and Hawaii. She currently works as a librarian and cultural diversity advocate. Her poems appear in *Poetry London, Shenandoah, Southwest Review,* and other journals. She lives in Michigan.

Simon Barker holds a Ph.D. in philosophy from the University of Sydney. He has worked as a community college instructor in northern California and as a philosophy lecturer at the University of New South Wales. His 2009 story, "Tarzan of the Danube," was nominated by *decomP* for a Pushcart Prize. His short stories have appeared in *Identity Theory, Storyglossia, Faultline,* and elsewhere. He lives in Sydney and works in administration.

Wendy Barker has published five books of poetry, including her most recent, *Nothing Between Us,* a novel in prose poems that was a runner-up for the Del Sol Prize (Del Sol Press, 2009). Her third chapbook, *Things of the Weather,* was also published in 2009. Her poems and translations have appeared in many magazines, including *Poetry, The Georgia Review, The Southern Review,* and *The Gettysburg Review.* She has received fellowships from the NEA and the Rockefeller Foundation, and is poet-in-residence at the University of Texas at San Antonio.

Richard Bausch is the author of eleven novels, including *Thanksgiving Night* and *Peace,* winner of the American Library Association's W. Y. Boyd Prize for Excellence in Military Fiction and the Dayton Literary Peace Prize, and eight collections of stories. His short stories have appeared in *The Atlantic Monthly, Esquire, Harper's, The New Yorker, The Best American Short Stories, O. Henry Prize Stories,* and *The Pushcart Prize Stories.* He currently serves as The Moss Chair of Excellence in the Writing Program at the University of Memphis.

L. Annette Binder has fiction published or forthcoming in *One Story, American Short Fiction, The Southern Review, Fairy Tale Review,* and others. Her collection, *Rise,* received the 2011 Mary McCarthy Prize in Short Fiction and will be published by Sarabande Books in August 2012. She is a student in the Programs in Writing at the University of California, Irvine.

Karina Borowicz is the author of *The Bees Are Waiting,* selected by Franz Wright for the 2011 Marick Press Poetry Prize. She also has published work in *AGNI, Poetry Northwest,* and *The Southern Review.*

Grace Brogan has published writing and photographs in *Studio One, Camas,* and the publications of a variety of organizations. She is inspired by place and determined to cultivate healthy, just communities and environments through communication, education, and thoughtful work done by hand. She is a graduate student in the University of Montana's Environmental Studies program, with emphases in creative writing and sustainable food systems.

Philip S. Bryant teaches at Gustavus Adolphus College, where he is currently a professor of English. His books of poetry include *Stompin' at the Grand Terrace,* a collection of jazz poems with accompanying CD; *Sermon on a Perfect Spring Day;* and a chapbook, *Blue Island.* He has published poems in *The Iowa Review, Indiana Review, The American Poetry Review,* and *Nimrod,* and in the anthology *Where One Voice Ends Another Begins: 150 Years of Minnesota Poetry,* edited by Robert Hedin.

Mary Cappello is the author of four books of literary nonfiction: *Night Bloom; Awkward: A Detour* (a *Los Angeles Times* bestseller), *Called Back;* and *Swallow: Foreign Bodies, Their Ingestion, Inspiration and the Curious Doctor Who Extracted Them.* A recipient of the Dorothea Lange/Paul Taylor Prize from Duke University's Center for Documentary Studies and the Bechtel Prize for Educating the Imagination from Teachers and Writers Collaborative, Cappello is a former Fulbright lecturer at the Gorky Literary Institute (Moscow) and currently professor of English and creative writing at the University of Rhode Island. A 2011 Guggenheim Fellow in Nonfiction, she is at work on a book-length essay on "mood."

Geoff Collins lives in a small town in Wisconsin, where he works in the local schools. His poems and stories have appeared in *Whitefish Review, Blue Earth Review, Amoskeag, SLANT,* and elsewhere.

Kathleen Coskran is the author of a collection of short stories, *The High Price of Everything,* winner of a Minnesota Book Award, and co-editor of *Tanzania on Tuesday: Writing by American Women Abroad.* Her short fiction and essays have appeared in numerous publications and anthologies. She is the recipient of numerous artists' fellowships and residencies, including an NEA Fellowship, a Bush Foundation Fellowship, and two grants from the Minnesota State Arts Board.

Todd Davis teaches creative writing and environmental studies at Penn State University's Altoona College. He is the author of four books of poems, most recently *The Least of These* (Michigan State University Press, 2010) and *Some Heaven* (Michigan State University Press, 2007). He is also co-editor of *Making Poems: Forty Poems with Commentary by the Poets* (State University of New York Press, 2010).

David Allen Evans, the poet laureate of South Dakota, has received grants from the NEA and the Bush Artist Foundation and been nominated for a Pushcart Prize. He was a Fulbright Scholar twice in China. His poems have appeared in such publications as *Prairie Schooner, Esquire, Poetry Northwest, Southern Poetry Review, Splash: Great Writing About Swimming and Diving, The Norton Book of Sports, Best Poems of 1969 (The Borestone Awards),* and *The HBJ Treasury of Literature.* He lives with his wife, Jan, in Sioux Falls, SD.

Kerry James Evans is currently pursuing a Ph.D. in creative writing at Florida State University. His poems have appeared or are forthcoming in *Agni, Beloit Poetry Journal, Narrative, New England Review, New Letters, Ploughshares, Prairie Schooner,* and elsewhere. His new book, *Bangalor,* is forthcoming from Copper Canyon in 2013.

Nimo H. Farah embraces her experiences as a refugee Muslim woman living in America but believes the human spirit is too multidimensional to categorize and classify. Exposed to many cultures and struggles, she is inspired to write about and celebrate the resilience, complexity, and compassion of the human spirit. She aspires to be a keeper of her ancestors' rich oral traditions and mother tongue; both are at the brink of endangerment.

Sarah Fox edits Fuori Editions and contributes to the multiauthor blog *Montevidayo*. Her book of poetry, *Because Why*, was published by Coffee House Press. Recent work has appeared in *Conduit, Action Yes, Eleven Eleven, Spout, Rain Taxi*, and elsewhere. Her awards include fellowships and grants from the NEA, the Bush Foundation, the Minnesota State Arts Board, and the Jerome Foundation. She was also the recipient of a 2010 Academy of American Poets James Wright Prize. With John Colburn she co-founded the Center for Visionary Poetics. She teaches English and creative writing at the University of Minnesota, where she's currently pursuing an M.F.A. in poetry.

Rebecca Fremo is associate professor and chair of English at Gustavus Adolphus College. Her poems have appeared or are forthcoming in *County Lines: 87 Minnesota Counties, 130 Minnesota Poets, Tidal Basin Review, Naugatuck River Review, River Poets Journal*, and *Poetica: A Magazine of Jewish Arts and Culture*. A native of Richmond, VA, Fremo lives in Minneosta with her husband and three sons.

George Friend has had a range of careers: prison counselor, university instructor, landlord, livestock farmer, real estate broker, atomic energy technical writer, small businessman, and consultant. He lives and writes in Spring Mills, MA, and summers on Otsego Lake, NY.

Madelyn Garner has worked as as a creative writing instructor, administrator, and editor. Her awards include the Colorado Governor's Award for Excellence in the Arts and Humanities, an Aspen Writers' Conference Fellowship, the D.H. Lawrence Award from the University of New Mexico and the Jackson Hole Writers Conference Poetry Prize for 2010. Recent work has appeared in *Margie, Harpur Palate, Saranac Review, PMS poemmemoirstory, American Journal of Nursing*, and the anthology *Beyond Forgetting, Poetry and Prose about Alzheimer's Disease*.

Dobby Gibson is the author of *Polar* (Alice James Books, 2005), winner of the Beatrice Hawley Award, and *Skirmish* (Graywolf Press, 2009). His new collection of poetry, *It Becomes You*, is forthcoming from Graywolf Press in 2013. He lives in Minneapolis.

Sarah Gilbert received her degree in English and journalism from Washington and Lee University, and her M.B.A. from the Wharton School. Once an investment banker, she now writes and keeps home in Portland, OR. She has been published in many online publications and in *Hemispheres*, United Airlines' in-flight magazine, and *Oregon Humanities* magazine. She is working on a book about feeding her family.

Rigoberto González is the author of three books of poetry: *So Often the Pitcher Goes to Water Until It Breaks*, a National Poetry Series selection; *Other Fugitives and Other Strangers*, winner of San Francisco State University's Poetry Center Book Award; and, most recently, *Black Blossoms*. His prose includes two bilingual children's picture books; the story collection *Men Without Bliss*; the novel *Crossing Vines*; the YA novel *The Mariposa Club*; and the memoir *Butterfly Boy: Memories of a Chicano Mariposa*, winner of the American Book Award from the Before Columbus Foundation. Other awards include fellowships from the Guggenheim and NEA Foundations, and the Shelley Memorial Award of the Poetry Society of America. He is an associate professor of English at Rutgers-Newark.

Rae Gouirand has published poems and essays in *American Poetry Review, Boston Review, Columbia, The Kenyon Review: KROnline, Seneca Review, Bateau, Memoir, Best New Poets 2009*, and on *Verse Daily*. She is the recipient of a 2009 award from the Dorothy Sargent Rosenberg Foundation for outstanding work by emerging poets. Her first collection of poems, *Open Winter*, was recently selected by Elaine Equi for the 2011 Bellday Poetry Prize and will be published in fall 2011. Gouirand lives in Davis, CA, and serves as writer-in-residence for the Cache Creek Conservancy.

Lisa Graley received her M.F.A. from McNelse State University and her Ph.D. from the University of Louisiana at Lafayette, where she currently teaches English and the humanities. Her stories have appeared in *Glimmer Train*.

Jonathan Greenhause has published poetry in more than a hundred literary reviews around the world, most recently in *Cream City Review, Dos Passos Review, Nimrod,* and *Reed,* and has been nominated for a Pushcart Prize. He works as a Spanish interpreter and lives with his wife and their dog, Antigone.

Alamgir Hashmi has published eleven books of poetry and several volumes of literary criticism in the United States, Canada, England, Australia, India, Pakistan, and elsewhere. He has won numerous national and international awards and honors, and his work has been translated into several European and Asian languages. For over three decades he has taught in European, Asian, and American universities. He has served as a judge of the Commonwealth Writers Prize and the Neustadt International Prize for Literature. He is founding president of The Literature Podium.

Ames Hawkins received a Ph.D. in composition and rhetoric from Wayne State University. She is an associate professor in the English department at Columbia College Chicago. In 2006, she became the first faculty fellow for Critical Encounters, a nonhierarchical, volunteer, civic-engagement art and activism initiative at the college. Her work has appeared in *Q Review, Midway Journal, Fourth Genre, The Broome Review,* and elsewhere. Her hybrid essay—a manifesto—appears in *RAW: (Reading and Writing) New Media.* She was a 2010 Lambda Literary Writers' Retreat fellow. Hawkins lives in Oak Park, IL.

Kathleen M. Heideman is a 2011 fellow of the Helene Wurlitzer Foundation, and a past fellow of the National Science Foundation's Antarctic Artists & Writers Program. In 2010, she served as artist-in-residence at Badlands National Park, Andrews Experimental Forest, Aspen Guard Station, and Necedah National Wildlife Refuge. She is the recipient of awards from the Bush, Jerome, and McKnight Foundations and the Minnesota State Arts Board, and she has been nominated for a Pushcart Prize. Her work has appeared in *Artifice, Conduit, Cream City Review, Exquisite Corpse, Folio, Fringe, Passages North, Sundog, Willow Springs,* and elsewhere. She resides in Upper Michigan.

Brenda Hillman is the author of eight collections of poetry, including the most recent, *Practical Water* (Wesleyan, 2009). She is the Olivia Filippi professor of poetry at Saint Mary's College of California.

Richard Jarrette is the author of *Beso the Donkey* (MSU Press), winner of the 2010 Midwest Book Award and a finalist for *ForeWord Reviews* Book of the Year Award. His work has appeared in *Connotations, The Mas Tequila Review, Blind Donkey,* and *Great Granny Press.* Jarrette is a member of The Frisch Studio and recently appeared in a production of Clifford Odets's *Awake and Sing.* He lives in Los Olivos, CA, and works as a psychotherapist specializing in pain management, post-traumatic stress disorder, and coping skills for illness.

Hershman John is a poet and a short-fiction writer. He is Navajo—born for the Deer Spring People and the Bitter Water People. He received his M.F.A. in creative writing from Arizona State University. He teaches at Phoenix College. His work has been published in *Arizona Highways, Flyway-A Literary Review, Hayden's Ferry Review, Journal of Navajo Education, Puerto del Sol, Wicazo Sa Review, O Taste and See: Food Poems,* and elsewhere. His first collection of poems, *I Swallow Turquoise for Courage,* was published by University of Arizona Press.

Reeves Keyworth has recently published work in *Rattle, Terrain.org,* and *Slate.* Her work has been nominated for a Pushcart Prize, and she received a fellowship in fiction from the New York Foundation for the Arts. Her chapbook, *My Daphne Phase,* was published by Finishing Line Press in 2010. She lives in Tucson, AZ.

Mary Jane LaVigne, winner of The Loft Mentor Series, has written for *A View from the Loft, Minnesota Monthly, Twin Cities Daily Planet,* and *Black Rock Beacon* under her playa name, Mrs. Lucky.

Ed Bok Lee was raised in South Korea, North Dakota, and Minnesota. A former bartender, phys. ed. instructor, journalist, and translator, he has studied in the U.S., South Korea, Kazakhstan, and Russia, and earned an M.F.A. from Brown University. Lee has shared his work in journals and anthologies, and on stages, public radio, and MTV. He teaches part-time at Metropolitan State University in St. Paul. His first book, *Real Karaoke People,* was the winner of the PEN Open Book Award. His second book of poems, *Whorled,* is forthcoming in fall 2011 from Coffee House Press.

Eleanor Lerman is the author of five books of poetry and two short-story collections. She has been nominated for a National Book Award, received an NEA Fellowship, and won the 2006 Lenore Marshall Prize for the year's best book of poetry. In 2011 she received a Guggenheim Fellowship in poetry. Her novel, *Janet Planet*, will be published by Mayapple Press in September 2011.

Joel Long is the author of two books of poetry: *Winged Insects*, winner of the White Pine Press Poetry Prize, and *Knowing Time by Light* (Blaine Creek Press, 2010). His chapbooks, *Chopin's Preludes* and *Saffron Beneath Every Frost*, were published from Elik Press. His poems have appeared in *Gulf Coast, Bitter Oleander, Crab Orchard Review, Bellingham Review, Sou'wester, Prairie Schooner, Willow Springs, Quarterly West*, and *Seattle Review* and anthologized in *American Poetry: The Next Generation, Essential Love, Fresh Water*, and *I Go to the Ruined Place: Contemporary Poems in Defense of Global Human Rights*.

Matt Mauch is the author of *Prayer Book* (Lowbrow Press) and the chapbook *The Book of Modern Prayer* (Palimpsest Press). His poems have recently appeared in *Salt Hill, Leveler, InDigest, Connotation Press, H_NGM_N, Poetry Daily*, and elsewhere. The editor of *Poetry City, USA*, Vol. 1, and curator of the annual Great Twin Cities Poetry Read, Mauch teaches writing and literature in the A.F.A. program at Normandale Community College. He lives in Minneapolis.

June Melby has been published in *McSweeney's Internet Tendency, Versal*, the *LA Weekly, Kafee.Satz.Lesen* (Hamburg, Germany), and elsewhere. As a poet and a spoken-word artist she has performed at CBGB and Knitting Factory in New York; the UCLA Hammer Museum in Los Angeles; the Seattle Bumbershoot Arts Festival; and in London, Munich, Hamburg, Bonn, and Amsterdam. She is currently writing a memoir, *Little House on the Astroturf*. She lives in a log cabin in Iowa.

Alison Morse is the founder of TalkingImageConnection, a reading series that brings together writers, contemporary visual art, and new audiences. Her poetry and prose have been published in *Water~Stone Review, Natural Bridge, The Pedestal, Rhino, Opium Magazine, mnartists.org, Potomac Review, Flashquake*, and elsewhere. She received her M.F.A. in creative writing from Hamline University, where her thesis won the Outstanding Fiction Award.

Travis Mossotti received his M.F.A. in poetry from Southern Illinois University Carbondale. He has been a faculty lecturer at the University of California Santa Cruz and McKendree University, and his poetry is published widely. Mossotti was awarded the James Hearst Poetry Prize from the *North American Review* in 2009, and his poem "Decampment" was adapted to screen in 2010 as an animated short film. His first collection of poems, *About the Dead* (Utah State University Press), was awarded the 2011 May Swenson Poetry Award by contest judge Garrison Keillor. Mossotti resides in St. Louis with his wife, Regina.

Sheila O'Connor is the author of three novels, including her most recent, *Sparrow Road* (G.P. Putnam, 2011). Her second novel, *Where No Gods Came*, won the Minnesota Book Award and the Michigan Award for Literary Fiction and was selected as a Barnes & Noble Discover Great New Writers title. Her poems, stories, and essays have appeared in anthologies and magazines, including *Riding Shotgun: Women Write About Their Mothers; The Next Parish Over; Mothers and Daughters;* and others. She has received fellowships and grants from the Bush and Loft-McKnight Foundations and the State Arts Board. The fiction editor of *Water~Stone Review*, she teaches in the M.F.A. program at Hamline University.

Andre Perry lives and works in Iowa City.

Mark Robert Rapacz is the author of many short stories that have appeared in online and print journals. His story "The Stone the Builder's Refused," published in *Water~Stone Review*, received a Special Mention in the *2011 Pushcart Prize* anthology. His first novella, *Buffalo Bill in the Gallery of the Machines*, is forthcoming from Burnt Bridges Press in early 2012. He lives and works as a writer and editor in Minneapolis.

William Reichard is the author of four books of poetry, most recently *Sin Eater* (2010) and *This Brightness* (2007), both from Mid-List Press. He is the editor of the anthology *American Tensions: Literature of Identity and the Search for Social Justice* (New Village Press, 2011). He directs the Writing for Social Change and City Arts programs for the Higher Education Consortium for Urban Affairs and lives in Saint Paul.

Alberto Ríos, a recent finalist for the National Book Award, is the author of ten books and chapbooks of poetry, including *The Theater of Night*—winner of the PEN/Beyond Margins Award—three collections of short stories, and a memoir about growing up on the border, *Capirotada*. Ríos is the recipient of numerous awards and his work is included in over 200 national and international literary anthologies. His next book, *The Dangerous Shirt*, is forthcoming. His work is regularly taught and translated, and has been adapted to dance and both classical and popular music. Ríos is a Regents' Professor and the Katharine C. Turner Chair in English at Arizona State University.

José Rodríguez is a former editor of Harpur Palate. His work has received the 2009 Allen Ginsberg Poetry Award and been nominated twice for a Pushcart Prize. His poetry collection, *The Shallow End of Sleep*, was published by Tia Chucha Press in 2011. Recent work is forthcoming in *Green Mountains Review*, *Upstreet*, *Platte Valley Review*, *Big Muddy*, *The New York Quarterly*, and *Paterson Literary Review*. José holds a Ph.D. in English and creative writing from Binghamton University.

Lee Rossi is a staff interviewer and reviewer for the online literary journal *The Pedestal*. His poems have appeared in the *Harvard Review Online, EscapeIntoLife .org*, and *Green Hills Literary Lantern*. Originally from Missouri, he recently relocated from California to cyberspace.

Stan Sanvel Rubin has published three full-length collections of poetry, including *Hidden Sequel*, winner of the Barrow Street Book Prize. His work has appeared in many magazines, including *The Georgia Review, The Iowa Review, The Kenyon Review, Chelsea, Virginia Quarterly Review, The Laurel Review, Beloit Poetry Journal*, and, most recently, *The Louisville Review*. His work is also included in the anthologies *Long Journey: Contemporary Northwest Poets* and *The Poet's Guide to the Birds*. He is director of the Rainier Writing Workshop low-residency M.F.A. at Pacific Lutheran University.

Michael Schmeltzer earned an M.F.A. from the Rainier Writing Workshop at Pacific Lutheran University. His awards include three Pushcart Prize nominations, the *Gulf Stream* Award for Poetry, *Blue Earth Review's* Flash Fiction Prize, and the Artsmith Literary Award. He helps edit *A River & Sound Review* and has been published in *Natural Bridge, Mid-American Review, New York Quarterly, Crab Creek Review, Fourteen Hills,* and elsewhere. He is a stay-at-home father in Seattle.

SJ Sindu is an M.A. student at the University of Nebraska–Lincoln studying English with a concentration in creative writing. Sindu is an activist and writer, focusing on traditionally silenced voices, the immigrant, the poor, the queer, the female-bodied, the non-Christian, the non-white. Her work has appeared or is forthcoming in *Brevity, Harpur Palate, Sinister Wisdom,* and elsewhere.

Joyce Sutphen is the author of four books of poetry, including her most recent, *First Words* (Red Dragonfly Press). Her first book, *Straight Out of View,* won the Barnard New Women's Poets Prize. Her third book, *Naming the Stars,* won the Minnesota Book Award in Poetry. Other awards include a Minnesota State Arts Board Fellowship, two Jerome Fellowships, a Salzburg Fellowship, a Loft-McKnight Award in poetry, and numerous artist residencies. She teaches literature and creative writing at Gustavus Adolphus College in St. Peter, MN.

Loren A. Taylor is a senior librarian at Ridgedale Library in Minneapolis, MN. In 2009 he served as the assistant editor in fiction for *Water~Stone Review.* He has an M.F.A. in creative writing from Hamline University.

Norma Tilden is director of the Writing Program at Georgetown University in Washington, D.C., where she has taught for many years. She is currently completing *The Indigenous Essay,* a critical study of the contemporary nature essay, and is at work on a chapbook of lyric essays, *Animal Watch.* Her writing has received recognition and awards from numerous publications, including *The Yale Review, New Letters,* and *Biography.*

Francine Marie Tolf is the author of *Rain, Lilies, Luck,* her first full-length collection of poetry, and *Joliet Girl,* a memoir, both from North Star Press (2010). Her poems and essays have appeared in *Rattle, Spoon River, Poetry East, Southern Humanities Review,* and elsewhere. Her awards include grants from the Minnesota State Arts Board, the Elizabeth George Foundation, The Loft Literary Center, and the Barbara Deming Memorial Fund for women writers.

Kathleen Weihe teaches developmental writing at Anoka-Ramsey Community College and lives in Minneapolis with her family. She has received an artist's assistance fellowship from the Minnesota State Arts Board, a Loft-McKnight Award, and a Loft Mentor Award. She graduated from Hamline University with an M.F.A. in creative writing and has completed a new poetry manuscript, *Selves and Gods.*

Mary Wharff has published stories in *Room Magazine, Connecticut Review, Mochila Review,* and *The Class That Fell in Love with the Man,* an essay collection honoring author Tom Spanbauer. She is the co-founder of "Big Tent at the Raven," a monthly reading series, and the fiction editor of *Coal City Review.* In 2006 she won the Langston Hughes Award for Fiction. She lives in Lawrence, KS, with her husband and their adopted four-legged family.

Morgan Grayce Willow has received awards in poetry and prose from the Minnesota State Arts Board, the McKnight Foundation, the Jerome Foundation, and elsewhere. In 2009, she published the poetry collections *Between* (Nodin Press) and *Silk* (Shu Kuang Press), as well as a letterpress chapbook, *The Maps Are Words* (Red Dragonfly Press). Her memoir, "Riding Shotgun for Stanley Home Products," appeared in *Riding Shotgun: Women Write about Their Mothers.* Her essay "Double Language" was published in *Third Coast* in 2004. A former sign language interpreter, she lives in Minneapolis.

Francine Witte received an M.F.A. from Vermont College and has worked as a high school teacher for the past seventeen years. Her poetry chapbook, *First Rain,* was published by Pecan Grove Press. Her flash-fiction chapbook, *Cold June,* was the winner of the Thomas A. Wilhelmus fiction contest and was published by Ropewalk Press. She lives in New York City.

Lidia Yuknavitch is the author of the memoir *The Chronology of Water,* as well as *Allegories of Violence: Tracing the Writing of War in 20th Century Novels,* and three books of short stories. Her fiction, nonfiction, and critifiction have appeared in journals such as *The Iowa Review, Ms., Exquisite Corpse, Another Chicago Magazine, Zyzzyva,* and *Critical Matrix,* as well as in the anthologies *Life As We Show It, Wreckage of Reason, Forms at War,* and the upcoming *Men Undressed.* She is the editor of Chiasmus Press and teaches writing, literature, film, and women's studies in Oregon. Her debut novel, *Dora: A Head Case*, is forthcoming from Hawthorne Books in 2012.

Photographers' Notes

Anna Beeke is a documentary and event photographer based out of Brooklyn, NY. She is a graduate of the International Center of Photography's photojournalism and documentary photography certificate program and is currently an M.F.A. candidate at the School of Visual Arts. She was selected as a participant in the Eddie Adams Workshop in 2009, and her work was chosen to be included in the reGeneration2: Tomorrow's Photographers Today traveling exhibition and book by the Musée de l'Élysée in Lausanne, Switzerland. Her work has been exhibited around the world, including in New York, Washington, D.C., Milan, and Paris.

Debbie Carlos was born in Los Angeles and grew up in Manila, Philippines. She moved back to the U.S. to study photography at the School of the Art Institute of Chicago, graduating in 2007.

Anne Golaz was born in Switzerland in 1983 and is currently working toward a master in photography degree at Taik in Helsinki, Finland. She has exhibited in several places, mainly in Switzerland and France, with individual shows in the Photoforum Pasquart Museum, the 2008 European Photo Month in Paris, and the 2009 Quinzaine Photographique Nantaise. She was recently selected by the Musée de l'Élysée in Lausanne for the international traveling exhibition, *reGeneration2: Tomorrow's Photographers Today*. Her series *Chasses, Enquête Photographique Fribourgeoise* was published by *inFolio Editions* in 2010.

David Goldes has exhibited his work nationally and internationally. It is included in the collections of the Whitney Museum of American Art, the Walker Art Center, the Museum of Modern Art, and the Art Institute of Chicago. He is the recipient of the Guggenheim Memorial Fellowship, an NEA Fellowship, two

Bush Foundation Fellowships, and six McKnight Foundation Fellowships. He is currently a member of the faculty in Media Arts at the Minneapolis College of Art and Design.

Sarah Hobbs was born in Lynchburg, VA, and received an M.F.A. in photography (graduating with honors) from the University of Georgia. Her work has been exhibited at the Art Institute of Chicago, the Knoxville Museum of Art, and Silver Eye Center for Photography. Her work is included in public collections of the Art Institute of Chicago, the Brooklyn Museum of Art, the Los Angeles County Museum of Art, and the Museum of Fine Arts, Houston. Her new book, *Small Problems in Living*, is forthcoming from Charta Books in 2012.

Chang Kyun Kim was born in 1974 in South Korea. He holds an M.F.A. in photography from Parsons The New School for Design. He has exhibited around the world and is included in collections such as the Musée de l'Élysée in Lausanne and Michaelis Galleries of University of Cape Town, South Africa. His work has been published by *PDN, American Photo, Photographer's Forum, SHOTS,* and *Photographie.* He currently lives and works in New York City.

Ani Kington was born in Columbus, OH, and received a B.F.A. in photography from Tisch School for the Arts at NYU. Her work has been included in several group exhibitions, including *reGeneration2: Tomorrow's Photographers Today*, which continues to travel internationally. She lives and works in Brooklyn.

Karen Knorr was born in Frankfurt am Main, Germany, and was raised in San Juan, Puerto Rico. She finished her education in Paris and London, studying at the University of Westminster, and has taught, exhibited, and lectured internationally, including at Tate Britain, Tate Modern, the University of Westminster, Goldsmiths, Harvard, and the Art Institute of Chicago. She is currently professor of photography at the University for the Creative Arts in Farnham, Surrey.

Richard Misrach has exhibited individually at the National Gallery of Art, the Art Institute of Chicago, the Los Angeles County Museum of Art, and the Centre Pompidou, Paris, amongst others. His work is included in the collections of most major institutions, including the Museum of Modern Art, the Whitney Museum of American Art, and the Metropolitan Museum of Art in New York. In 2010, the exhibition *Untitled [New Orleans and the Gulf Coast, 2005]* made its debut at the New Orleans Museum of Art and the Houston Museum of Fine Arts. In 2002 he was given the Kulturpreis for Lifetime Achievement in Photography by the German Society for Photography, and in 2008 the Lucie Award for Outstanding Achievement in Fine Art Photography. *Image: Copyright © Richard Misrach, courtesy Fraenkel Gallery, San Francisco, Marc Selwyn Fine Art, Los Angeles, and Pace/ MacGill Gallery, New York.*

Rachael Victoria Nelson was born in Greenville, Pennsylvania. She received her B.F.A. in photography from the Minneapolis College of Art and Design, and currently lives in upstate New York. *Image: From an ongoing series in which the artist and her collaborators photograph each other.*

Andrea Star Reese is a photojournalist/documentary photographer based in New York who holds an M.F.A. from California Institute of the Arts School of Film. In 2007, she began *The Urban Cave,* a three-year project on long-term, unsheltered men and women living in makeshift housing in New York City. *The Urban Cave* has been awarded Best Social Documentary from the New York Photo Festival, received three Honorable Mentions from the International Photography Awards, was a finalist for Picture of the Year: World Understanding and was a 2010 Visa d'Or feature nominee. She has exhibited around the world, most recently in the traveling exhibition, *reGeneration2: Tomorrow's Photographers Today.* She is a 2010 fellow in photography from the New York Foundation for the Arts.

Carla Alexandra Rodriguez is a first-generation Venezuelan-American, born and raised in Houston, TX. She received her B.F.A. in photography from the Minneapolis College of Art and Design, and is currently living in St. Paul, MN.

Jeff Wall studied art history at the University of British Columbia, Vancouver, and at the Courtauld Institute, London. His work has been exhibited in numerous international exhibitions, including a touring solo retrospective at the Museum of Modern Art, New York; the Art Institute of Chicago; and the San Francisco Museum of Art. He has been the recipient of numerous prizes, including The Paul de Hueck and Norman Walford Career Achievement Award for Art Photography; Ontario Arts Council, Canada; Erna and Victor Hasselblad Foundation

International Award in Photography; and the Roswitha Haftmann Prize for the Visual Arts. *Image: Jeff Wall, After Invisible Man by Ralph Ellison, the Preface, 1999-2001, transparency in lightbox, 174 x 250.5 cm, courtesy of the artist.*

Augusta Wood is an artist currently living and working in Los Angeles. Originally from the greater Boston area, she earned a B.F.A. from The Cooper Union and an M.F.A. from CalArts. Her work has been featured in exhibitions at the Torrance Art Museum, Cherry and Martin Gallery, China Art Objects Galleries, and Anton Kern Gallery, among others. She was included in the Fotofest 2010 Biennial in Houston, TX, and most recently has been the subject of a solo exhibition at Angles Gallery. Her work has been written about in *Modern Painters, The Huffington Post, Art Lies: A Contemporary Art Quarterly,* and the *Los Angeles Times,* and has appeared on the cover of *Black Clock.* She is represented by Angles Gallery in Los Angeles. *Image: Copyright © Augusta Wood*

Shizuka Yokomizo was born in Tokyo and received an M.F.A. from Goldsmiths College, London. She has exhibited at Museo d'Arte Contemporanea, Rome; the San Diego Museum of Art; and Wako Works of Art, Tokyo; as well as other venues in Europe, the United States, and Japan. In 2003, her work was included in the Venice Biennale; the First ICP Triennial at the International Center for Photography, New York; and the Tate Triennial, Tate Britain, London. Her work recently appeared in *Exposed: Voyeurism, Surveillance and the Camera* at Tate Modern and *Talent Show* at Walker Art Center, Minneapolis and MoMA PS1, Long Island City, NY. *Image: Copyright © Shizuka Yokomizo*

Alchemic Symbols

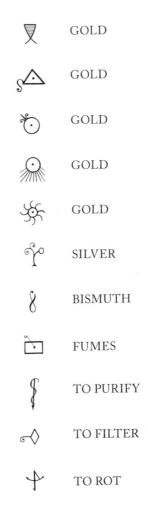

GOLD

GOLD

GOLD

GOLD

GOLD

SILVER

BISMUTH

FUMES

TO PURIFY

TO FILTER

TO ROT

Call For Submissions

Water~Stone Review, an annual review of literature at Hamline University, is seeking submissions for our Fall 2012 issue. All submissions should be original, unpublished work.

* Submissions accepted from October 1 through December 1, 2011. (*Work is read between Dec. 1, 2011 and April 1, 2012.*)
* Manuscripts must be typed or printed in proper format on white paper, in English, one side only, double-spaced for prose. Cover letters should be brief. Author's name should not appear on the manuscript.
* Fiction and creative nonfiction manuscripts must be limited to 8,000 words.
* Novel and memoir excerpts are acceptable as long as they stand on their own.
* Poetry submissions must be limited to three poems or less.
* Simultaneous submissions are acceptable, but the writer must withdraw the manuscript immediately if it has been accepted elsewhere.
* Entrants may submit only one submission per category.
* Please include SASE for results. Manuscripts will be recycled, not returned.
* Payment is in two copies of the Fall 2012 issue.

The Fall 2012 issue of *Water~Stone Review* will be available for purchase in October, 2012. Submissions should be sent to:

Water~Stone Review, The Creative Writing Programs, Hamline University, MS-A1730, 1536 Hewitt Ave., St. Paul, MN 55104-1284.

Submission Guidelines and information about the review, including the latest *W~SR* news, subscription, merchandise, donation information, and back issues can be found at *www.waterstonereview.com*.

2012 Jane Kenyon Poetry Prize

$1,000 Prize & Publication, Poetry Prize Judge: Alberto Ríos

Water~Stone Review announces the 2012 Jane Kenyon Poetry Prize in honor of Jane Kenyon, a distinguished poet who died in April 1995. Jane Kenyon is the author of five books of poetry, the most recent being *Otherwise: New & Selected Poems* (Graywolf Press).

- All submissions should be original, unpublished work. Submissions accepted October 1 through December 1, 2011. (*Work is read Dec. 2011–April 2012.*)
- Manuscripts must be typed or printed in proper format on white paper, in English, one side only. Cover letter should be brief. Author's name should not appear on the manuscript.
- Submit up to three poems. (*Total number of pages may not exceed 10.*) Please send three copies of your submission.
- Please include a self-addressed, stamped envelope (*SASE*) for notification of results. Manuscripts will be recycled, not returned.
- An entry fee of $15 (check made payable to *Water~Stone Review*) must accompany your submission. (*Only one submission per person.*)

Submissions should be sent to:
Poetry Prize, Water~Stone Review, The Creative Writing Programs, Hamline University MS-A1730, 1536 Hewitt Avenue, St. Paul, MN 55104-1284

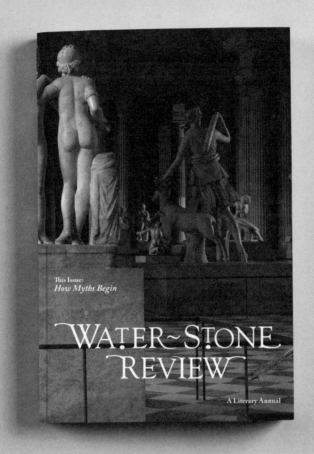

Thank you, *Water~Stone Review*, for many great
years of writers, reading, inspired teaching, and
a creative collaboration second to none.

MCAD DesignWorks
2501 Stevens Avenue
Minneapolis, MN 55404

www.mcad-designworks.com

Sustaining Patrons

$1,000+

Peggy Shumaker and Joe Usibelli

Friends of Water~Stone Review

$100

Lon Otto and Kathleen McKown
Garvin and Bernice Davenport
John Bessler and Amy Klobuchar
Stephen Seidel and Deborah Keenan
Stan Rubin and Judith Kitchen
David Grothe and Margaret Hasse
Mary and Garth Rockcastle
Marilyn C. Anderson
Sarah (Sally) French
Frieda Gardner
Carol Ellingson
Bruce Lebus
Jeffrey Scherer
James Lenfestey
Ginny Thompson
Margot Galt
Joe and Beth Windler
Ron Koertge
Deborah Bancroft
Lois Welshons
Robert Ready
Loren Taylor
Suzanne Swanson
Norita Dittberner-Jax
Lisa McLean
Marie Stolte
Marc Conklin
Lisa Higgs and Tobias Kohler

The 14th annual *Water~Stone Review* was printed in Minneapolis, MN, by Modern Press. The cover of this book is printed on New Page Producolith Matte 80lb Cover, and the literary content is printed on Cougar Opaque Natural Smooth 80lb. The photography section is printed on New Page Producolith Matte 80lb Text. This issue of the review was designed using the typeface Adobe Caslon Pro, a variant of the typeface Caslon which was featured in such historic documents as the first printed version of the United States *Declaration of Independence.*